Practical Industrial Internet of Things Security

A practitioner's guide to securing connected industries

Sravani Bhattacharjee

BIRMINGHAM - MUMBAI

Practical Industrial Internet of Things Security

Commissioning Editor: Gebin George
Acquisition Editor: Prachi Bisht
Content Development Editor: Dattatraya More
Technical Editor: Sayali Thanekar
Copy Editor: Safis Editing
Project Coordinator: Shweta H Birwatkar
Proofreader: Safis Editing
Indexer: Priyanka Dhadke
Graphics: Jisha Chirayil
Production Coordinator: Arvindkumar Gupta

First published: July 2018

Production reference: 1260718

Published by Packt Publishing Ltd.
Livery Place
35 Livery Street
Birmingham
B3 2PB, UK.

ISBN 978-1-78883-268-7

www.packtpub.com

To my eternal parents

`mapt.io`

Mapt is an online digital library that gives you full access to over 5,000 books and videos, as well as industry leading tools to help you plan your personal development and advance your career. For more information, please visit our website.

Why subscribe?

- Spend less time learning and more time coding with practical eBooks and Videos from over 4,000 industry professionals

- Improve your learning with Skill Plans built especially for you

- Get a free eBook or video every month

- Mapt is fully searchable

- Copy and paste, print, and bookmark content

PacktPub.com

Did you know that Packt offers eBook versions of every book published, with PDF and ePub files available? You can upgrade to the eBook version at `www.PacktPub.com` and as a print book customer, you are entitled to a discount on the eBook copy. Get in touch with us at `service@packtpub.com` for more details.

At `www.PacktPub.com`, you can also read a collection of free technical articles, sign up for a range of free newsletters, and receive exclusive discounts and offers on Packt books and eBooks.

Foreword

When the internet was invented almost 40 years ago, security was not on anyone's radar. No one considered it at all. There was no need—the application in mind was to share documents across labs at CERN, and those documents were not secret. The internet was person-to-person, and these were persons who wanted to share.

The critical invention, the URL, is now used in a person-to-business manner. We can bank online, book flights and hotel rooms, and provide our credit card details over the internet. Since the internet is no longer a simple document-sharing scheme, security is now a major concern. Moreover, health records are often online and we (sometimes unwittingly) provide huge amounts of personal data via social media and sites that provide specific services, such as dating. We want that data to be kept private. Privacy is now definitely a major concern.

We are now connecting things to the internet. We can control physical devices in the real world; the internet is business-to-thing. Consequently, safety is a concern. Moreover, autonomous vehicles, for example, must not only be safe in the "airbag" sense, but they also need to be resilient and reliable in terms of their autonomous technology so that they don't break down at 65 miles an hour; they need to be resilient so that when they do break down, they degrade gracefully.

This **Industrial Internet of Things (IIoT)** is an internet of things, machines, computers, and people that will transform economies and societies. But only if it is trustworthy.

Trustworthiness is a combination of security (it's not just cyber- any more!), privacy, safety, reliability, and resilience across both the **Information Technology (IT)** and **Operational Technology (OT)** domains. This convergence involves people from many different areas with different vocabularies ("security" means different things to an IT specialist and a plant manager) and different timelines (IT is updating my phone as we speak, while a chemical plant requires many compliance checks). It requires careful thought and reconciliation of culture, processes, values, and emphasis.

Trustworthiness is therefore a complex, expansive subject that encompasses multiple dimensions and disciplines. It requires comprehensive groundwork to promote awareness, expertise, and practical actions. It ties directly to safety, environmental damage, and ethics—the entire economy and society worldwide. Yet there's a lack of comprehensive understanding of trustworthiness among business stakeholders and technical professionals, including system developers, integrators, and manufacturers. Industrial users looking to adopt IIoT need comprehensive guidance.

This book, *Practical Industrial IoT Security*, takes the IIC's work, existing standards, and best practices and combines them into a security practitioner's handbook. It is widely applicable across verticals, targeting solutions architects and anyone else responsible for IIoT security, allowing them to digest a single volume to consume the breadth of the security issues in IIoT. The book seamlessly aligns with these frameworks and demonstrates their practical applicability to various IIoT uses cases.

The industry today is much in need of such a resource. This book fills the gap between conceptual frameworks and practice. It addresses the security roles and responsibilities across the life cycle, from business case and requirements definition, development, and integration, right the way to deployment and live operations. In addition to IIC resources, readers will also find several useful industry references, including works done by the IEEE, IEC, OMG, Cloud Security Alliance, NIST, research organizations, and academics. As such, this book is very closely tied with the IIC's vision and initiatives.

This book is not the conclusion for IIoT security, but rather the start of a journey to realize a digitally connected world, enabling it to evolve to meet the security challenges of the foreseeable future.

Stephen J Mellor

CTO

Industrial Internet Consortium

La Jolla, CA, USA

2018-06-27

Contributors

About the author

Sravani Bhattacharjee has been a data communications technologist for over 20 years. As a technology leader at Cisco till 2014, she led the architectural planning and security evaluations of several enterprise cloud/datacenter solutions. As the principal of Irecamedia, She currently collaborates with Industrial IoT innovators to drive awareness and business decisions by creating industry whitepapers and a variety of editorial and technical marketing content. She is a member of the IEEE IoT chapter, a writer, and a speaker. She has a master's degree in Electronics Engineering.

I sincerely acknowledge the insights, valuable time, and support of my industry colleagues toward this book. Special thanks to Arjmand Samuel (Microsoft), Stan Schneider (RTI), Dean Weber (Mocana), Stephen Mellor (IIC), Paul Didier (Cisco), and Rebecca Lawson (GE). I was humbled by the active support of Rajive Joshi (RTI) and Steve Hanna (Infineon). My loving thanks to all my family members and friends for their continuous support to complete the book.

About the reviewer

Sven Schrecker is the Chief Architect for Intel's IoT Security Solutions Group. He is responsible for open, standards-based platforms and strategy to enable end-to-end IoT security across both legacy and new technologies, leveraging hardware and software solutions to demonstrably increase security focused at embedded and industrial deployments. He is also the Chair of the IIC's Security Working Group, where he seeks to improve security capability across IIoT. He is an inventor of over four dozen security-related patents either pending or granted.

Packt is searching for authors like you

If you're interested in becoming an author for Packt, please visit `authors.packtpub.com` and apply today. We have worked with thousands of developers and tech professionals, just like you, to help them share their insight with the global tech community. You can make a general application, apply for a specific hot topic that we are recruiting an author for, or submit your own idea.

Disclaimer

The information within this book is intended to be used only in an ethical manner. Do not use any information from the book if you do not have written permission from the owner of the equipment. If you perform illegal actions, you are likely to be arrested and prosecuted to the full extent of the law. Packt Publishing does not take any responsibility if you misuse any of the information contained within the book. The information herein must only be used while testing environments with proper written authorizations from appropriate persons responsible.

Table of Contents

Preface

The **Industrial IoT (IIoT)** is ushering in enormous social and economic opportunities. It has introduced a new era of autonomous machines and intelligent processes. However, an undeniable side effect of connectivity is exposure to cyber intrusions. Security is therefore a top concern in IIoT adoption. IIoT security is intricately linked to the reliability of physical systems, as well as human and environmental safety.

This book provides a comprehensive understanding of the entire gamut of IIoT security and practical techniques to build and adopt secured IIoT solutions. In this book, readers will find expert insights into the foundational tenets of IIoT security, threat models, reference architectures, and real-world case studies.

This book covers practical tools for designing risk-based security controls, and goes into depth regarding multi layered defense techniques involving IAM, endpoint security, connectivity technologies, and edge- and cloud-based applications, such that you gain a solid grasp of this crucial security discipline. Developers, architects, plant managers, manufacturers, and business leaders are just some of the people who should be concerned with securing IIoT life cycle processes, standardization and governance, and assessing the applicability of emerging technologies (for example, blockchain, AI/machine learning, TSN, and quantum) with a view to implementing resilient and socially beneficial connected systems at scale.

Who this book is for

This book targets IIoT practitioners, including IIoT researchers, security professionals, architects, developers, and business stakeholders. Anyone who needs to have a comprehensive understanding of the unique safety and security challenges of connected industries, and who needs to learn practical methodologies to secure industrial assets, will find this book immensely helpful. This book is uniquely designed to benefit professionals from both IT and industrial operations, backgrounds.

What this book covers

Chapter 1, *An Unprecedented Opportunity at Stake*, introduces you to the foundational IIoT concepts, definitions, and unique challenges in securing ICS/SCADA/DCS systems. The chapter also dives into security assessment of a few prominent IIoT use cases.

Chapter 2, *Industrial IoT Dataflow and Security Architecture*, gives you an in-depth understanding of data flows in industrial applications, reference architectures, and risk management methodologies for IIoT. Finally, it establishes an end-to-end IIoT security architecture based on the **industrial internet security framework (IISF)**.

Chapter 3, *IIoT Identity and Access Management*, helps you develop comprehensive insights in terms of identity and access control technologies and their evolutionary developments to protect IIoT architectures.

Chapter 4, *Endpoint Security and Trustworthiness*, introduces you to the crucial subject of endpoint security and provides a solid understanding of the importance, challenges, and solutions to secure IIoT endpoints.

Chapter 5, *Securing Connectivity and Communications*, introduces the **Industrial Internet Connectivity Framework (IICF)**, and covers the breadth and depth of IIoT connectivity technologies and architectures, giving you an expert insight into their security postures.

Chapter 6, *Securing IIoT Edge, Cloud, and Apps*, explains the security technologies that are designed to protect IIoT applications, from the edge to the cloud, using real-world IoT cloud examples.

Chapter 7, *Secure Processes and Governance*, covers the critical role of the management and governance aspects of IIoT security, in order to provide some guidance to business leaders and industry players.

Chapter 8, *IIoT Security Using Emerging Technologies*, helps you to understand many emerging technologies and evaluate their relevance to securing connected industrial use cases.

Chapter 9, *Real-World Case Studies in IIoT Security*, builds on various dimensions of IIoT security discussed in this book with real-world use cases.

Chapter 10, *The Road Ahead*, summarizes the technical findings presented in this book and provides some concluding remarks and insights on what to do next.

To get the most out of this book

This book has been uniquely designed to cater to the needs of technical professionals with either an IT or operational background, and also for organizational business leaders. Chapter 3, *IIoT Identity and Access Management*, Chapter 4, *Endpoint Security and Trustworthiness*, Chapter 5, *Securing Connectivity and Communications*, and Chapter 6, *Securing IIoT Edge, Cloud, and Apps*, have advanced-level information and expect a certain degree of technical proficiency in IT technologies and a knowledge of industrial operations. The remaining chapters have been developed to provide crucial insights for IIoT practitioners with both technical and business backgrounds.

Download the color images

We also provide a PDF file that has color images of the screenshots/diagrams used in this book. You can download it here: https://www.packtpub.com/sites/default/files/downloads/PracticalIndustrialInternetofThingsSecurity_ColorImages.pdf.

Conventions used

There are a number of text conventions used throughout this book.

CodeInText: Indicates code words in text, database table names, folder names, filenames, file extensions, pathnames, dummy URLs, user input, and Twitter handles. Here is an example: "Default passwords are usually easy-to-guess phrases (such as password123), and are meant to be replaced by stronger passwords when the device has been deployed."

Bold: Indicates a new term, an important word, or words that you see on screen. For example, words in menus or dialog boxes appear in the text like this. Here is an example: "The security program for their automated fleet and **industrial automation control system (IACS)** was operationalized to protect valuable assets and ensure the safety of rig personnel."

Warnings or important notes appear like this.

Tips and tricks appear like this.

Get in touch

Feedback from our readers is always welcome.

General feedback: Email `feedback@packtpub.com` and mention the book title in the subject of your message. If you have questions about any aspect of this book, please email us at `questions@packtpub.com`.

Errata: Although we have taken every care to ensure the accuracy of our content, mistakes do happen. If you have found a mistake in this book, we would be grateful if you would report this to us. Please visit `www.packtpub.com/submit-errata`, selecting your book, clicking on the Errata Submission Form link, and entering the details.

Piracy: If you come across any illegal copies of our works in any form on the internet, we would be grateful if you would provide us with the location address or website name. Please contact us at `copyright@packtpub.com` with a link to the material.

If you are interested in becoming an author: If there is a topic that you have expertise in and you are interested in either writing or contributing to a book, please visit `authors.packtpub.com`.

Reviews

Please leave a review. Once you have read and used this book, why not leave a review on the site that you purchased it from? Potential readers can then see and use your unbiased opinion to make purchase decisions, we at Packt can understand what you think about our products, and our authors can see your feedback on their book. Thank you!

For more information about Packt, please visit `packtpub.com`.

An Unprecedented Opportunity at Stake

1

"Any sufficiently advanced technology is indistinguishable from magic."
- Arthur C. Clarke

Network connectivity has fundamentally changed the world as we know it. In the last four decades, connected computing has fueled a global economy centered around the internet and internet-based applications, and most notably the World Wide Web. It has redefined human communications and our experiences with shopping, banking, and travel. However, when this same connectivity concept extends beyond the human boundaries to otherwise dumb devices and machines, the value latent in these machine data creates unprecedented opportunities, much of which we are probably only anticipating at this point and are yet to harness completely.

The present era of smart connected machines has ushered new markets with enormous growth potential, especially with almost every industrial company being under pressure to exploit the benefits of digital intelligence. In the last five years, most industrial verticals, notably manufacturing, transportation, retail, and healthcare, have begun to embrace connected technologies at scale. These technologies collectively is known as the **Industrial Internet of Things (IIoT)**.

Securing IIoT deployments against cyber threats, however, remains a major challenge. The consequences of an IIoT security breach are much more severe than compromises of traditional IT deployments. In the case of a hack in IIoT systems, in addition to the usual IT-based fallouts such as reputation damage and financial loss, there could be loss of life and/or environmental damage. Since IIoT systems interact with the physical environment, the security paradigms of e-commerce and IT infrastructures significantly differ in the cyber-physical domains in terms of attack vectors, threat actors, and impact.

Nevertheless, while cyber-insecurity is the undeniable flip-side of connectivity, security-by-obscurity is no longer an option. The benefits of industrial data and cloud connectivity offer enormous advantages that cannot be ignored. Industries will embrace these new technologies and must therefore balance them with adequate safety and security controls.

For any connected industry use case, security is a business and moral imperative. Much research, innovation, and investment are being directed world-wide to secure connected industries. This book combines these developments to provide a comprehensive understanding of IIoT security, and will equip the reader with practical know-how and tools to tackle both its technical and business aspects. Readers will find the important concepts and techniques needed to plan, design, and build resilient IIoT systems and can benefit from the experiences of IIoT security experts on these topics.

In this chapter, we shall establish a solid foundation by discussing the following topics:

- Defining the Industrial IoT
- Industrial IoT security – a business imperative
- Cybersecurity versus cyber-physical IoT security
- Industrial "things," connectivity, and **operational technologies** (OT)
- IT and OT convergence – what it really means
- Industrial IoT deployment architecture
- Divergence in IT and OT security fundamentals
- Industrial threats, vulnerabilities, and risk factors
- Evolution of cyber-physical attacks
- Industrial IoT use cases – examining their cyber risk gap

Defining the Industrial IoT

Security is a foundational element of IIoT adoption. Before diving into the paradigms of the IIoT security framework, let's first define and fathom the expanses of IIoT.

The Internet of Things in itself is gaining a pervasive scope, resulting in the many ways that it is defined and described. The **Internet Engineering Task Force (IETF)**, states that *"in the vision of the IoT, "things" are very various such as computers, sensors, people, actuators, refrigerators, TVs, vehicles, mobile phones, clothes, food, medicines, books, etc."* (Minerva, Biru, and Rotondi 2015 (`https://www.tandfonline.com/doi/full/10.1080/23738871.2017.1366536`) Minerva, R., A. Biru, and D. Rotondi. 2015. "Towards a Definition of the Internet of Things (IoT)." IEEE Internet Initiative, Torino, Italy, 1. (Google Scholar)).

However, for the scope of our discussion in this book, we shall primarily lean on the following definition of the Internet of Things, which has been excerpted from (IEEE-IOT):

"An IoT is a network that connects uniquely identifiable "things" to the internet. The "things" have sensing/actuation and potential programmability capabilities. Through the exploitation of the unique identification and sensing, information about the "thing" can be collected and the state of the "thing" can be changed from anywhere, anytime, by anything."

(`https://iot.ieee.org/images/files/pdf/IEEE_IoT_Towards_Definition_Internet_of_Things_Revision1_27MAY15.pdf`)

This definition mentions the collection of information about the **thing** and also the possibility of changing the state of the thing from anywhere, anytime, and by anything. In other words, the connected **things** are, by design, vulnerable to harvesting and subjugation without the need for authority. This highlights the importance of security to protect IoT, a topic that will be delved deeper into in the rest of this book.

From a functional perspective, IoT is essentially an enabler to digitize and interconnect physical assets. By embedding the communication protocol stack and software logic (or smarts), otherwise dumb entities such as appliances, sensors, actuators, or any device or machinery can intelligently communicate data without any human intervention. The enormous quantity of data (rather big data) generated by things can be analyzed to gain data-driven insights and to offer value-added products and services.

Industrial IoT, Industrial Internet, and Industrie 4.0

The IIoT digitally transforms industrial and enterprise operations by adding smarts and connectivity to machines, people, and processes. IIoT converges technical advancements in multiple areas, including:

- Innovations in network connectivity (low energy wireless, edge and cloud technologies)
- Low-cost sensing and computing with machine learning
- Sensor-generated big data
- **Machine-to-machine** (**M2M**) communications
- Automation technologies those have existed in the industry for many years

IIoT is also interchangeably referred to as the **Industrial Internet**, a term originally coined by **General Electric** (**GE**). GE defines the Industrial Internet as (GE-IIoT) *"the convergence of the global industrial system with the power of advanced computing, analytics, low-cost sensing and new levels of connectivity permitted by the internet."*

GE's Industrial Internet refers to the third wave of innovation in industrial environments, the first two waves being the industrial revolution, followed by the Internet revolution, as shown in the following diagram:

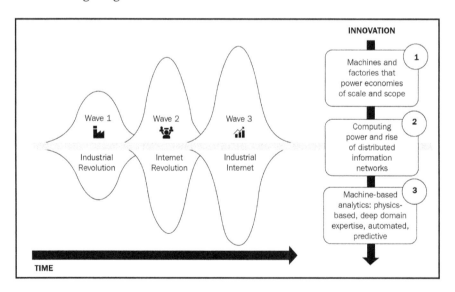

Figure 1.1: Industrial Internet—the third wave of industrial innovation; Source: Adapted from https://www.i-scoop.eu/industry-4-0/

Industrie 4.0 is a digital transformation project that was launched (`https://www.i-scoop.eu/industry-4-0/`) by Germany in 2011 and widely referenced in Europe (ISP-4IR). It refers to connected cyber-physical systems (discussed later in this chapter). The Industrial Internet concept is comparable to the fourth revolution, as illustrated in figure 1.2.

Industrie 4.0 is primarily focused on the digital transformation of manufacturing by leveraging technologies such as big data/analytics and IoT. This transformation is catalyzed by the convergence of **information technology** (**IT**) and OT, robotics, data, artificial intelligence, and manufacturing processes to realize connected factories, smart decentralized manufacturing, self-optimizing systems, and the digital supply chain in the information-driven, cyber-physical environment of the fourth industrial revolution, sometimes called 4IR (ISP-IIoT):

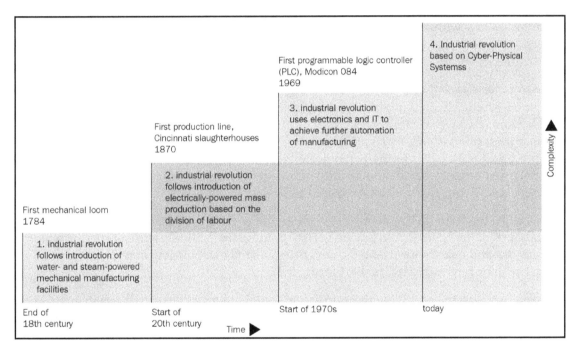

Figure 1.2: Industrie 4.0 as the fourth Industry Revolution (4IR); Source: Partially adapted from DKFI 2011 www.dfki.de

According to top analyst firms, over the next decade, the number of connected machines is estimated to be in the order of tens of billions, while through accelerated productivity growth, the global **gross domestic product** (**GDP**) is estimated to expand in double digits. Increases in efficiency, data management, productivity, and safety are the core drivers for IIoT adoption.

Interestingly, this wave of digital transformation in various industry verticals is also a key driver for safety and security technologies in order to realize reliable systems and architectures.

Consumer versus Industrial IoT

The value of sensor-embedded connected devices took a giant leap with the ubiquity of smartphones. Hand-held mobile phones morphed from being just a data and voice communication device to a versatile commodity that assists in navigation, news, weather, health, and so on. The iPhone itself boasts of a number of sensors for proximity, motion/accelerometer, ambient light, moisture, a gyroscope, a compass, and so forth. Apple watch, Fitbit, Amazon Echo, and so on have heralded a whole new era of smart, personal wearables, along with ingestible and home controls, thus opening up entirely new market segments. These home and personal devices together are most commonly understood as the Internet of Things.

However, these same principles when applied at scale—in enterprises and industries—multiply both in terms of complexity and benefits. The **Industrial Internet Consortium (IIC)** was established in March 2014 with the mission to accelerate the industrial adoption of IoT, by creating standards to "connect objects, sensors and large computing systems." This formally delineated IIoT from consumer IoT, the latter being more focused on personal and home automation gadgets and appliances, and dealing with different security postures when compared to IIoT.

In this book, the term IIoT refers to scalable internet of things architectures that are applicable to enterprises across a wide variety of industry verticals, such as energy, water, farming, oil and gas, transportation, smart cities, healthcare, building automation and so on, and will be referred to by its short form, IIoT.

In many contexts, the use of the term IIoT is limited to being a connectivity enabler, just like the internet enabled the connection of computers. However, we look at IIoT as more than connectivity. It encompasses the entire industrial value chain, which involves embedded intelligence, network connectivity, harnessing big data, machine learning/AI, the smart supply chain, and advanced analytics-driven business insights.

 Conventions such as (ISP-IIoT), (ISP-4IR), (GE-IIoT), and so on, is the reference to the Appendix I.

Industrial IoT security – a business imperative

Digital connectivity of industrial machinery and equipment (or any physical asset) with advanced IT platforms is a unique advancement that opens up unprecedented social and economic opportunities. This convergence of the physical and cyber worlds at an industrial scale translates to managing operations thousands of miles away, preventing critical machine failures through proactive detection and remediation, digitally tracking the supply chain, providing elderly care remotely, and many similar use cases.

The use cases are promising, no doubt. However, cyber threats are the bane of ubiquitous connectivity, and currently it is a major deterrent to IIoT adoption.

At the Industry of Things 2017, 62% of industrial participants cited cybersecurity and data privacy as their concern in regards to adopting IoT. The lack of standards for interoperability and interconnectivity comes next at 39% (IOT-WLD).

In traditional industrial settings, obscurity has ensured security. Air-gapping has been a prevalent security strategy for protecting sensitive industrial systems. By definition, an air-gapped system is not connected to any external network or system. Air-gapping as a strategy seems questionable in a digital era where assets are never fully immune to intrusion.

Connecting enterprise systems to boost productivity and efficiency came at a price. The Equifax cybersecurity breach in August 2017 reportedly exposed the identity of several million users, and this is just one of many instances of DDoS attacks, ransomware, fraudulent transactions, and even meddling with national administration and governance.

While the impact of enterprise cybercrimes has been mainly limited to loss in finances, brand reputation, and privacy, the impact of a security breach for mission critical assets is feared to be much more severe. For example, a breach in an airline database can expose confidential passenger records and personal data. However, by compromising an aircraft's flight control system, highly sensitive aviation data can be manipulated in real time; for example, the navigation dashboard could display the plane as traveling at a higher altitude than it actually is. A breach in an airline database is serious enough; however, loss of altitude (and safety) could have much worse consequences (WLT-ICS). A cybersecurity intrusion in a connected nuclear facility, manufacturing plant, smart energy grid, or connected hospital environment could cause massive damage in infrastructure and cost human lives.

That's why security is such an important criteria in every IIoT use case. In any IIoT deployment, security can neither be considered in isolation, nor can it be an afterthought. Processes, people, and things—the three components of any IIoT architecture—dictate its safety and security requirements. IIoT security encompasses the full solution life cycle, and this book provides security guidance across most of it. Awareness and proper cognizance of the unique security characteristics of connected industries, risk evaluation, mitigation across a product's life cycle, and "security by design" principles are central to any successful IIoT business strategy. Otherwise, costly security compromises could far outweigh the social and economic promises of IIoT.

Cybersecurity versus cyber-physical IoT security

Cybersecurity is the foster child of the internet. With the proliferation of networks and networks of networks, information (data) and intelligence (software programs and applications) stored in a given network domain became vulnerable to unauthorized access. To prevent such access and its consequences, cybersecurity and information security became an indispensable discipline. Cybersecurity can be generally defined as a technology stack of processes, protocols, and practices to protect computing systems (servers, application endpoints), data, and networks from unauthorized access, malicious attacks, and other forms of intentional and unintentional damage.

Securing the Industrial Internet can be considered as a superset of cybersecurity, since now we are talking about protecting cyber-physical systems.

What is a cyber-physical system?

A **cyber-physical system** (**CPS**) refers to any network-connected instrumentation that also interacts with the physical world. Consider the example of a thermostat that's connected to a data network. In the industrial context, a common example of a cyber-physical system is an industrial control systems or ICS. An ICS is a general term used to describe a wide variety of control systems and instrumentation that's used to control industrial processes. This ranges from small panel-mounted controller modules with few control loops to several geographically distributed controllers.

Large-scale ICS is usually deployed using **supervisory control and data acquisition (SCADA)** systems, or **distributed control systems (DCS)** and **programmable logic controllers (PLCs)**. All systems receive data from remote sensors that measure **process variables (PVs)**, compare these with desired **set points (SPs)**, and derive command functions that are used to control a process through the **final control elements (FCEs)**, such as control valves.

When a CPS is connected to an external network (let's say to a centralized cloud infrastructure), we can refer to it as a cyber-physical IoT. The following diagram is a generalization of an ICS or a cyber-physical system. The system could be controlling engine performance and acceleration in an automobile, or the temperature-based controls in a power grid:

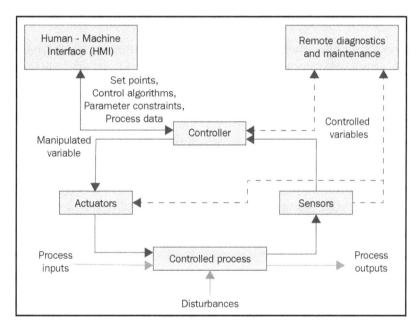

Figure 1.3: Industrial control system (ICS) functional flow diagram; Source: (NIST-800-82r2)

In the case of cybersecurity, the prime focus is to protect the data itself. Data privacy and identity protection are the top priorities. In the case of cyber-physical security, visibility into the controls is important. For example, if a temperature sensor in a power generation plant is hacked remotely, it can incorrectly output very high temperature values, which would cause the control system to shut down the entire power plant. In the reverse case, that is, if the sensor output is much lower than what it should be, the control action may result in much more dangerous consequences.

General characteristics of any CPS/ICS system include:

- Ability to interact with the physical environment over a communication channel to receive inputs (for example, temperature) and/or feedback. In this case, unlike a cyberattack, an attacker can cause damage without breaking into the system by remotely triggering a set of physical actions. These actions can be sensed, causing the CPS to exhibit unexpected behavior. This highlights the need to secure the communication channel and the end devices.
- Management and control are typically distributed.
- Uncertainty regarding readings, status, and trust.
- Involves real-time control loops with deterministic performance requirements.
- Can be geographically spread over a large area, with components in locations that lack physical security.

These characteristics render cyber-physical security more complex than cybersecurity. In CPS, due to environmental interactions, a security breach has physical safety implications.

This necessitates cyber-physical control systems being inherently resilient. A control system is characterized as resilient when it can maintain state awareness and an accepted level of steady state behavior (operational normalcy) when exposed to abnormal conditions, which include intentional and unintentional errors, malicious attacks, and disturbances (RIE-GERT).

 Barry Boehm, Axelrod, W. C., Engineering Safe and Secure Software Systems, p.61, Massachusetts, Artech House, 2013 elegantly correlated safety and security as follows (IOT-SEC): **Safety**: The system must not harm the world. **Security**: The world must not harm the system

Industrial "things," connectivity, and operational technologies

In ITU-T Y.2060, we came across the following definitions for devices and things in the context of IoT (ITU-IOT): *"Device: A piece of equipment with the mandatory capabilities of communication and the optional capabilities of sensing, actuation, data capture, data storage, and data processing. Thing: An object of the physical world (physical things) or the information world (virtual things), which is capable of being identified and integrated into communication networks."*

In the IoT context, the capability to communicate and decipher data is an intrinsic property of things. With increasing digitization and connectivity in industries, industrial "things" include a wide spectrum of equipment and devices, starting with low memory, power, and computing footprints. In addition to physical assets, things include virtual objects, too. For example, certain IoT cloud platforms uses the concept of a digital "twin", which is an exact digital replica of its physical counterpart (for example, a wind turbine), to gain greater visibility and easier access to a CPS for efficient fault detection and remediation.

Technologies and platforms that come under the umbrella of IIoT are, in a sense, laying the foundations for greater levels of process efficiency and optimization, ushering in new business models and revenue paradigms. Connectivity is an inseparable dimension of these advancements, and one of the fundamental facets of connectivity is cyber threats, however unfortunate that may sound. As standard-based connectivity technologies replace proprietary industrial protocols, threats commonly seen in IT domains, for example, malware, data exfiltration, unauthorized remote access, and so on, become increasingly applicable to industrial networks as well.

Operational technology

OT refers to the hardware and software dedicated to detect or induce changes in physical processes. OT involves technologies that are used to directly monitor and/or control physical devices such as valves, pumps, and so on. As an example, consider the computing and connectivity technologies involved in an ICS/SCADA system of a power station or a railway locomotive manufacturing facility, which monitors and controls the various physical systems and plant processes.

By adopting IoT, as industries accelerate into the future, it is important to evaluate the current industrial assets and technologies in a typical industrial deployment, and to determine practical mechanisms to transition to greater efficiencies without compromising resiliency. So, before diving deeper into the subject of IIoT security, the prevalent industrial devices, systems, and technologies are discussed in this section.

Machine-to-Machine

Though often incorrectly confused with IoT, digital M2M has existed in industries for the last two to three decades. Broadly speaking, M2M refers to any technology that enables machines to exchange information and perform actions without any human mediation. From that end, M2M is foundational to the development of IoT.

To quote from (GART-IOT) ,"*The key components of an M2M system are: Field-deployed wireless devices with embedded sensors or RFID-Wireless communication networks with complementary wireline access includes, but is not limited to cellular communication, Wi-Fi, ZigBee, WiMAX,* **wireless LAN (WLAN),** *generic* **DSL (xDSL),** *and* **fiber to the x (FTTx).**"

The cellular M2M communications industry can be traced back to when Siemens developed and launched a GSM data module called **M1** in 1995. M1 was based on the Siemens mobile phone S6, which was used for M2M industrial applications; it enabled machines to communicate over wireless networks.

In industries, telemetry was a very common use case for M2M, in addition to remote monitoring and the control of field assets.

An overview of SCADA, DCS, and PLC

SCADA is a distributed control system architecture used to control geographically dispersed assets. Distribution systems such as electrical power grids, oil and natural gas pipelines, water distribution, railway transportation, and so on heavily rely on centralized data acquisition and control. A SCADA control center monitors alarms and processes data for field sites, usually over long-distance communications networks. This information from the remote stations is used to push automated or operator-driven supervisory commands to remote field devices (which will be discussed later in this section) to control local operations such as the opening/closing of valves, breakers, collecting sensor data, and so on (NIST-800-82r2).

A DCS is functionally similar to SCADA, though it is typically used for localized control in continuous manufacturing process use cases, for example, a fuel or steam flow in a power plant, petroleum in a refinery, and distillation in a chemical plant. As DCS localizes control functions near the process plant, it is a more cost-effective, secure, and reliable option for uses cases where the control room is not geographically remote.

PLCs are extensively used in most industrial processes. PLCs are solid-state closed-loop control system components that are used in SCADA and DCS to provide operational control of discrete processes such as automobile assembly lines.

Being localized within a factory or plant, DCS and PLC communications use reliable and high-speed **local area network** (**LAN**) technologies. On the contrary, SCADA systems cover larger geographical territories, and need to account for long-distance communication challenges, delays, and data loss in remote sensor networks.

An ICS is an overarching industrial technology that usually includes SCADA, DCS, and PLC functionalities.

Industrial control system architecture

An ICS is a generic term used for all industrial systems that perform data acquisition, monitoring, and supervisory control of local and remote devices and assets. In the previous section, we talked about SCADA, DCS, and PLCs, which are the basic building blocks for centralized monitoring and control of distributed assets and operations, which are sometimes scattered over thousands of square kilometers. The following diagram shows the various functional levels of a manufacturing control system:

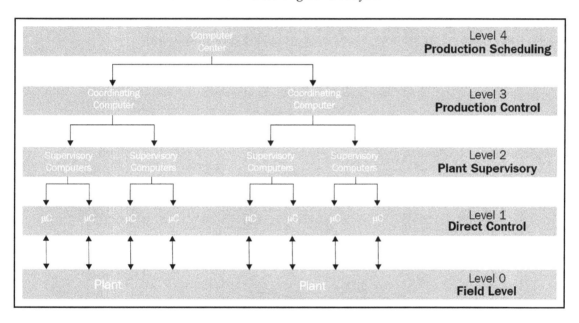

Figure 1.4: Functional levels of computerized manufacturing

From the preceding diagram, we come to know of the following:

- Field devices such as sensors and control valves in level 0
- Industrial microcontrollers and **input/output** (**I/O**) modules, which are shown in level 2
- Control room elements, including supervisory computers with consolidated process information and operator control screens, which are in level 2

- Production control, which is shown in level 3, is mainly concerned with the monitoring of production activities and assets
- Production scheduling functions are captured in level 4

Field devices are remote station control devices that can act on either automated or operator-driven supervisory commands from central control stations. These control stations generate commands, such as for opening or closing valves and breakers, collecting data from sensor systems, monitoring local environments for alarm conditions, and so on, based on information received from other remote stations (NIST-800-82r2).

These are industry-specific components that interface with digital or analog systems and expose data to the outside digital world. They provide machine to machine, human to machine, and machine to human capabilities for ICS to exchange information (real-time or near real- time), thus enabling other components of the IIoT landscape. This includes sensors, interpreters, translators, event generators, loggers, and so on.

Plant devices and equipment include sensors and actuators, control valves, and so on, which sense and act on commands from ICS.

The following diagram shows the various components of an ICS/SCADA system:

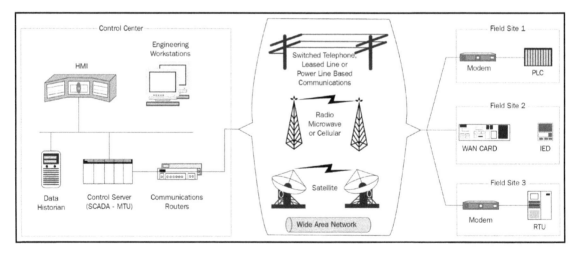

Figure 1.5: Functional components of a SCADA system; Source: (NIST-800-82r2)

ICS components and data networks

An overview of the various ICS/SCADA control components is provided here:

- **Control server**: The control server hosts supervisory control software (for DCS and PLC), which communicates with subordinate control devices over an ICS network.
- **Master terminal unit** (**MTU**): MTU or the SCADA server acts as the master in a SCADA system, while remote terminal units and PLC devices, which are located at remote field sites, act as slaves.
- **Remote telemetry unit** (**RTU**): The RTU supports data acquisition and control in SCADA remote stations. As field devices, RTUs are equipped with both wired and wireless (radio) interfaces.
- **Intelligent electronic devices** (**IED**): These are **smart** sensors/actuators containing the intelligence required to acquire data, communicate to other devices, and perform local processing and control. An IED could combine an analog input sensor, analog output, low-level control capabilities, a communication system, and program memory in one device.
- **Human-machine interface** (**HMI**): The HMI is usually stationed in centralized control rooms, and includes the software and hardware that allow human operators to monitor the state of a process under control, modify control settings, configure set points and control algorithms, and manually override automatic control operations in the event of an emergency. The HMI displays process status information and reports to supervisory personnel, who usually have internet access.
- **Data historian and IO server**: The data historian is a centralized database for logging all processed information within an ICS and supports various planning and report generation functions, while the IO server collects and buffers information from PLCs, RTUs, and IEDs.

ICS network components

Industrial control networks involve a lot of connectivity across the various levels of the control hierarchy, as shown in the following diagram:

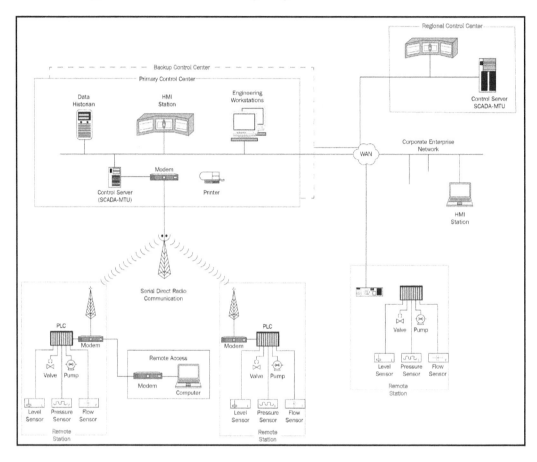

Figure 1.6: Distributed ICS/SCADA connectivity diagram; Source: (NIST-800-82r2)

Field devices and sensors usually communicate with a Fieldbus controller, which can uniquely identify them. For long-distance SCADA communications, routers are used to connect the LAN and WAN segments. Network segregation strategies are implemented using industrial firewalls. Firewalls enable fundamental network-based access control of resources on a particular network segment. Furthermore, depending on **deep packet inspection** (**DPI**) capabilities, there is the potential to get into protocol-level filtering as well. Consider an example of a firewall with DPI that is looking at Modbus traffic to manage read versus write versus read/write privileges based on the data source.

Considering the nature of OT traffic and the protocols involved, these firewalls are quite different from IT or next-gen firewalls, which we will discuss in greater depth in subsequent chapters. And yes, modems are still used to enable long-distance serial communications between MTUs and remote field devices in SCADA systems. DCS and PLCs use modems and remote access points to gain remote access to field stations for command, control, and configuration changes for operations, maintenance, and diagnostic purposes. Examples include using a **personal digital assistant** (**PDA**) to access data over a LAN through a wireless access point, and using a laptop and modem connection to remotely access an ICS system.

Fieldbus protocols

ICS networks involves deterministic, tight control loops. **Fieldbus** refers to the family of ICS networks used for real-time distributed control. These protocols are usually defined to satisfy the requirements of specific industry verticals, are proprietary, and as such have limited interoperability. Examples include the **Common Industrial Protocol** (**CIP**), Modbus (Modbus-serial, Modbus-TCP), DNP3, Profibus, Profinet, Powerlink Ethernet, OPC, EtherCAT, HTTP/FTP, GOOSE, GSSE for automated power substations (defined in the IEC 61850 standard), and so on.

Many of these protocols support both serial and Ethernet-based TCP/IP stacks, and have been in deployment since as far back as the 1960s. Many vulnerabilities exist in these protocols, and these will be examined in Chapter 5, *Securing Connectivity and Communications*.

To sum up this section, OT technologies have evolved over a very different runway than information technologies, with a life cycle that runs into decades. In industrial operations, maximizing equipment uptime is critical. So, many industrial deployments today adhere to age-old technologies, which were never designed with security and interoperability in mind. Understanding these technologies is important for planning and designing secured IIoT architectures.

Even though security technologies for OT deployments exist today, the Industrial Internet pushes the boundaries much further with state-of the-art software, firmware, and connectivity paradigms, thus calling for a major shift in mindsets. How does IIoT provide an evolutionary path for existing ICS systems? Let's discuss that now.

IT and OT convergence – what it really means

Industrial systems generate a lot of data. The introduction of the Industrial Internet and Industrie 4.0 is driving a shift in the context for this field generated data. In a manufacturing plant, for example, the data generated by a sensor can pertain to control and actuation, and it may contain telemetry and diagnostics data. The latter may not be immediately consumed by the control level devices, but this telemetry and diagnostics data can be analyzed by higher business application functions for process optimization, anomaly detection, predictive maintenance, and other value-added applications.

This compelling dimension of IIoT is a main driver for organizations to redefine and transform their existing control and information architectures.

Traditionally, industrial enterprises have kept their operational and IT domains separate. The operational dynamics of OT and IT domains have also been discreet. This has two major implications with respect to the Internet of Things:

- An IIoT solution involves connectivity and hardware-software solutions provided by a rather complex ecosystem of vendors. Some IIoT solutions such as connected cars, fleet management, and so on that involve technologies from more than one industry vertical; this calls for the greater need for system interoperability. These factors are driving OT environments to transition to open, standards-based, IT-based solutions, such as the internet protocol stack, containerized software platforms, and so on.
- The main value proposition of IIoT centers on harnessing the value of machine and sensor data to create efficient processes and services. Centralized cloud platforms performing advanced analytics are essential components of IIoT architectures. OT platforms and ICS/SCADA networks now connect to the cloud using IP-based connectivity. This ubiquitous connectivity exposes enterprises to new cyber risks and attack vectors, raising the need to securely interconnect enterprise IT and OT networks.

While legacy industrial deployments (brownfield) may continue to coexist, IIoT is also a major driver for prioritizing security and integrating security into newer architectures.

From a security standpoint, the convergence of IT and OT translates to intertwining the principles of safety and reliability from the OT environment with those of cybersecurity from the IT environment. Now is the time to drive sufficient clarity on the expanded significance of industrial security, and to make it easy for industrial end users to understand and identify security as a critical issue that needs systematic investment.

Industrial IoT deployment architecture

Although IIoT architectures have many use case-specific variations, in this section, we shall consider a basic example architecture to establish the context. Subsequent chapters present multiple IIoT reference architectures and architecture-based case studies.

Most IIoT deployments are brownfield, and involve both new and legacy technologies. In the following diagram, the main components of the architecture are:

- Sensor networks (communicating over Wi-Fi/BLE)
- A controller/aggregator
- An edge gateway connecting the industrial systems to cloud-based platforms for analytics
- Business applications used for data visualization and insights:

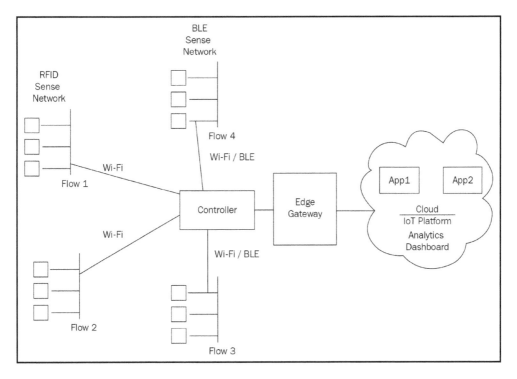

Figure 1.7: A typical IIoT deployment architecture

In this book, the terms **greenfield** and **brownfield** are used often. A greenfield refers to an IIoT use case that is developed from scratch rather than built on top of an existing deployment; the latter is referred to as a brownfield.

In the case of a brownfield deployment, as shown in the following diagram, the SCADA network is connected to the cloud via an edge gateway. Traffic needs to be securely controlled both at the ingress and at the egress of the edge device:

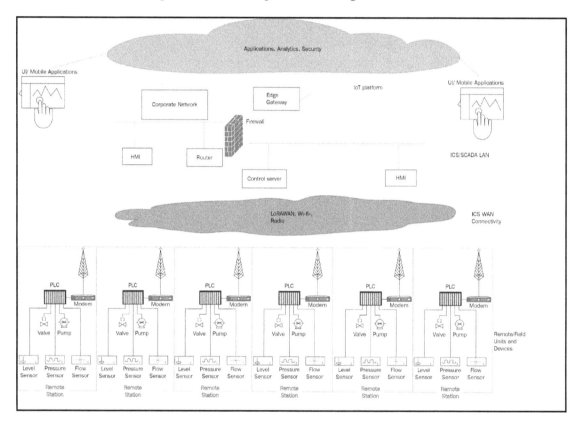

Figure 1.8: A brownfield IIoT architecture for an ICS/SCADA system

In the case of a large wind farm, several remote windmill units are controlled by the ICS/SCADA system. With the adoption of IIoT, the wind farm gets connected to a cloud-based IoT platform. Data from the wind turbines is sent up to a data center to do analytics and so on in the cloud. The turbine data has to go through an edge device, which can be a gateway, center hub, or edge controller. This edge device collects telemetry and diagnostics information from the wind farm sensors. In this edge device, a lot of protocol handshakes and translations occur, and as such, it provides a sweet spot for attackers to inject malware. The vulnerable edge device needs to be fortified with security counter measures. For example, deep inspection of packet flow to inspect both IT and OT protocols (MODBUS, TCP, and UDP) to detect anomalies is important.

Such deployments involving multiple vendors and technologies provide a favorable environment for mistakes, oversight, and misconfigurations. So, there must be enough visibility to see exactly what's happening in the OT network. In traditional OT networks, there is a serious lack of traffic visibility as compared to IT networks, in terms of traffic flows, source destination information, and so on. That's because historically, OT environments were considered immune to cyberattacks. Besides that, proprietary technologies and "security by obscurity" principles were erroneously deemed to be secure by design.

Divergence in IT and OT security fundamentals

In order to effectively comprehend the scope of IIoT security, we need to keep the divergent operational dynamics and priorities of IT and OT in perspective, and mainly those that have evolved over the past decades. This divergence impacts the approach to security as well. The adoption of standard-based IT technologies in OT environments necessitates the adoption of IT security best practices as well. However, these practices must preserve if not enhance the safety and reliability capabilities of industrial systems, and the ability to protect physical assets and processes. These distinguishing characteristics render IIOT security a considerably challenging feat that we must achieve.

Operational priorities

The following diagram illustrates a side-by-side comparison of priorities in IT and OT environments in the context of securing operations:

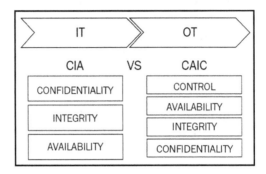

Figure 1.9: Divergent priorities of IT and OT

In the case of securing ICS and SCADA networks, the protection of the plant, people, and processes takes precedence. Industrial controls involve engineered processes (for example, the opening/closing of valves, turning energy levels higher/lower, and so on). These controls and commands must function in a deterministic fashion. Thus, although industrial controls are not technically integral to a security framework, security measures must align with industrial control requirements.

In IT networks, it may suffice to inspect network layer traffic, but to secure OT environments, industrial firewalls are expected to perform deep-packet inspection to monitor and analyze actual commands in the application layer.

The availability of OT systems and infrastructure is shown next in terms of priority. With the introduction of data-centric models and the Internet of Things, data integrity is arguably more important than availability in certain use cases.

In IT environments, data confidentiality, integrity, and system availability are the main priorities (not necessarily in any particular order, as in some use cases, system availability takes precedence over confidentiality).

Attack surface and threat actors

Attack surfaces differ considerably in IT and OT environments. IT is characterized by ever-evolving and intertwined technology stacks, which makes the attack surface rather fluid and dynamic. IT data traffic is primarily hierarchical, north-sound bound. The IT cybersecurity approach is usually threat-based, constantly plugging holes for new malware and viruses. The threat actors in IT typically target monetary gains and, as such, range from miniscule to large, organized cybercriminals.

In the case of OT, although the processes and controls are deterministic, the attack surfaces can be vast and scary. Their diverse deployments foster several avenues of intentional and unintentional cyber incidents. An attack surface in the case of OT is laterally spread, as there is not much traffic traversing north-south across the DMZ. OT cyber threats involve a completely different type of adversary. Threat actors in the case of ICS are usually not after money, and often involve nation state actors whose prime motivation is to inflict large-scale disruption in business, national, or political arenas.

The following diagram illustrates the diverse attack surfaces in a typical industrial use case:

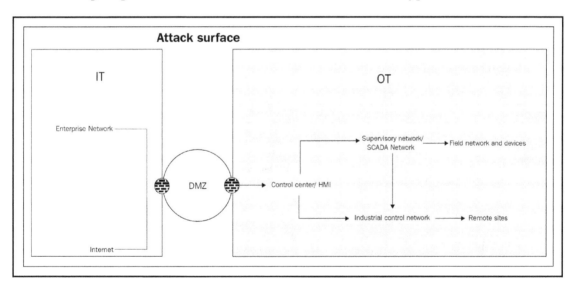

Figure 1.10: Attack surfaces in IT and OT domains

Interdependence of critical infrastructures

Industrial systems are highly interconnected and mutually dependent in complex ways, both physically and through a host of information and communications technologies. This dependency often leads to the interplay of more than one organization or business entity.

In the case of critical infrastructure, this collaborative model is often referred to as a **system of systems**. The Industrial Internet and Industrie 4.0 further enhance this concept, as IIoT solutions typically involve multiple technologies, systems, and ecosystem collaborators. A failure in any one part of the system of systems can directly or indirectly cascade into other connected systems, thereby intensifying the consequences.

Consider the example of an electric power transmission SCADA system, where a cascading failure can be initiated by disrupting the wireless communications network. In the absence of adequate monitoring and recovery capabilities, such failures could take one or more generating units offline. This event can, in turn, lead to the loss of power at a transmission substation, which could subsequently cause a major imbalance, triggering a cascading failure across the power grid. This would ultimately result in large-scale blackouts and could potentially impact dependent operations such as oil and natural gas production, refinery operations, water treatment systems, wastewater collection systems, pipeline transport systems, and so on, which rely on the grid for electric power.

The following table summarizes the divergent characteristics of IT and ICS security (in a pre-IIoT context) (NIST-800-82r2):

Category	IT system	ICS/OT technology system
Performance requirements	High throughput and typically less deterministic. Latency and jitter are acceptable in the majority of use cases.	Deterministic industrial control loops require real-time performance with low latency and jitter. Modest throughput is acceptable.
Availability requirements	Availability deficiencies (for example, reboot, power cycle) can often be tolerated, depending on the system's operational requirements.	Responses such as rebooting may not be acceptable because of process availability requirements. Availability requirements may necessitate redundant systems. Outages must be planned and scheduled days/weeks in advance. High availability requires exhaustive pre-deployment testing.

Risk management requirements	Data confidentiality and integrity is paramount. Fault tolerance is less important, and momentary downtime is not a major risk. A Major risk impact is the delaying of business operations.	Human and environmental safety are paramount, followed by protection of the processes and other physical assets. Fault tolerance is essential; even momentary downtime may not be acceptable. Major risk impacts are regulatory noncompliance, environmental impacts, loss of life, equipment, or production.
Security architecture focus	Primary focus is protecting the IT assets, and the information stored on or transmitted between these assets.	Primary focus is the protection of humans/environment and physical assets, for example, plant equipment, field devices, process controllers, supervisory servers, and so on.
Unintended consequences	Security solutions are designed around typical IT systems.	Security tools must be tested (for example, offline on a comparable ICS) to ensure that they do not compromise normal ICS operation.
Time-critical interaction	Tightly restricted access control can be implemented to the degree necessary for security.	Response to emergency interaction is critical. Access to ICS should be strictly controlled, but should not hamper or interfere with human-machine interaction.
System operation	Systems are designed for use with typical operating systems. Upgrades are straightforward with the availability of automated deployment tools.	Proprietary operating systems, often without security and upgrade capabilities. Specialized control algorithms, software, and hardware require updates to be carefully made, usually by software vendors.
Resource constraints	Systems are specified with enough resources to support the addition of third-party applications such as security solutions.	Systems are designed to support the intended industrial process and may not have enough memory and computing resources to support third-party cybersecurity solutions. Additionally, in some instances, third-party security solutions are not allowed due to vendor license and service agreements, and a loss of service support can occur if third-party applications are installed.

Communications	Standard communications protocols. These are primarily wired networks with some localized wireless capabilities. Typical IT networking practices are followed.	Many proprietary and standard communication protocols. Several types of communication media is used, which include dedicated wire and wireless (radio and satellite). Networks are often high-loss and low-speed, and complex enough to require the expertise of control engineers.
Component lifetime	Asset lifetime is in the order of 3-5 years.	Asset lifetime is in the order of 15-20 years or more.
Access to components	In most cases, components are local and easy to access.	Depending on the industry, components could be isolated, remote, and often inaccessible.
Cybersecurity expertise	IT stack-specific.	Domain-specific.
Visibility	Usually sufficient visibility into connected assets, servers, and traffic patterns using third-party cyber solutions.	Lacks visibility into assets and traffic. There may be a network connected server with traffic that can maliciously find inroads into the industrial network.
Security technologies	Off-the-shelf IT firewalls and malware scanners are designed with IT requirements in mind.	Deep packet inspection of ICS traffic and protocol-specific capabilities. Focus is more on traffic across the lateral databus rather than north/south traffic.

Table 1.1: A comparison of the security priorities in IT and ICS

In spite of these differences, it is important to note that there are areas where IT and OT security overlap and converge. According to Gartner's 80/20 rule of thumb (GART-IIoT), with the growing adoption of IT technologies in OT, 80 percent of the security issues faced by OT are almost identical to IT, while the remaining 20 percent are diverging and involve critical assets such as people, environment, and systems.

On the topic of air-gapping OT environments, here's some comprehensive guidance excerpted from GE-Wurldtech' s research paper (WLT-ICS):

"The common notion that industrial assets are immune to cyber-attacks if parts of them are isolated from the internet (or other vulnerable corporate networks) is no longer practical in a hyper-connected enterprise. Although total air-gapping of an industrial network is possible, there are several reasons why this may not be a reliable security measure for industrial enterprises. For example, Wi-Fi, Ethernet ports, and USB ports present vulnerable attack surfaces. File transfers between the company and outsiders are inevitable as a hacker can infiltrate the organization's network by installing malicious software through such file transfers. An increasing number of companies are encouraging their employees to adopt the **bring-your-own-device** *(**BYOD**) trend; however, the probability of a cyberattack through compromised personal devices is high. Even if an industrial network is completely air-gapped, it is still vulnerable to potential threats from accidental or intentional damage from its internal workforce. The only way to control this internal attack vector is by continuously monitoring the network and by implementing rigid access control mechanisms."*

To summarize this section, the differences in operational dynamics and risk patterns between ICS and IT systems necessitates careful consideration when building IIoT security strategies. To counteract these new attack vectors that have been exposed by IIoT adoption, industrial enterprises need to factor in these differences. Merely applying legacy IT security in OT may cause more problems than what it solves. Vulnerabilities and attack surfaces that are specific to the OT infrastructure need to be assessed; advanced security best practices that exist in the IT side of the house, for example, increased visibility into assets and traffic, need to be adopted. The measurement of "security success criteria" between IT and OT need to be aligned by accounting for human and environmental safety. OT-specific vulnerabilities would need to be prioritized, and existing security gaps would need to be addressed.

Industrial threats, vulnerabilities, and risk factors

As we saw in the previous section, any discussion of IIoT security needs to factor in the pillars of **information assurance (IA)**, in addition to physical safety and resiliency. In IIoT, the confidentiality and integrity of data is as relevant as the resiliency of controls and the safety of physical assets and people. In this context, let's define the pillars of IIoT security as follows:

- **Confidentiality**: Protecting sensitive information from disclosure and maintaining data privacy

- **Integrity**: Information is not modified, accidentally or purposefully, without being detected
- **Authentication**: Data is accessed by known entities, while making sure that that data belongs to a known identity or endpoint (this generally follows identification)
- **Non-repudiation**: Ensuring that an individual or system cannot later deny having performed an action
- **Availability**: Ensuring that information is available when needed

In addition to these pillars, the disciplines of resiliency and safety are defined as:

- **Resilience**: Ensuring the industrial control system maintains state awareness and an accepted level of operational normalcy in response to disturbances, including threats of an unexpected and malicious nature
- **Safety**: Ensuing in the event of an attack that the affected system does not cause injury, harm, or damage to the environment or people

In the foundation of these tenets of IIOT security, let's examine the typical threats, vulnerabilities, and risk factors that are pertinent to connected industrial systems.

Threats and threat actors

A threat can be defined as the potential of an exploit for a given system. Threat actors refers to the adversaries who trigger or inflict the exploit. In the case of an industrial system, such as a wind turbine, a threat actor could be either natural or man-made.

In the IIoT context, threats impact both the information and physical domains. The privacy and integrity of machine data—both control and payload—have the potential to be exploited. Unauthorized access and manipulation of IoT platforms, software, and firmware are also potential threats. On the other hand, IoT devices and control systems are exposed to physical reliability, resilience, and safety threats. Control system transfer functions, state estimation filters, sensing, feedback loops, and so on can also be targeted by malicious players. For example, manipulating a sensor/actuator system can cause a control valve to transmit dangerous levels of chemicals that may damage the immediate environment or interdependent system.

There is no silver bullet for industrial security, even though some brands lay claim to it. The adoption of digital technologies expose new types of attack vectors, and newer attack surfaces. A practical approach for IIoT security is to adopt a defense in depth strategy for security, wherein each defense mechanism makes it so much more formidable for the attacker.

Defense in depth (also known as the Castle Approach) is a concept found in IA, where multiple layers of security controls (defense) are placed throughout the architecture to be protected. Its intent is to provide redundancy in the event if any one security control fails or a vulnerability is exploited, the system will still be protected. These defenses can cover aspects of personnel, procedural, technical, and physical security for the duration of the system's life cycle. For any specific use case, system architects need to consider how the data flows and how to secure the data flow. Determining which data is important and needs protection within a given context is also vital.

Threat actors, in the case of IIoT systems, include:

- **Cyberattackers**: The sophistication of attacks is growing worldwide and monetary gains associated with the dark web are also on the rise. Even if no monetary gains are involved, a cyberattacker may spy, spoof, inject malicious malware, or launch a DDoS attack.
- **Bot-network operators**: These actors launch coordinated attacks to distribute phishing schemes, spam, malware leading to DDoS, or ransomware attacks.
- **Criminal and terrorist groups:** Nation state actors, international corporate spies, and organized crime organizations also pose a threat and could take control of processes, identity, and so on, and are often motivated by geopolitical interests.
- **Insiders**: Exploits from insiders can be both intentional and unintentional. While disgruntled insiders can be threat actors causing serious damage, Wi-Fi/Ethernet/USB ports/BYOD can unintentionally result in a malicious event. In fact, unintentional human errors contribute to a high percentage of incidents in enterprises.

Other threat actors include phishers, spammers, malware/spyware authors, industrial spies, and so on.

Vulnerabilities

Vulnerabilities refer to the software and hardware weaknesses that are inherent in the system and can expose the system to threats. System vulnerabilities can be the outcome of how it was designed, implemented, tested, or is operated. While vulnerabilities are unavoidable, proper assessment and proactive remediation techniques need to be employed to combat them.

Vulnerability in any part of the deployment can be subject to an exploit. Experienced cyberattackers are aware of potential vulnerabilities. This makes the attack surface complex and scary. In subsequent chapters, IIoT security strategies and countermeasures will deal with this topic in greater depth.

The following subsections contain a categorized list of common vulnerabilities that are applicable to any cyber-physical IoT security plan (NIST-800-82r2).

Policy and procedure vulnerabilities

The following is a list that gives some insight into policy and procedure vulnerabilities:

- Inadequate ICS security policy
- Lack of formal ICS security training and awareness program
- Inadequate security architecture and design
- Lack of documented security procedures that have been developed based on ICS security policy
- Absent or deficient ICS equipment implementation guidelines
- Lack of administrative mechanisms for security enforcement

Platform vulnerabilities

The following is a list that gives some insight into platform vulnerabilities:

- OS and vendor software patches may not be developed until after security vulnerabilities are found
- OS and application security patches are not maintained
- OS and application security patches are implemented without exhaustive testing
- Critical configurations are not stored or backed up
- Inadequate authentication and authorization, inadequate testing of security changes
- Inadequate physical protection (location, unauthorized access) for critical systems
- Insecure remote access on ICS components
- Lack of redundancy for critical components

Software platform vulnerabilities

The following is a list that gives some insight into software platform vulnerabilities:

- Buffer overflow and installed security policies are not enabled by default, including **Denial of Service (DoS)**, lack of password encryption, and the mishandling of undefined, poorly defined, or "illegal" conditions.
- Detection/prevention software not installed, lack of sandboxing, inadequate authentication and access control for configuration and programming software, intrusion detection/prevention software, insufficient logging, incidents not detected, and so on.

Network vulnerability

The following list explains the main considerations regarding network vulnerability:

- Vulnerable legacy protocols with insufficient security capabilities
- Weak network security architecture
- Network device configurations not stored or backed up
- Unencrypted passwords, lack of password expiration policies
- Inadequate access controls applied
- Inadequate physical protection of network equipment
- Unsecured physical ports
- Non-critical personnel have access to equipment and network connections
- Lack of redundancy for critical networks
- No security perimeter defined, firewalls not used adequately, and control networks used for non-control traffic
- Lack of integrity checking for communications

- Inadequate data protection between clients and access points:

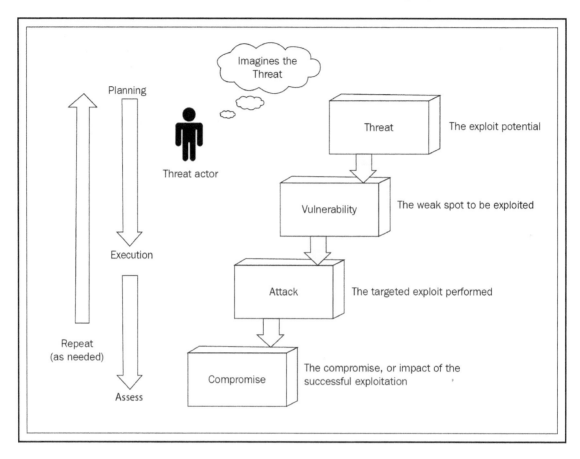

Figure 1.11: The flow sequence of threat and risk assessment; Source: Practical IoT Security Book, Packt Publishing

Risks

Risk can be defined as the probability of a successful exploit and the associated loss thereafter. While a security vulnerability is innate to a platform, risk refers to the chances of that vulnerability being exploited to cause the anticipated damage. For example, an industrial computer used to process accounting data may be running an application with known authentication and remote access control defects. If this computer is air-gapped, the risk associated with these defects is almost negligible. However, when connected to the internet, the associated risk increases by a great degree (IOT-SEC).

Risks can be managed by using threat modeling (which will be described in `Chapter 2`, *Industrial IoT Dataflow and Security Architecture*), which helps to ascertain the possible exposure, impact, and overall cost associated with an exploit. It also helps to estimate the importance of the exposure to the attackers, their skill levels to launch the attack, and so on. Risk management practices help to deploy mitigation strategies proactively.

Some examples of ICS risks that have been introduced by brownfield IoT deployments are:

- The adoption of open-standard protocols and technologies with known vulnerabilities
- The connectivity of the control systems to external networks and data centers
- Insecure and rogue connections
- Widespread availability of technical information about control systems

Evolution of cyber-physical attacks

Over the last decade, the frequency and sophistication of industrial cyberattacks have evolved remarkably.

Prior to the year 2000 and the related Y2K concerns, cyberattacks were much less frequently reported and less sophisticated, and generally involved breaking into computers by cracking the passwords. In the past decade, the attacks have become more sophisticated, involving ransomware, malware injected denial of service attacks, data spoofing, and so on. Increased coordination and the formation of botnets of up to 100,000 nodes paints a bleak picture as to what to expect in the future. Nation state actors and cyber criminals backed by major funding are in a position to exploit a nation's social, financial, and critical infrastructures.

The cybersecurity for the C-Level fact sheet (DHS-NCCIC) from the **Department of Homeland Security** (**DHS**) entreats industrial enterprise leaders to prioritize cybersecurity strategies in increasingly connected industry environments. It highlights the growing rate and sophistication of malware attacks, citing Havex and BlackEnergy as examples. Havex, which operates as a **Remote Access Trojan** (**RAT**), can inject unauthorized control commands onto ICS/SCADA devices and cause denial of service in critical infrastructures (for example, water, and energy); BlackEnergy, another Trojan-type bug, can compromise HMI software to gain access to control systems:

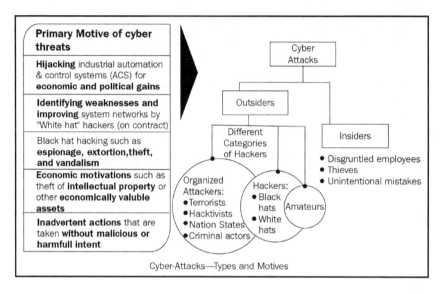

Figure 1.12: Categories of cyberattackers—types and motives; Source: Adapted from frost and sullivan (FSV-IoT)

Industrial IoT use cases – examining the cyber risk gap

Based on the discussions so far, you can probably appreciate the enormity of the opportunities the Industrial Internet presents. The unique convergence of Moore's law with mobile and cloud-based technologies is enabling several breakthroughs in predictive services, intelligent processes, efficient control, ubiquitous connectivity, newer streams of revenue, and above all better living standards.

As the network moves from the last mile to the last micron, field sensors, water irrigation pumps, and automobile engines are digitally transforming into data sources and sinks. Just as the orchestration of connectivity, analytics, and control varies across industry sectors, so does the nature of security vulnerabilities, attack surfaces, and cyber threats. In this section, cyber risk gaps are discussed for a few industry-specific IIoT use cases, which sets the IIoT security methodologies discussed in the rest of this book into perspective.

Energy and smart grids

IoT connectivity in power generation and distribution (smart grids) is an important use case that enables utility companies to communicate with their retail and enterprise consumers. This bidirectional communication enables demand-based variable energy production, as well as fuel and cost optimization (NIST-SMG). With smart metering, utility workers no longer need to physically visit consumer premises to obtain meter readings. This makes metering and billing more accurate and cost-efficient. Accuracy in tracking and reporting usage enables utility companies to gain better insights into customer energy usage profiles, which enables them to optimize usage and defer usage away from peak hours.

A power generation utility is a typical example of a system of systems, with highly distributed control systems and networks. Smart grids are, in general, implemented in a way that depends massively on TCP/IP networks, both wired and wireless.

In many power generation facilities around the globe, the cyber defense practices utilized today are often outdated. Inadequate use of risk management practices and security controls such as industrial firewalls with DPI capabilities and access control render these facilities exposed to cyber risks.

As critical infrastructures, the impact of a cyberattack in these facilities could potentially cascade onto other interdependent systems, such as water purification facilities, smart city traffic control systems, and so on. In Chapter 9, *Real-World Case Studies in IIoT Security*, the anatomy of a power grid cyberattack is discussed elaborately.

Data suggests that energy sectors are more prone to cyberattacks and more than 15% of industrial cyberattacks target the energy sector (ENER-SYMT). Stuxnet, Duqu, Shamoon, and Night Dragon are infamous security incidents that targeted the energy sector. Internet threats are one of the prime concerns in the energy sector, compounded with the ubiquity of legacy systems, which were originally designed as air-gapped systems and still remain to be fortified with security controls.

Manufacturing

In manufacturing plants, unscheduled downtime has always been the top reason for lost productivity. Critical asset failures largely contribute to these unplanned shutdowns. Finding effective ways to predict and prevent asset failures on the factory floor has always been a **hard-to-win** battle. Today, the evolving framework of IoT enables us to better manage physical assets using smart sensing, scaled connectivity, and data-driven predictability. Using the IIoT framework, manufacturing plants can deploy instrumentation across the factory processes to establish a **digital continuum**, which connects information and utilizes actionable data. Real-time analysis of this data enables early fault detection and data-driven decision making, which in turn helps minimize unplanned downtime and improve performance, and therefore increase profits.

In manufacturing, legacy technologies, inadequate cybersecurity skills among OT operators to conduct timely patches, upgrades, segmentation, perimeter-based defense, and so on pose a serious cyber risk. The interplay of multiple vendors owning the various components of an IIoT solution and the vulnerabilities in third-party systems, such as unsecured APIs, lack of permission-based access, the use of clear text, and so on, need to be carefully examined:

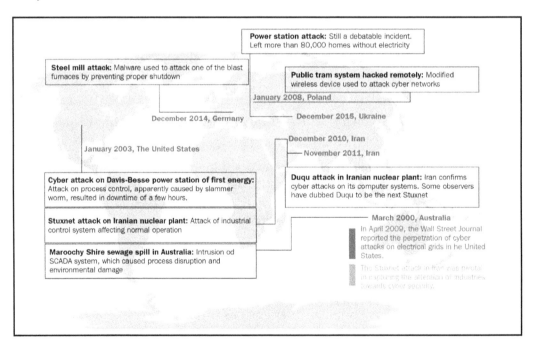

Figure 1.13: Chronology and global spread of industrial cyberattacks: Source: Frost and sullivan (FSV-IoT)

Cyberattack on industrial control systems – Stuxnet case study

In June 2010, 14 industrial sites, including a uranium-enrichment plant, were infected by a 500 KB computer worm called Stuxnet. The worm entered one of the computers through a USB stick, and feigned a trustworthy digital certificate to evade automated detection systems. It proliferated via the enterprise LAN and infected air-gapped computers, owing to its ability to be transmitted through a USB drive.

Event flow

The worm attacked in three phases:

- **Phase 1**: Targeted Microsoft Windows machines and networks.
- **Phase 2**: Checked whether the ICS was controlled by Siemens Step7, a Windows-based application used to control centrifuges in Iranian nuclear plants. If the system was not a target, Stuxnet did nothing except spy on its sensitive information.
- **Phase 3**: It attacked PLCs that controlled the centrifuges.

The Stuxnet worm was unusually smart and exploited four zero-day vulnerabilities, namely:

- **The LNK vulnerability**: LNK is a file shortcut in Microsoft Windows
- **Shared printer-spooler vulnerability**: Used to spread in shared printers in a LAN
- **Privilege escalation vulnerability**: To gain system-level privileges even in thoroughly locked down computers

After infecting the controller system, the worm would relay false feedback information to upstream controllers to evade threat detection until it was too late. The Stuxnet worm was estimated to have destroyed 984 uranium enriching centrifuges, which is estimated to have contributed to a 30% decrease in enrichment efficiency (STN-REP).

Key points

From the flow of the attack, it seemed obvious that financial gain was not the goal of this attack. The sophistication of the attack suggests the involvement of nation state actors. Although the exact motive of the attack is debatable, the worm specifically targeted the Siemens systems used in the Iranian nuclear plants. To be able to slow down the Iranian fuel enrichment program is also widely accepted as a possible motive.

Risk gap summary

The Stuxnet cyberattack amply testifies to the impact of a breach in mission-critical industrial control systems, which are widely used in power generation, manufacturing, automobiles, and so on.

A few key takeaways from this incident are as follows:

- Industrial systems can be infected, even if they are air-gapped. LAN connectivity accentuates this risk. The internet and cloud connectivity allow for much easier proliferation, thus multiplying the risk by many factors.
- Financial gain is usually not the goal of industrial attacks. Reports indicate that subverting the Iranian fuel enrichment program was the motive of Stuxnet. In any case, the role of nation state actors in industrial cyberattacks is amply showcased in this case and the impact of such breaches can potentially lead to warfare-like consequences, often dubbed the "Cyber-Pearl-Harbor."

Smart city and autonomous transportation

Driverless, autonomous vehicles taking over the city's roads is the grandest human dream of this decade. Fuel efficiency, hassle-free commuting, parking efficiencies, traffic and road safety, reduction in harmful fuel emissions, and so on are the advantages associated with the vision of autonomous vehicles. While we may have to wait some more years before we can live in this dream, internet-enabled connected vehicles and fleet management are very much a reality. Connected sensor meshs, communications using **vehicle to vehicle** (**V2V**) and **vehicle to infrastructure** (**V2I**), telemetry, AI and machine learning, cloud connectivity, and so on are the building blocks to make connected vehicles a reality. General Motor's OnStar, Ford's Sync, and Chrysler's Uconnect are some examples of early-stage connected vehicle technologies that are already in use.

Road safety, mobility, and the environment are the top priorities of the connected vehicle program that the US **Department of Transportation** (**DOT**) is driving, in partnership with state and local transportation agencies. The **National Highway Traffic Safety Administration** (**NHTSA**) estimates that connected vehicles can reduce the 5 million recorded crashes on US roads by 80% (DOT-VHC). According to DOT, surface transportation loses nearly 4 billion gallons of gas each year due to traffic congestion, which also significantly adds to the **greenhouse gases** (**GHG**) that vehicles emit. Smart traffic controls thus equate to both fuel and environmental efficiency.

Nextgen connected vehicle communication uses **dedicated short-range communications** (**DSRC**), in addition to cellular, GPS, Bluetooth, and so on, to gain 360-degree road awareness. **Forward Collision Warning** (**FSW**) doesn't depend on line-of-sight. Considering a driver's data privacy, vehicle information—heading, position, speed, and so on—are communicated using **Basic Safety Messages** (**BSM**), which eliminates any **personal identifying information** (**PII**) regarding the vehicle or the driver.

In connected vehicles, several complex technologies intricately interplay. The software and hardware often involve multiple vendors. Cloud connectivity provides inroads for black hat hackers. Vulnerabilities in an automobile's **control area network** (**CAN**) databus, use of insecure APIs in the software modules, lack of permission control for third-party applications, inadequate "security by design" practices, and penetration testing provide a wide attack surface that can very well shatter our smart transportation dreams.

By exploiting a software bug, security experts Charlie Miller and Chris Valasek demonstrated the fatal consequences of an on-the-road hack when they wirelessly sabotaged a 2014 Jeep Cherokee. The full exploit is explained in Miller and Velesek's report (`http://illmatics.com/Remote%20Car%20Hacking.pdf`)

Healthcare and pharmaceuticals

Several IoT applications are digitally transforming healthcare systems around the world. Some of the common IoT use cases are connected hospitals, where connected medical devices are simplifying critical patient monitoring instruments. In hospitals, smart medical equipment provides accurate data and reduces cluttered wiring, thus reducing human error-related accidents. Remote monitoring of patients, particularly the elderly, is also a promising use case.

Real-time tracking of medical devices and personnel (such as doctors) in large healthcare facilities is possible by using **Bluetooth low-energy** (**BLE**) and RFID. Real-time OS and high throughput data buses allow the cloud connectivity of medical equipment to optimize equipment usage, reduce cost, and improve patient care with instant reports and health analytics. In the pharmaceutical industry, robotics and biosensors are improving the quality of drug manufacturing. IoT also improves visibility into the supply chain of pharmaceuticals, ensuring improved drug quality and patient safety.

In November 2017, for the very first time, the **Food and Drug Administration** (**FDA**) approved a digital pill (FDA-MED). A digital pill is a medication that's embedded with a sensor that can tell doctors whether and when patients take their medicine. Since critical medical devices and drugs are linked to human life/death conditions, conformance to FDA regulation is a helpful safety gate. Although regulatory intervention holds the reins for healthcare digitization, connected medical devices and hospitals are a reality today. Black hat incidents in hospitals also testify to the fluid attack surfaces that have been exposed with the adoption of internet connectivity in this slow-moving sector.

May 2017 saw one of the worst cyberattacks in medical history, which crippled the UK's National Health Service with the WannaCry ransomware. Outdated software and applications, legacy systems, and inadequate cybersecurity practices pose major risks for black hat exploits. Inadequate cybersecurity awareness among hospital staff, and the lack of security disciplines such as regular patch cycles, and so on add to the risk factors. In the case of a cybersecurity breach, loss of confidential information such as a patients' medical and financial records is bad enough, but an OT cyber incident can also temper with medication and monitoring devices, which could cost human lives.

The ransomware attack on the healthcare enterprise – "WannaCry" case study

In May 2017, WannaCry ransomware spread across enterprises in 150 countries. The ransomware was combined with a Microsoft Windows **Server Message Block** (**SMB**) protocol exploit called EternalBlue (ETN-WRD). The IT infrastructure in enterprises including Telefonifa, Santander, Deutsche Bank, Fedex, and so on was infected. However, the biggest impact was seen in hospitals belonging to the UK's **National Health Service** (**NHS**), where swathes of computers were infected, forcing hospitals to turn away patients and cancel surgeries.

The EternalBlue exploit, when successfully delivered, grants admin access to every connected system in an Enterprise IT infrastructure. The vulnerability existed in legacy Miscrosoft Windows versions—Windows 7 and 8, XP, and 2003.

Cyber risk gap summary

The WannaCry cyberattack went viral quickly and proved the notion of multipliers in force in a connected business world. The impact on the UK's NHS hospitals exposed two facts:

- **The cyber risk gaps prevalent in OT environments:** The lack of a security patch that exposed the NHS's network to the WannaCry cyberattack, which had been released by Microsoft two months prior to the attack. Threats such as WannaCry highlighted the gap in organizations' priorities and understanding to apply security patches in a timely manner. Newer operating system versions integrate many security fixes over their predecessors. WannaCry affected deprecated Windows operating systems, which meant that Windows 10 escaped unscathed. Lack of enterprise-wide software and hardware upgrades and the use of outdated legacy software is often seen in industrial enterprises. This extends the attack surface in OT environments.

- **How a cyber incident can impact healthcare processes and patients:** Although there has been no reports of fatal consequences, the attack reportedly locked out numerous devices in acute care facilities (trusts), blood testing and diagnostic equipment, and MRI scanners, leading to the cancellation of thousands of appointments and operations (DIG-HLT).

 In this book many companies/vendors have been referenced as practical examples to illustrate the theoretical concepts. The author is unaffiliated and unbiased to any of these vendors. The references are only meant to provide the readers with a source to find more information on the practical implementation of the technology being discussed. The author fully acknowledges that there could be more than one vendor excelling in that technology space, but including all brands is not practically possible; nor the purpose of this book. We hope that the readers find these vendor examples as useful references to promote their understanding on the subject.

Summary

This chapter acts as a foundation to the subsequent discussion of IIoT security methodologies. This chapter presented the enormity of the opportunities that IIoT offers, and established the need for securing IIoT deployments and investments.

Many foundational concepts of industrial systems and security were laid down in this chapter. Readers now understand the unique characteristics of ICS/SCADA/DCS systems, the implications of OT and IT convergence in the context of their divergent operational paradigms, and the prevailing cyber risk gaps in some prominent industrial use cases with real-world case studies.

As we continue to build an actionable blueprint for secured IIoT deployments, Chapter 2, *Industrial IoT Dataflow and Security Architecture,* will introduce the IIoT security framework for protecting industrial data flows and architecture. Readers will also find valuable information on IIoT threat modeling, and practical disciplines to decompose and design security architectures for highly sophisticated IIoT deployments.

2
Industrial IoT Dataflow and Security Architecture

"Ensuring that the devices and systems connected to the internet are secure is a key to ensuring the safety and reliability of industrial operations."
– Dr. Richard Soley, Executive Director, Industrial Internet Consortium (IIC)

The sheer scale and complexity of IIoT demands a systematic approach to secure the system architecture. When the degree of complexity is high, decomposing the security paradigm into subdomains helps to manage and mitigate risks. This decomposition is particularly useful to use cases involving several technologies, and spanning across multiple organizational boundaries (a common scenario in IIoT).

Industrial systems last for decades. This further necessitates to plan for protecting industrial IoT systems and assets against both current and future threats.

This chapter presents in-depth insights into IIoT (big) data flows and IIoT reference architectures, and introduces the industrial internet security framework developed by the IIC. These discussions subsequently lead the reader to a simplified four-tier IIoT security model, which decomposes the essential IIoT security measures into four main layers.

But, before getting into those details, we shall present a primer on IIoT attacks, countermeasures, and threat modeling.

The main topics covered in this chapter are as follows:

- A primer on IIoT attacks, countermeasures, and threat models
- Trustworthiness of an IIoT system
- Industrial big data pipeline and architectures
- Building blocks of the industrial IoT security architecture

Primer on IIoT attacks and countermeasures

Understanding the dynamics involved in industrial IoT attacks is crucial to perform security risk analysis and mitigation. Threat modeling is commonly used as a security countermeasure, and has been discussed later in this chapter. Attack and fault trees are two methodologies useful to develop security threat models and to communicate the risk of an attack.

In the real world, most attacks are highly customized to target specific vulnerabilities in IoT products and connectivity. Many attacks target zero-day vulnerabilities. In the case of zero-day vulnerabilities, an exploit already exists and can be easily proliferated through the internet or corporate networks to create a snowball effect. Since IIoT involves significant investment and skills, most attacks involve nation state threat actors, who are motivated to create a major impact.

Some common types of attacks in the IIoT context are as follows:

- Malware-triggered ransomware
- Wired and wireless scanning and mapping attacks
- Network protocol attacks
- Infecting ICS and SCADA intelligence
- Cryptographic algorithm and key management attacks
- Spoofing and masquerading (authentication attacks)
- Unauthorized endpoint control to trigger unintended control flows
- Data corruption attacks
- Operating system and application integrity attacks
- Denial of service and service jamming
- Physical security attacks (for example, tampering or interface exposure)
- Access control attacks (privilege escalation)

More attack types can be added to this list. Today, ransomware attacks are rising steeply. In IIoT, if malware encrypts the data of any control system, it can directly trigger a physical catastrophe. For example, encrypting medical data in a hospital (refer to the WannaCry case study in Chapter 1, *An Unprecedented Opportunity at Stake*) could potentially lead to lethal consequences at scale. So, possible attacks in every deployment need to be carefully studied in order to better manage security risks.

Figure 2.1 shows the correlation of vulnerabilities, attacks, and countermeasures:

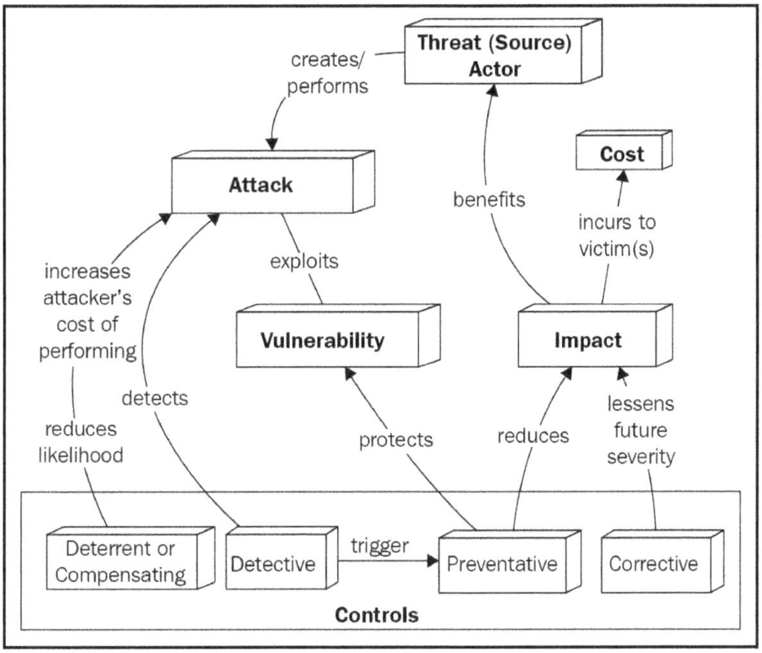

Figure 2.1: Dynamics of attacks and countermeasures; Source: Practical IoT Security, Packt Publishing

Attack surfaces and attack vectors

Industrial security risk was discussed in Chapter 1, *An Unprecedented Opportunity at Stake*. To assess the risk of an attack to a system, two commonly used terms are **attack surface** and **attack vector**. Both of these terms are closely tied to the industry the system was designed for, the specific deployment use case, and the associated business objectives.

The **attack surface** spans across the system components that can potentially contribute to an attack. For example, in a traditional ICS system connected only to the SCADA network, the attack surface includes exposure to the insider threats, physical threats, vulnerabilities in proprietary SCADA protocols, and so on. However, when an ICS system is connected to a cloud platform, vulnerabilities in the cloud technologies, for example, IP-based WAN connectivity, remote configuration, and device management, and so on. get added to the equation. To sum up, IIoT significantly expands the attack surface of industrial systems and infrastructure.

An **attack vector** includes the tools and technologies that can contribute to an attack. This too is closely tied to the industry and the technologies involved. A threat actor can utilize a variety of mechanisms to launch an attack to compromise a system. So, attack vectors for an IIoT system could be physical, or network-, software-, or supply chain-related. Examples of common cyberattack vectors are phishing campaigns, insecure wireless networks, removable media, mobile devices, malicious web components, viruses, and malware.

Given the cyber-physical nature of the risks involved in IIoT, security practitioners must factor in the physical consequences of threats, attack surfaces, and attack vectors while assessing the overall risk associated with any IIoT deployment.

OWASP IoT attack surfaces

As part of OWASP's IoT Project, a non-exhaustive list of attack surfaces has been identified for IoT systems (OWASP-IoT). The list is included here to provide a basic idea of attack surfaces for IoT systems, and it is applicable to IIoT as well and can be used in attack surface-based analysis. You also can visit the OWASP website, provided in the reference section, for further elaboration:

• Attack surface ecosystem (general)	• Third-party backend APIs
• Device memory	• Update mechanism
• Device physical interfaces	• Mobile application
• Device web interface	• Vendor backend APIs
• Device firmware	• Ecosystem communication
• Device network service	• Network traffic
• Administrative interface	• Authentication/authorization
• Local data storage	• Privacy
• Cloud web interface	• Hardware (sensors)

Attack trees

Attack trees provide a structured and hierarchical way to collect and document the potential attacks on a given organization, in order to perform threat analysis. Fundamentally, an attack tree allows us to derive the possible ways in which an asset or target could be attacked.

Attack trees have been used in a variety of industries, especially to analyze threats against tamper-resistant electronic systems, and in digital control systems in power grids. This concept can also be extended and utilized for connected industries.

As shown in *Figure 2.2*, attack trees are multi-level diagrams consisting of one root, and multiple leaf and child nodes. From the bottom up, child nodes are conditions that must be satisfied to make the direct parent node true. Following each path from the bottom up, when the root is satisfied, the attack is complete. Each node may be satisfied only by its direct child nodes:

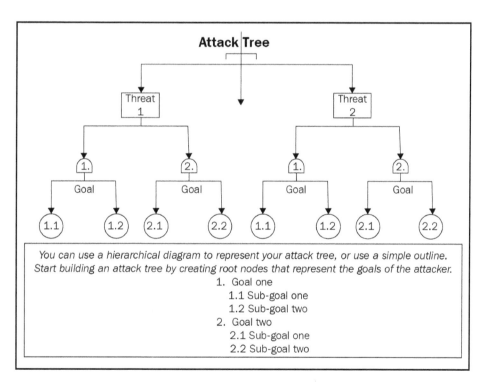

Figure 2.2: Illustration of an attack tree

Attack trees exploit the power of deduction to cover the entire spectrum of attacks and threats that exist in the wild. The deductions can be integrated with other threat models to create a transparent and direct mode of analysis of attacks and attackers.

In traditional cyber incidents, the goals could be identity theft, data exfiltration, denial of service, and so on. However, for use cases involving cyber-physical systems, the goals could involve physical catastrophe *"ranging from turning off a light bulb to turning off a human heart"* (IOT-SEC). Similarly, new threats and attack flavors for the root nodes also need to be accounted for, due to possible interactions with the physical world.

Fault tree analysis

In the case of IIoT, where attacks are cyber- physical in nature and closely correlates with safety and reliability engineering, fault tree analysis can be used as an effective tool.

IIoT systems and technologies involve a degree of complexity. As a result, a failure at the system level can be the result of faults occurring in any of the subsystems. The likelihood of failure, however, can often be reduced through improved system design. In **fault tree analysis** (**FTA**), logic diagrams are created for the overall system to map the relationship between faults, subsystems, and redundant safety design elements. *Figure 2.3* shows an example of a fault tree diagram:

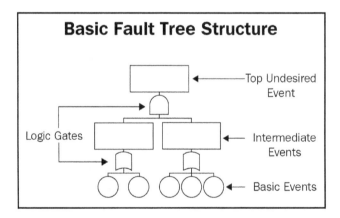

Figure 2.3: Logical structure of a fault tree

Unlike attack trees, FTA is top-down. Here, we analyze by combining a series of lower-level events (involving subsystem failures). Using Boolean logic, these events are combined to analyze an undesirable state of a system. This is also a deductive failure analysis method commonly used in safety and reliability engineering to understand how systems can fail, and hence to find ways to reduce risks of failure.

FTA was first used in the aerospace industry, where safety assurance is mandated at very high levels. For commercial aircraft, the probability of failure is 10^{-9} (one in a billion) (IOT-SEC). Nowadays, in addition to aerospace, FTA is used in many other industries such as nuclear power, chemical engineering, pharmaceuticals, energy grids, and so on. FTA is also used in software engineering, for debugging purposes, and is closely related to the cause elimination technique, used to detect bugs.

Several industry and government standards describe the FTA methodology, such as:

- NUREG–0492 for the nuclear power and aerospace industry
- SAE ARP4761 for civil aerospace
- MIL–HDBK–338 for military systems
- IEC 61025 for cross-industry usage

Threat modeling

It is not possible to eliminate threats. Threats exist regardless of the security measures employed to mitigate the risks of an attack. In real-world deployments, security measures are all about managing risks while acknowledging the existence of threats. However, unless we know the threats for a specific use case, we cannot mitigate them (OWA-TRM).

Threat modeling is a systematic technique to effectively manage and communicate risks. In threat modeling, based on a solid understanding of the architecture and implementation of a system, we identify and rate the threats according to their probability of occurrence. This allows us to mitigate risks in a prioritized order, which can be both cost-effective and efficient (MST-TRM).

Microsoft developed a threat modeling approach for applications, which can also be applied to IIoT systems. So, we shall treat IIoT threat modeling in this section according to Microsoft's approach, which involves the steps shown in *Figure 2.4*:

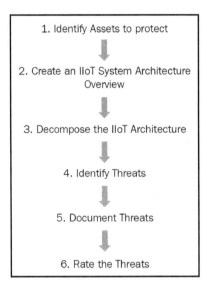

Figure 2.4: Microsoft threat modeling process applied to IIoT architecture

The steps are explained as follows:

1. **Identify assets:** Identify a list of assets that must be protected.
2. **Create an architecture overview**: Document the overall IIoT system architecture, which includes subsystems, platforms, applications, trust boundaries, control and data flows, and so on.
3. **Decompose the architecture:** Decompose this architecture into system (application, IoT endpoints) and infrastructure (communication protocols, data centers, network protocols) components. Use this to create a security profile for this specific IIoT use case with the goal to uncover vulnerabilities in the design, implementation, or deployment configuration.
4. **Identify the threats**: Based on the attack surfaces and vectors, and by using attack trees and FTA (discussed earlier in the chapter), identify the threats. Two commonly used threat identification techniques are STRIDE and DREAD (discussed in upcoming sections). Both of these techniques were developed by Microsoft, and can be used at this stage.

5. **Document the threats**: Document each threat, using a common threat template that defines a core set of attributes to capture for each threat.

6. **Rate the threats**: Rate each threat and prioritize the threats based on their impact. The rating process weighs on the probability of the threat against the damage that could result from an attack. This allows us to effectively direct investments and resources.

   Rating and ranking of threats can be done using several factors. *Figure 2.5* shows a risk-centric approach that can be applied at a high level for IIoT deployment use cases:

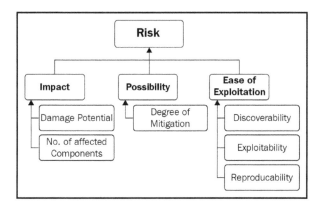

Figure 2.5: Risk-based threat ranking

STRIDE threat model

STRIDE, developed by Microsoft, is a model to identify and classify threats. The STRIDE model has also been extended to include IoT threats (MST-STR), and can be applied to IIoT use cases. The STRIDE acronym represents the following types of threat:

- **Spoofing identity**: A type of threat where a person or device uses another person's credentials, for example, login and password, certificate, and so on, to gain access to an otherwise inaccessible system. A device can use a spoofed device ID.

- **Tampering with data**: Altering the data to mount an attack. The data could be related to a device, protocol fields, unencrypted data in motion, and so on.

- **Repudiation**: When a person or a device is able to refuse to be involved in a particular transaction or event; and when it is not possible to prove otherwise. In the case of a security breach, the inability to trace it to the responsible person or device is in itself a threat.

- **Information disclosure**: Exposure of information to individuals who are not authorized to have access to it. In the IIoT context, this could mean when sensor or operational data is accessible to an adversary planning to launch an attack.
- **Denial of service**: These threats prevent legitimate users or devices from accessing server (compute) or network resources. Exploits that slow down system performance to unacceptable levels can also be considered as a form of denial of service attack.
- **Elevation of privilege**: An unprivileged user penetrates the security defenses to gain a sufficient level of trust and access privileges to compromise or damage the targeted system.

DREAD threat model

After the threats have been identified and classified, it is also important to rank and prioritize them. Higher priority threats must be addressed. The DREAD method is designed to rank the threats (MS-DREAD). Although originally developed for subsystem components (software, firmware, and so on), the DREAD concept can be utilized in threat assessment at various levels of granularity of an IIoT system.

DREAD is an acronym that represents five criteria for threat assessment:

- **Damage**: Assessing the damage that could result if the threat advances to a security attack. In the case of cyber-physical systems, the damage could be data exfiltration, environmental damage, human injury, and so on.
- **Reproducibility**: A measure of how frequently the specific threat would mature into a successful attack. An easily reproducible threat has a higher chance of being exploited.
- **Exploitability**: An assessment of the effort, monetary investment, and expertise required to launch the exploit. Threats requiring low levels of skill and experience are more exploitable than those that require highly skilled personnel and great expense to carry out. In the case of IIoT, the exploits usually involve a high degree of complexity and expertise. If an industrial threat can be remotely exploited, then it is more exploitable than an exploit requiring on-site, physical access and special credentials.
- **Affected users**: The number of users that could be affected by an attack is a measure to prioritize threats. This criteria can also be extended to include the number of devices and assets impacted by the attack.
- **Discoverability**: The likelihood a vulnerability can be taken advantage of.

In the DREAD classification scheme, threats are quantified, compared, and prioritized based on their risk value. The risk value is computed using the following formula:

Threat risk using DREAD = (Damage potential + Reproducibility + Exploitability + Affected Users + Discoverability) / 5

Trustworthiness of an IIoT system

As already noted in this book, the concept of securing cyber-physical systems is a superset of what we normally understand by cybersecurity and information security.

To properly represent the scope of IIoT security, the term **trustworthiness** is used (NIST-CPS) (IIC-IISF). A working definition of trustworthiness for CPS, according to NIST-CPS, is:

> *"Trustworthiness is the demonstrable likelihood that the system performs according to designed behavior under any set of conditions as evidenced by characteristics including, but not limited to, safety, security, privacy, reliability and resilience."*

Trustworthiness of an IIoT system is an important stakeholder expectation. To make an IIoT system trustworthy, security characteristics of both IT and OT domains must be combined (IIC-IISF). As shown in *Figure 2.6*, the key characteristics of a trustworthy IIoT system combine the elements of IT trustworthiness (privacy, security, reliability, and resilience) and OT trustworthiness (safety, reliability, security, and resilience). All references to IIoT security in this book are founded on this concept of IIoT trustworthiness:

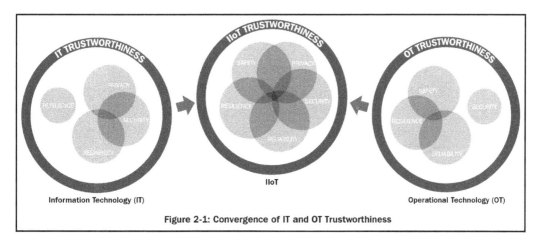

Figure 2-1: Convergence of IT and OT Trustworthiness

Figure 2.6: IIoT trustworthiness converges IT and OT trustworthiness; Source: IIC-IISF

In an organization, risks are perceived quite differently by the enterprise IT and OT teams. A balanced consideration between OT and IT is needed to ensure the trustworthiness of IIoT systems. The control and data flows, in the case of IIoT, may span across multiple intermediaries. Trust should also permeate across the system life cycle, involving various actors and functional entities, starting from hardware and software component builders, system and platform builders, and the supply chain, all the way to the operational users. Chapter 7, *Secure Processes and Governance*, further elaborates on this critical concept.

In the subsequent sections of this chapter, we shall analyze the industrial big data flows, discuss the various IIoT architectural patterns, and subsequently develop a simplified 4-tier security model as a practical foundation for IIoT trustworthiness.

Industrial big data pipeline and architectures

Data is the prime asset in the IIoT value chain. Industrial devices such as sensors, actuators, and controllers generate state and operational data. The information inherent in this industrial big data enables a variety of descriptive, prescriptive, and predictive applications and business insights. This end-to-end flow of data, from the point of ingestion, through information processing using various **extract, transform and load (ETL)** functions, applying AI and machine learning intelligence, up to the point of data visualization and business application, is collectively referred to as the industrial big data pipeline (shown in *Figure 2.7*):

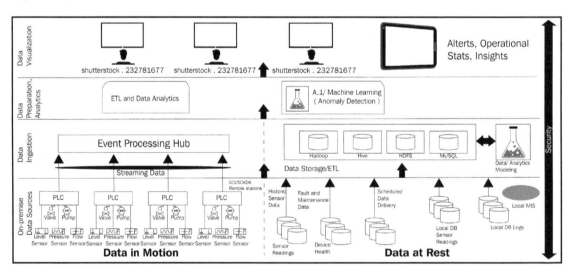

Figure 2.7: Schematic illustration of the stages in Industrial Data flows

The preceding diagram is explained as follows:

- **On-premise data sources**: On-premise data includes usage and activity data – both real-time streaming data (data in motion) and historical/batch data from various data sources. Sensors and controllers embedded in remote sites or plant floors generate big data. This data reflects sensed parameters, controller action, and feedback signal data; from which we can gain granular visibility into real systems. This raw data can be both structured and unstructured, and can be stored in data lakes for future processing or streamed for (near) real-time stream analytics. Data at rest is stored in transient or persistent data stores and includes historical sensor data, fault and maintenance data reflecting device health, and event logs. This data is sent upstream to canonical data stores in platforms, either on-premise or in the cloud, for batch processing.
- **Data ingestion**: Event processing hubs are designed to ingest high data rates and send the data for real-time analytics. In the case of batch data, canonical data stores and computing clusters such as Hadoop/HDFS, Hive, SQL, and so on perform ETL functions and may direct the data to machine learning applications.
- **Data preparation and analytics**: In this stage, feature engineering and ETL can be performed on the data to prepare it for analytics.
- **Stream analytics**: It provides real-time insights based on the sensor data, for example, the device health of a steam turbine. The data can be stored here in long-term storage for more complex, compute-intensive batch analytics. The data can be transformed for consumption by machine learning applications that can predict, for example, the remaining useful life of the steam turbine.
- **Data visualization**: Enterprise-tier applications such as **customer relationship management** (**CRM**), **enterprise resource planning** (**ERP**), and so on consume the data. **Business intelligence** (**BI**) analytics software such as Tableau, Pentaho, and so on can be used to develop data visualization applications to gain a variety of BI insights (for example, performance, remaining useful life, and so on) or create alerts and notifications based on anomalies.

The exact implementation of the big data pipeline and data flows can vary based on specific data governance and data ownership models. The end-to-end pipeline can be fully owned by the industrial organization (for example, a smart windmill) or can leverage private or public cloud infrastructures to leverage application and business domain efficiencies.

In the cases where the assets are dispersed and remote, for example, turbine engines in a wind farm and oil rigs in an oil field, data processing and computational capability may be needed at or near the assets for local analytics and control. This process is further elaborated in the subsequent sections of this chapter.

From an IIoT system trustworthiness perspective, each element of the big data pipeline needs to be designed by integrating data privacy, reliability, and confidentiality controls; and at the same time keeping in view safety, availability, and resilience implications.

Practical mechanisms to integrate security controls such as secure transport, storage and updates, security monitoring, and so on across this industrial data pipeline and data flows are discussed in the subsequent chapters.

Industrial IoT security architecture

In 2015, the IIC released the **Industrial Internet Reference Architecture** (**IIRA**) for IIoT systems (IIC-IIRA). It uses "ISO/IEC/IEEE 42010:2011 Systems and Software Engineering–Architecture Description" for architectural conventions and common practices. IIRA provides an architectural framework to analyze concerns, views, models, and so on with certain degrees of abstraction. The use of reference architectures helps to incorporate security by design. Architects can build use case-specific IIoT architectures on top of these reference architectures.

In this section, the four viewpoints of IIC's reference architecture are briefly discussed. These viewpoints simplify the understanding and decomposition of IIoT architectures. You can find an in-depth treatment of these viewpoints in (IIC-IIRA).

Business viewpoint

The business viewpoint of an IIoT architecture helps to analyze and evaluate business-oriented concerns, such as the business objectives of adopting an IIoT solution and its value, return on investment, lifecycle maintenance costs, and so on. It further identifies how the IIoT system achieves the stated objectives through its mapping to fundamental system capabilities. According to IIC:PUB:G1:V1.80:20170131:

> *"To verify that the resultant system indeed provides the desired capabilities meeting the objectives, they should be characterized by detailed quantifiable attributes such as the degree of safety, security and resilience, benchmarks to measure the success of the system, and the criteria by which the claimed system characteristics can be supported by appropriate evidence."*

Usage viewpoint

The activities and workflows involved in the usage of an IIoT system to achieve the key system and business objectives are analyzed in this viewpoint. An example workflow would be:

1. Register new device to the edge gateway
2. Register the new device in the cloud-based management platform by automatic discovery and querying of all gateways
3. Run remote test procedure appropriate for this device type and verify that values generated are within expected range and consistent with similar devices in the proximity

This analysis maps the usage elements to their functional and implementation counterparts in the overall architecture. Safety is an important trustworthiness factor of IIoT system usage—in addition to data integrity, data confidentiality, and resilience—that needs to be factored in across the usage cycle.

Functional viewpoint

The functional viewpoint provides a basic abstraction to design the important functional components of an IIoT end-to-end architecture. IIoT involves multiple mission-critical functional components with complex structures, mutual interactions, interfaces, and connectivity. These need to be properly designed to ensure safety and resilience.

IIRA decomposes this functional viewpoint into five function domains to better tackle analysis, design, and security integration. These functional domains are applicable across industry verticals. While there can be other ways to decompose function-specific use cases, the following five domains provide a starting point to conceptualize a functional architecture:

- **Control domain**: This focuses on the sensing and actuator functions. Interaction with external physical objects and the environment is the main aspect of this domain, which also deals with environmental safety, resilience, and data protection. Common examples are control units in a wind turbine or autonomous vehicle, or an ICS in an energy grid.

- **Operations domain:** In an industrial internet architecture, traditional industrial controls which are typically focused on one local physical plant, evolves to a higher level. The operations domain includes functions around provisioning, management, monitoring, and optimization across multiple plants, asset types, fleets, or customers. As an example, instead of optimizing one train, IIoT operation domain factors in data combined from multiple fleets owned by different railroads. This can optimize the rail network utilization across an entire country.

- **Information domain**: Represents a collection of functions to gather data from various domains, most significantly from the control domain. This data is then transformed, persisted, and modeled to acquire high-level intelligence about the overall system; which in turn helps us obtain data-driven insights and dynamic optimization. For example, using cost, demand, and logistics, the output of an automated production plant can be dynamically altered. Since these functions mostly belong to the IT domain, proper cybersecurity controls must be integrated in the planning and in design.

- **Application domain**: This includes functions to implement business functionalities, such as application logic and rules, APIs, dashboards, and so on.

- **Business domain**: Functions integrate the IIoT systems with traditional or new business applications such as ERP, CRM, **Product Lifecycle Management (PLM)**, **Manufacturing Execution System (MES)**, **Human Resource Management (HRM)**, asset management, service lifecycle management, billing and payment, work planning and scheduling systems, and so on.

These functional domains cross-cuts multiple system trustworthiness characteristics, as shown in *Figure 2.8*. Depending on the specific use case requirements, these functional domains can be concentrated or dispersed, both logically and physically. For example, the information domain can be provisioned either at the edge of the industrial premises (for faster processing and decisioning), or in remote data centers or with cloud service providers:

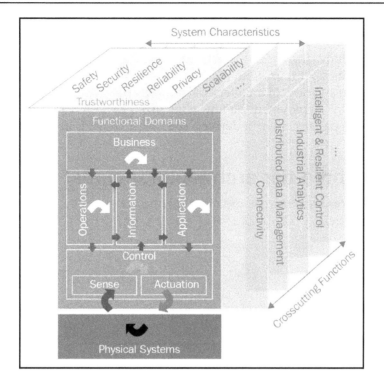

Figure 2.8: Functional domains and cross-cutting IIoT trustworthiness; Source: IIC-IIRA

Implementation viewpoint

The implementation viewpoint is the culmination of the other three viewpoints. This viewpoint needs to factor in the business objectives, such as cost and time-to-market constraints, activities related to product usage, protocols, network topologies, and so on, necessary to meet the functional characteristics.

This is also the viewpoint where security strategies such as security by design, defense in depth, and threat-based risk analysis need to be implemented.

In the next section, we shall review a few common IIoT architectures to establish a baseline understanding before we dissect the security analysis into subcomponents.

IIoT architecture patterns

IIoT deployment includes the various functional domains (control, operations, information, application, and business) discussed in the previous section. Implementation of these domains can result in a variety of architectural patterns (IIC-IIRA). By abstracting the specifics of various IIoT deployments, a few generalized patterns can be derived. We shall discuss two common patterns to help derive a security architectural model.

Pattern 1 – Three-tier architectural model

Three-tier architectures are quite common and involve connectivity, data, and control flows across the following tiers:

1. Edge tier
2. Platform tier
3. Enterprise tier

Figure 2.9 shows a three-tier IIoT architecture:

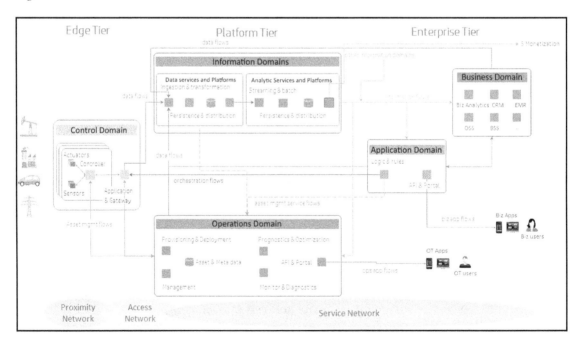

Figure 2.9: Functional domain representation in a three-tier IoT architectural pattern; Source: IIC-IIRA

The three-tier pattern combines the major components of IIoT, such as sensing and control, data processing and transformation, intelligence, communications and connectivity, and also management services and business applications. It also maps to the functional viewpoint. For example, in *Figure 2.8*, the control domain functionality is mapped in the edge tier, information and operations in the platform tier, and application and business in the enterprise tier.
This mapping can vary, depending on the implementation. For example, in some use cases, to enable intelligent edge computing, some functions related to information processing and certain application logic and rules could be implemented in or close to the edge tier.

Connectivity in the edge tier is provided by a proximity network that connects field devices, sensors, actuators, and control systems, also known as edge nodes. Connectivity can be wired or wireless. A proximity network may utilize mesh or LAN network topologies, creating one or multiple clusters, which are then connected to the edge gateway that bridges to WAN or corporate networks. Data is collected from the edge nodes at the edge tier, which can be processed locally or sent via the gateway to cloud-based platforms.

The access network connects the edge and platform tiers. The platform tier consolidates and analyzes data flows originating in the edge tier. The platform tier also forwards management and control management commands from the enterprise to the edge tier. The access network can be a corporate network or a WAN **virtual private network** (**VPN**) over the public internet, or a 3G/4G/5G cellular network.

The enterprise tier is an abstraction of management functionalities. It receives data flows that originate in the edge tier and are processed in the platform tier. This data can be used for visualization or analytics for business decisioning. Operational users in the enterprise tier can also generate control, configuration, and device management commands, which are transported downstream to the edge nodes. The platform and enterprise tiers are connected over the service network. The service network may use a VPN either over the public internet or a private network equipped with enterprise-grade security.

Pattern 2 – Layered databus architecture

A databus is a logical abstraction of connectivity that implements a common set of schemas and a common data model. In a layered databus model, each endpoint in a given layer communicates using that common set of schemas.

The layered databus architecture provides low-latency (real-time), secure, peer-to-peer data communications both within and across the logical layers of an IIoT deployment. This pattern is useful in industrial use cases where control and monitoring are distributed at various operational layers. For example, in a SCADA system in an oil rig, smart machines and controllers deployed in the remote field locations need to directly communicate control and monitoring data, which can also enable faster local analytics.

Supervisory controls, monitoring, and analytics are contained in the supervisory layer.

A separate databus can connect a series of systems for coordinated control, monitoring, and analysis at the next higher level.

In a layered architecture, the databus at various layers may have a different set of schemas or data model. To allow communication across different layers using different data models, a lower-level databus exports only a controlled set of internal data.

To match data models across different layers, databus gateways or adapters may also be used. The adapters may also separate and bridge security domains, or act as interface points for integrating legacy systems or different protocols (IIC-IISF).

The transitions between the layers may filter and reduce data. Since the scope of control and analysis increases at every layer from the bottom up, it is important to reduce the amount of data transmitted across layers to match the increase in scope, latencies, and also level of abstraction.

The data-centric publish-subscribe communication model is very common to data buses, where applications in a given layer simply "subscribe" to data they need as inputs and "publish" information they produce. This publish-subscribe communication model is effective for quickly distributing large quantities of time-critical information, especially when the delivery mechanisms are not very reliable.

Object Management Group's (OMG) data distribution service (DDS) standard utilizes this layered databus model. **Message Queuing Telemetry Transport (MQTT)** uses a broker-based publish-subscribe model. DDS and MQTT, and their security capabilities, are discussed in `Chapter 5`, *Securing Connectivity and Communications*.

In *Figure 2.10*, a representation of large SCADA systems used for oil monitoring and operation control is shown as an example implementation of the layered databus architecture:

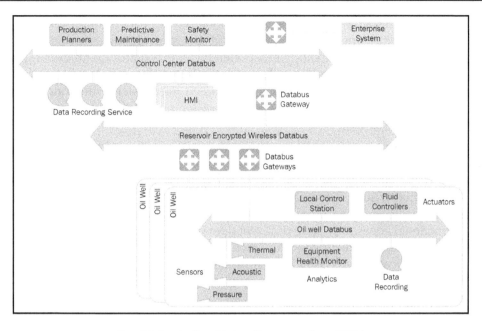

Figure 2.10: Example of layered databus architecture pattern; Source: IIC-IIRA

Building blocks of industrial IoT security architecture

For the three-tier architecture discussed in the previous section, the IIoT security architecture has to span end-to-end across the three tiers – from device endpoints at the edge, through the platform tier, and ultimately to the enterprise tier. In the case of layered databus deployments, the security framework needs to encompass the databus communication and schemas, the endpoints at each layer, and also the interlayer communication through the databus gateways. This proves the pervasive nature of IIoT security. Besides, security can't be bolted on as an afterthought, rather security risks should be evaluated early in the deployment lifecycle; and countermeasures must be built into the design. These security requirements are however, not always easy to implement in real-world industrial IoT deployments, due to some distinguishing characteristics of IIoT, as excerpted below from **IIC's Industrial Internet Security Framework (IIC-IISF)** document:

- Since IIoT involves both IT and OT, ideally security and real-time situational awareness should span IT and OT subsystems seamlessly without interfering with any operational business processes.

- Average lifespan of an industrial system is currently 19 years. Greenfield deployments using the most current and secure technologies are not always feasible. Security technology must often be wrapped around an existing set of legacy systems that are difficult to change. In both greenfield and brownfield deployments, all affected parties—manufacturers, systems integrators and equipment owner/operators—must be engaged to create a more secure and reliable IIoT system.

- As there is no single "best way" to implement security and achieve adequately secure behavior, technological building blocks should support a defense-in-depth strategy that maps logical defensive levels to security tools and techniques. Due to the highly segregated nature of industrial systems, security implementation needs to be applied in multiple contexts. Multiple sub-networks and differing functional zones may have different operating technologies and security requirements. Security tools and techniques built for IT environments may not always be well suited for OT environments.

- IIoT systems may have constrained system resources that need to meet various requirements, such as system safety and real-time execution. These factors may not allow implementing all security measures and controls to their fullest extent (as required by the defense-in-depth strategy). The security program implementation considerations should take into account all the required functional and non-functional aspects of the system behavior, including their relative priorities.

Based on the preceding distinguishing characteristics, *Figure 2.11* shows the functional building blocks for a multilayered IIoT security framework from edge to cloud proposed by (IIC-IISF). It maps to the functional viewpoint of IIC's reference architecture:

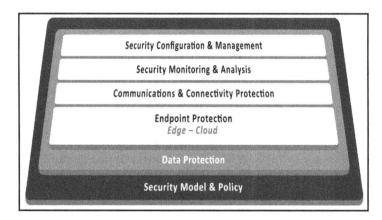

Figure 2.11: Security framework functional building blocks: Source: IIC-IISF

The functional viewpoint of the security framework is composed of six interacting building blocks. These building blocks are organized into three layers. The top layer consists of the four core security functions: endpoint protection, communications and connectivity protection, security monitoring and analysis, and security configuration management.

These four functions are supported by a data protection layer and a system-wide security model and policy layer.

A brief description of each of these layers has been excerpted from (IIC-IISF):

- **Endpoint protection**: This implements defensive capabilities on devices at the edge and in the cloud. Primary concerns include physical security functions, cyber security techniques, and an authoritative identity. Endpoint protection alone is insufficient, as the endpoints must communicate with each other, and communications may be a source of vulnerability.
- **Communications and connectivity protection**: This uses the authoritative identity capability from endpoint protection to implement authentication and authorization of the traffic.
Cryptographic techniques for integrity and confidentiality, as well as information flow control techniques, protect communications and connectivity.
Once endpoints are protected and communications secured, the system state must be preserved throughout the operational lifecycle by security monitoring and analysis, and controlled security configuration management for all components of the system.
These first four building blocks are supported by a common data protection function that extends from data at rest in the endpoints to data in motion in the communications. It also encompasses all the data gathered as part of the monitoring and analysis function and all the system configuration and management data.
- **Security model and policy**: The functional layer governs how security is implemented and the policies that ensure the confidentiality, integrity, and availability of the system throughout its lifecycle. It orchestrates how all the functional elements work together to deliver cohesive end-to-end security.

A four-tier IIoT security model

An industrial IoT system is highly complex and involves several moving parts. To simplify the security analysis and implementation, there are multiple ways we can decompose IIoT architecture into constituent components. Since most common deployment models consist of the edge, platform, and enterprise tiers, and security research and development are more aligned with the technology stacks, in this book, to facilitate security analysis, planning, and implementation, we shall dissect the overall architecture in a four-tier security model, with the following tiers:

1. Endpoints and embedded software
2. Communication and connectivity
3. Cloud platform and applications
4. Process and governance

This layering follows the unique security considerations of IIoT as discussed earlier, namely:

- Security integration needs to factor in IT and OT domain specific dynamics
- Security needs to address the industrial lifecycle (which may run into decades) and brownfield deployments (coexistence with older technologies)
- Resource constraints of industrial endpoints and their high availability requirements

This four-tier security model takes into account data protection layer functionality in the IISF (*Figure 2.11*), which encompasses data at rest, in use, and in motion. The functionalities in the top layer of the security framework map to tiers 1-3 of this four-tier security model. The security and policy layer of the security framework maps to the process and governance tier of this model:

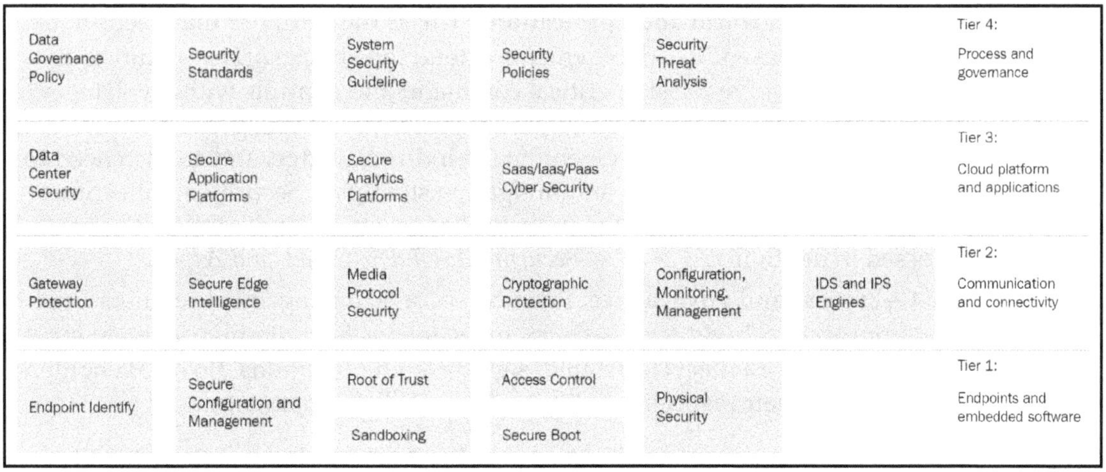

Data Governance Policy	Security Standards	System Security Guideline	Security Policies	Security Threat Analysis		Tier 4: Process and governance
Data Center Security	Secure Application Platforms	Secure Analytics Platforms	Saas/Iaas/Paas Cyber Security			Tier 3: Cloud platform and applications
Gateway Protection	Secure Edge Intelligence	Media Protocol Security	Cryptographic Protection	Configuration, Monitoring, Management	IDS and IPS Engines	Tier 2: Communication and connectivity
Endpoint Identify	Secure Configuration and Management	Root of Trust Sandboxing	Access Control Secure Boot	Physical Security		Tier 1: Endpoints and embedded software

Figure 2.12: Four-tier industrial IoT security model

The four-tier model is explained as follows:

- **Tier 1—Endpoints and embedded software**: In IIoT deployments, security must extend from the silicon to the software layers of device endpoints. IIoT endpoints range from resource-constrained field devices to enterprise-grade servers and routers with significant storage and compute capabilities. Many industrial deployments include legacy devices with insecure protocol stacks. This provides a unique environment where security must not be limited to the network perimeter, but extend up to the endpoints. Chapter 3, *IIoT Identity and Access Management*, and Chapter 4, *Endpoint Security and Trustworthiness*, discuss the challenges involved in IIoT endpoint security, and present various endpoint security methodologies and solutions, such as access and identity management, establishing root of trust and trust chains, secure boot and firmware/software upgrades, partitioning, and more.
- **Tier 2—Communications and connectivity**: This tier focuses on securing data in use and in motion through secured transport, deep packet inspection, intrusion detection and prevention, secured communication protocols, and more. In Chapter 5, *Securing Connectivity and Communications*, the challenges and solutions of securing IIoT connectivity and communication have been dealt with in depth.

- **Tier 3—Cloud platform and applications:** This is the third tier that needs to be secured. Cloud-based IIoT deployments extend the attack surface significantly. IIoT use cases involve mission-critical command and controls with low latency requirements, which presents a unique set of security challenges at this tier. Cloud platform services often extend to the industrial edge, and as such need to factor in special attack vectors and mitigation strategies. Security architectures and methodologies to protect the industrial edge, cloud, and applications are discussed in depth in Chapter 6, *Securing IIoT Edge, Cloud, and Apps*.
- **Tier 4—Process and governance**: Practical security management requires a risk-based approach to "right-size" security investments. Security management must cut across the entire lifecycle, from design through operations. IIoT stakeholders must also play their respective roles to secure IIoT deployments.

Every organization that adopts and implements industrial IoT would benefit by having policies and governance guidelines for threat prevention and risk management. This is an essential component of meeting security objectives and business goals with industrial IoT. Security standards developed by industry organizations such as NIST, IEEE, and so on, and also open industry standards, need to be evaluated and suitably adopted at the design and planning phase of any IoT deployment. In addition, use case specific security models and policies need to be developed around configuration and management, data protection, connectivity, endpoint protection, threat analysis, and so on.

Chapter 7, *Secure Processes and Governance*, provides more insights into the risk management aspects of industrial IoT. It also reviews existing standards and governance principles to develop a successful security governance model for businesses.

Summary

This chapter presented a primer of attacks, countermeasures, and threat modeling, which lays the foundation for effective risk analysis and mitigation. It also provided the readers with insights into the distinguishing characteristics of trustworthiness for IIoT systems and the functional components of the industrial big data pipeline.

IIoT systems are highly complex; this chapter presented IIoT architectural viewpoints and patterns as developed by the IIC to provide you with a crisp understanding of end-to-end IIoT system components. Based on usage, operations, and functional domains, the IIoT security architecture was decomposed into a four-tier security model, which has been further elaborated in the subsequent chapters of the book.

IIoT Identity and Access Management

3

"In spite of the size, power, and storage challenges in IIoT environments, it is critical that we build strong identities and the means to convey them."
- Dean Weber, Chief Technology Officer, Mocana

Designing a robust identity and access management framework has always been a top challenge for security professionals. In the electronic world, multiple technologies have evolved over the decades for access control, using both wired and wireless infrastructure. Access control in the industrial internet introduces a tougher set of challenges.

In the cyber-physical world, due to the direct impact on the environment, ensuring device integrity through mutual authentication is critical. It is important to ensure that the sensor or the field device is indeed what it claims to be. It is also important to ensure that the control commands to actuate downstream systems are generated by an authorized controller. Absence of human intervention in the M2M world makes access control particularly challenging. In addition, the number of such IIoT devices can easily be in the order of millions, which demands automated and reliable mechanisms for **identity and access management** (**IAM**).

The increasing shift to distributed autonomous systems, the sheer scale of IoT devices, and the increasing sophistication of cyberattacks have made IAM a crucial component of trustworthy IIoT architectures.

This chapter discusses and evaluates various access control technologies to provide the reader insights into developing a robust IAM strategy for their IIoT deployments. The following topics are discussed in this chapter:

- A primer on identity and access control
- Distinguishing aspects of industrial IoT IAM
- Identity management across IIoT device lifecycle
- Authentication and authorization frameworks for IIoT
- Trust models – PKI and digital certificates
- PKI certificate standards for IIoT
- Certificate management in IIoT deployments
- Extending OAuth 2.0 Authorization Framework for IoT access control
- IEEE 802.1x
- Identity support in messaging protocols
- Identity support in communication protocols
- Monitoring and management capabilities
- Building IAM strategy for IIoT deployment

A primer on identity and access control

One of the fundamental tenets of security is to ensure only authorized entities gain access to the information, systems, networks, and other protected assets. Identification and access control have been practiced since the early days of civilization; in the *Arabian Nights*, we come across interesting stories weaved around passcodes and message encoding schemes to protect hidden treasures. We have come a long way since then.

Access cards, biometrics, passwords, physical security keys, and so on are widely used to control access in the human world. With the advent of web and e-commerce, several new protocols and trust models have emerged. These trust models heavily rely on applied cryptography to secure transactions in the cyber world. In the last decade, we have seen wireless authentication and authorization techniques developing at a fast pace to secure enterprise mobility, particularly BYOD practices. In this chapter, we will focus on trustworthy identity and access control techniques for the cyber-physical world on the industrial scale. Before we do that, let's review the four main pillars of identity and access management, namely identification, authentication, authorization, and account management/accounting.

Figure 3.1 illustrates these pillars:

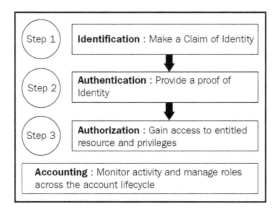

Figure 3.1: Four pillars of identity and access management

Identification

Identification is foundational to any access control system that requires entities (devices or people) to have a unique way to identify themselves to a system.

Definitions of the key terms are excerpted as follows from the Industrial Internet Security Framework (IIC-IISF):

- **Identity**: *"Identity is an inherent property of an entity that distinguishes it from other identities."*
- **Entity**: *"An item with recognizably distinct existence."*
- **Credential**: *"Evidence to support a claim of identity."*

Uniqueness is the key to a proper credential, so that the system will not confuse the entity with any other user of the system. Depending on the use case, there are a wide variety of identifiers. It can be as weak as a person's first and last name. A unique device identifier such as **media access control** (**MAC**) address is an example of a stronger credential. Some other common examples are usernames, electronic identification cards, and the IP address of a network endpoint.

To ensure an adequate level of trustworthiness, proper credentials should be created from strong cryptographic algorithms. Also, credentials must be securely used and stored. It is generally considered risky to transmit credentials without multiple layers of confidentiality and integrity controls in effect.

Authentication

Authentication validates the claim of identity using one or more authentication factors. In the information security world, these factors are classified as follows:

- **Something you know**: A secret such as a token, a password, or a passphrase
- **Something you are**: Biometric features such as fingerprints, facial geometry, or eye pattern
- **Something you have**: Physical possession of a device such as a smartphone, an email account, or an authentication token key fob

In a client-server environment, based on the use case, authentication of a client application or device can be performed by the server itself or by a separate authentication server. In the context of IIoT, we shall review some of these authentication mechanisms later in this chapter.

False acceptance rate (**FAR**) and **false rejection rate** (**FRR**) are two commonly performance measures for any authentication technology. False acceptance occurs when the system misidentifies an entity as an authorized user and grants access when it should have been denied. This causes a breach in confidentiality and integrity. In the case of false rejection, an authorized user is denied access, which impacts availability of systems and resources. Both these error rates need to be factored in when designing access management systems.

Authorization

In the authorization phase, an authenticated entity (application, device, or individual) is assigned privileges to access system resources and/or to perform various functions. Predefined access control policies are applied to the entity based on its identity, role, or group. From a confidentiality and integrity standpoint, a foundational authorization approach is the principle of least privilege, wherein the authenticated entity is assigned a minimum set of privileges (or none) to begin with. Another principle is separation of functions, wherein an entity is allowed some well-defined functions. In a server OS, containerization provides such separation.

The IAM system also allows associating policies that are role-specific or group-specific. This improves the scalability of the IAM system, where a new entity gets added to a role or group and the policies associated with the role get applied to it.

Account management

Once access is granted, the account associated with the user needs to be regularly monitored to evaluate activity logs. This is necessary to track resource usage by individual users, and also to detect malicious or erroneous activity that can impact the overall trustworthiness of the system. Account management also involves lifecycle maintenance functions such as role and group reallocation, permission updates, revocation, and deletion.

Now that we have a basic understanding of IAM principles in the cyber world, let's turn our focus to applying these mechanisms in the cyber-physical world, where the dynamics are significantly different.

Distinguishing features of IAM in IIoT

In Chapter 1, *An Unprecedented Opportunity at Stake*, we analyzed the divergent nature of IT and OT security priorities. While designing and implementing identity and access control mechanisms for IIoT systems, the unique characteristics of cyber-physical systems need to be factored in.

The protocols developed in the early days of IT—such as Telnet and TFTP—had very few security and cryptographic controls built in, as security was not a top concern back then. Besides, for IT software developers, getting "something to work" has historically been more important than integrating adequate security. So, in the IT world cybersecurity ended up being an incessant cat-and-mouse game where security is bolted on after compromises have already happened. This "patchwork" is not practical in OT domains. In fact, to satisfy the safety, reliability, and resilience standards of cyber-physical systems, bolting on security is simply not going to work.

In this section, the various distinguishing features of IIoT are presented to provide the reader with a contextual basis for implementing IAM for IIoT deployments.

Diversity of IIoT endpoints

An industrial IoT deployment includes a wide spectrum of endpoints that need to be uniquely identified and authenticated. The spectrum includes low-footprint, often battery-powered field devices such as connected sensors, oil pumps, and actuators, usually placed in remote locations. These devices interface with the physical environment and are susceptible to physical access and tampering. On the higher end of the spectrum are servers and gateways, which have high memory and processing capacities and are usually located in physically secured data center facilities.

Resource-constrained and brownfield considerations

Low-end industrial microcontrollers and IoT sensors have low memory and other resource constraints. To determine a suitable cryptographic framework for managing device identity, we must consider the memory and compute capacities of the endpoint. Asymmetric cryptography algorithms usually consume significant compute capacity, memory size, and power resources, whereas certain symmetric cryptography-based techniques are able to offer the benefits of mutual authentication with a much lower compute and power cost.

Unlike IT systems, industrial devices and equipment are designed to last for decades. As such, IIoT deployments are primarily brownfield, where identity and access controls must factor in both new and legacy systems. Even in the case of newly manufactured IoT devices, considering their extended lifespan, it is difficult to future-proof security; since security controls considered robust today may not suffice a decade from now.

Physical safety and reliability

The integrity of cyber-physical systems has direct consequences on system reliability, and also environmental and human safety. Unlike in IT infrastructures, the impact of a rogue endpoint can be catastrophic in OT settings. The data generated by a rogue sensor, or control commands from a rogue or compromised PLC, can result in serious consequences.

For greater reliability, IIoT device identity can also be integrated with an organization's existing **Physical Access Control System (PACS)** and **Logical Access Control System (LACS)** frameworks.

Autonomy and scalability

In enterprise IT networks, the endpoints (laptops, mobile devices, and so on) may be identified by a corporate credential tied to an employee (such as username and password, token, or biometrics). In the autonomous M2M world, device endpoints must be fingerprinted by means that do not require human interaction. Such identifiers include **radio-frequency identification (RFID)**, symmetric keys, X.509 certificates, or a public key burned in the silicon fuses of hardware-based root of trust.

Scalability is another key consideration, as the number of endpoints in any deployment can typically be in the order of thousands to millions. Strong password-based authentication techniques, which are prevalent in IT, may not be suitable in such cases, and we may need to explore passwordless alternatives and key-based authentication. The M2M world is not so conducive to passwords, anyway.

Event logging is a rarity

Traditional industrial devices usually do not generate log style data for reporting. In ICS and SCADA systems, maintaining history of event transactions is not the norm. The data historians maintain process history, but that's more to keep track of the controller command outputs (such as valve open/shutdown). This is not the event log style history that is needed for device visibility.

Account-related event monitoring is an integral part of IAM. Any malicious or erroneous activity or functional anomalies need to be flagged in a timely manner. This is an area that needs further innovation and hardening.

Subscription-based models

In the connected marketplace, there is a prevalence of subscription-based service models, where devices and equipment are leased and/or monitored by a different organization. Third-party organizations not only access data collected from the IoT devices, but they may also need to access the device itself. This calls for a dynamic IAM infrastructure, which can accommodate:

- Multiple organizational boundaries
- Fast access session setup and teardown with IoT devices
- Granting access at multiple levels of granularity

Consider the example of a turbine evaluator machine on lease, which generates test reports on turbine performance for a fixed number of cycles. To publish the test reports online, this evaluator needs to set up a secure communication channel from the lessee organization to its owning firm. This channel needs to allow only restricted access, which can make access control policies quite complicated for such deployments (IOT-SEC).

Increasing sophistication of identity attacks

IT departments in the financial industry are challenged by user-identity-related attacks, which are on a steady rise. According to a study (JSRS), in the year 2016, the financial losses in the USA alone had climbed to 16 billion USD. In the IIoT context, however, the goal of identity-based attacks is not always money. Well-funded nation state threat actors are involved to design and launch attacks to cause a long-term impact on corporate branding, or even cause a municipal or national crisis. Cyberattacks are usually coordinated; if one system fails, the impact cascades to other interconnected systems. An attack may compromise both the primary and backup systems. These days IoT botnets, involving millions of compromised IoT devices, are regularly used to inject malware and launch DDoS and ransomware attacks.

Sufficient funding and sophisticated techniques to leverage exploits and zero-day vulnerabilities make industries more susceptible to identity attacks, and security architects must factor this into their IAM strategy.

Since industrial systems are characterized by a long lifespan, what is safe today may not be safe 5 or 10 years from now. It is hard to improvise security during operations. Unlike IT, in OT environments patching is typically not a practical option, nor is device downtime or replacement. Safety tools—such as crypto algorithms RSA, AES, and ECC—also need updating as new attack types are exposed. So, IIoT stakeholders need to assess their current risks and project them out by 10-15 years, and plan for security by factoring in safety, reliability, and cost-effectiveness.

Risk-based access control policy

Identity and access control can be costly. That's why it is important to align IAM strategy with the level of risk by assessing and prioritizing the threats. It's important to remember that threat actors in industrial incidents have larger motives and funds. So, the risk of an identity breach in a small-scale smart wind farm can be much lower than that of a smart city energy grid.

IIoT deployment architecture often decides the boundary of edge premises and the cloud. In the case of using public data centers and cloud providers such as AWS and Microsoft Azure, the cloud provider might already have a shared security model, where managing identity and access control is partially taken care of. Evaluating the IAM implementation of the connectivity and cloud provider can help create a well-aligned IAM strategy that can be cost-effective and practical. This topic is discussed further in `Chapter 6`, *Securing IIoT Edge, Cloud, and Apps.*

Identity management across the device lifecycle

In IIoT identity management, the two important challenges are:

1. How to ensure digital uniqueness of devices
2. How to maintain digital uniqueness at the scale of millions (or forecasted billions) of deployed devices

In IT domains, the most common way to get an identity is to assign a unique username to an account, usually associated with a human user. Even in BYOD, the identity of mobile devices, such as tablets and smartphones, is tied to the owner's account, and they must be an authorized user of the corporate resources. The scale here is about two or three mobile devices per user. In a highly scaled IIoT use case involving millions of devices, to provision individual usernames would be anything but practical. Besides, IIoT devices typically don't have "users".

This requires the use of other forms of unique device identifiers. In addition to uniqueness, the more intrinsically the identifier correlates to the device, the better the scalability and reliability will be. Some unique identifier options are as follows.

UUID and ESNs: RFC 4122 defines a globally unique device namespace convention, known as a **universally unique identifier** (**UUID**), also known as a **globally unique identifier** (**GUID**). UUIDs are 128 bits in length, do not require any centralized authority to administer them, and are aligned with ISO/IEC 9834-8. UUIDs are unique and persistent; their generation algorithm supports very high allocation rates of up to 10 million per second per machine if necessary (RFC-4122).

Another option for *contextually unique* identifiers is **electronic serial numbers** (**ESNs**). A device manufacturing organization can also define their own device naming namespace, which can augment UUIDs and ESNs.

Unique device naming can also be achieved by combining multiple defining attributes for a device, such as manufacturer, serial number, type, deployment date, location, and so on. However, this may be less scalable from a provisioning standpoint. Even on a low scale, this presents a painful experience to maintain over time.

In the highly matrixed IIoT ecosystem, there are also a number of emerging identity vendors, who provide identity-as-a-service, where subscription-based randomly generated device identifier keys are made available.

IIoT deployments are predominantly brownfield, which means older machines and devices that are not individually upgradable to connect to the cloud will continue to coexist with newly manufactured IoT devices. Identity gateways need to be used to manage the identity for the older devices.

Now, let's evaluate some of the authentication and authorization techniques that have already been tried in enterprise IT networks.

Authentication and authorization frameworks for IIoT

While evaluating the practical applicability of IT-based authentication and authorization techniques for IIoT use cases, it is important that we keep in perspective the unique demands of the cyber-physical world (discussed in the *Distinguishing features of IAM for IIoT* section).

 Note: This section and all subsequent sections of this chapter assume that the reader has a basic familiarity with modern cryptography.

Figure 3.2 summarizes the three main approaches of authentication:

Know	Are	Have
Passwords	Fingerprint	Smart Card/Phone
Secrets	Eye Pattern	Token Generator
Private Information	Signature	Digital Keys
	Physical Coordinates	Email Account

Figure 3.2: Examples of authentication factors

Password-based authentication

Password-based authentication is the most widely used proof of identity for people to interact with a device or a system. It belongs to the "something I know" bucket as shown in *Figure 3.2*, and allows managing multiple levels of account privileges. In addition to the client-server applications, passwords are also used as secrets for securing access to operating system resources.

Many consumer and industrial IoT products manufactured today have factory default passwords. Default passwords are usually easy-to-guess phrases (such as `password123`), and are meant to be replaced by stronger passwords when the device has been deployed. Historically, these default passwords have often given the device owners/administrators a false sense of security, meaning they fail to replace the factory default password.

Most security breaches where comprised IoT devices are used as attack vectors trace back to default password exploits. Some security experts are of the opinion that, from a security perspective, it may serve the world well if manufacturers discontinue the practice of providing default passwords, thereby mandating that administrators provision new passwords.

Some of the IoT messaging and communication protocols have built-in support for password-based authentication. MQTT, a publish/subscribe messaging protocol designed mainly for scalable IoT infrastructures, has username/password fields in its CONNECT message (OASIS-OPEN). MQTT handles these fields in plaintext, so, for ensuring cryptographic security, TLS needs to be used in conjunction.

However, password-based authentication was never designed for the M2M world and, as such, this method presents multiple challenges for IIoT deployments. Some of the concerns are as follows:

- **Scalability**: Provisioning and managing usernames and passwords for a very large number of devices is a practical hurdle—both in terms of effort and accuracy.
- **Managing passwords**: It is hard to automate the initial deployment and periodic password updates in highly scaled use cases.
- **Secured storage**: Securely storing the passwords as secrets in the device is not easy and provides a backdoor for intrusion.
- **Defaulter syndrome:** When the barriers are high, operators rely on default options and do not bother to override the factory default passwords. However, the rise of IoT botnets proves the bad consequences of using default passwords.

In some small-scale and less vulnerable deployments, password-based authentication may still be applicable. If used, the following precautions are recommended:

- Implement password rotation policies in 30 or 40-day cycles for each device. Consider augmenting these policies with an alert mechanism that automatically prompts administrators when password updates for a group of devices are due.
- Establish event logging to monitor device account activity.
- Create privileged accounts to support administrative access to IoT devices.
- Segregate the password-protected IoT devices onto less trusted networks.
- Create a policy that disallows default passwords and enforces password strength requirements.
- Ensure password encryption is implemented in the transport layer.

Biometrics

The use of biometrics as an authentication factor is getting increasingly common. Biometrics not only provide the convenience of password-less authentication, but can also be used as a second factor in multi-factor authentication schemes. Fingerprints, facial geometry, voiceprints, and so on are various unique attributes used in biometrics-based authentication. It is true that biometrics comes into play in human-to-machine interfaces, for example, to authenticate an operator who accesses machines and resources. Consider the example of the transportation sector, where a field technician wants to repair a piece of **roadside equipment** (**RSE**). The technician can use voiceprints to access the device through a cloud connection to the backend authentication server (IOT-SEC).

So, in industrial IoT IAM strategies, biometrics are to be considered in conjunction with other schemes used for device authentication.

Biometric authentication involves a centralized biometric server that stores biometric data associated with various users. This database is used by the biometric authenticator. Having a centralized authentication has the vulnerability of being the single point of failure in the case of a malicious attack that targets this sensitive biometric data.

Biometric security companies such as Hypr (`www.hypr.com`) are promoting the concept of decentralized biometric tokenization. In a decentralized architecture, no two persons' biometric data is stored on the same server. Biometric tokenization allows the biometric data to be translated into a random token for safe storage on a user's mobile device. A cryptographic challenge-response function allows an action-specific or timestamped verifier to be drawn from the biometrics and sent via the cloud or local server to activate the login, vehicle start, or any other function the mobile app is designed to perform. The blockchain technology (discussed in `Chapter 8`, *IIoT Security Using Emerging Technologies*) is also increasingly being considered to develop decentralized biometrics solutions.

Biometrics-based security, also known as Bio-T, is finding faster adoption in the consumer IoT use case, which includes keyless home and automotive access, biometric locks, and so on. The FIDO alliance (`www.fidoalliance.org`) has developed the open standards that define the use of biometrics-based authentication.

Multi-factor authentication

At the beginning of this section, in *Figure 3.2*, three common authentication factors were shown. Authentication using any one of these factors is no doubt useful, but single-factor authentication has the vulnerabilities associated with the corresponding authentication factor it uses. For example, an attacker can compromise a password by launching a dictionary attack. However, if the authentication process requires two different authentication factors, such as a password and a smart-card-generated one-time token, the chances of a breach are drastically decreased. This illustrates the value of implementing multi-factor or two-factor authentication.

Multi-factor authentication is widely used in client-server sessions, and is also recommended for edge to cloud communications. IoT cloud providers such as AWS and Microsoft Azure use multi-factor authentication (primarily in human to machine use cases).

Key-based authentication

Key-based authentication is a fully automated authentication technique wherein encryption keys are used as secrets. This method heavily relies on cryptographic algorithms. Before we discuss key-based authentication, some of the key cryptography concepts are presented for completeness.

Cryptography utilizes encryption algorithms to perform two basic operations:

1. **Encryption**: Converts information from its plaintext form into an encrypted version, known as ciphertext, using encryption keys
2. **Decryption**: Performs the reverse transformation, to transform the encrypted ciphertext back into plaintext format

One of the challenges in choosing the right encryption algorithm is in determining the length of the key or key pair used for encryption and decryption without compromising key strength (in terms of resilience). Longer keys ensure greater security, as shown in the following graph:

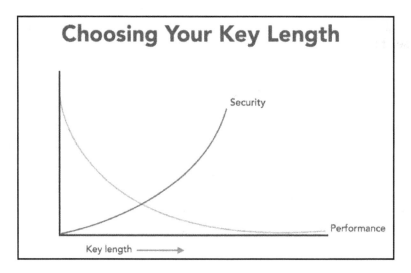

Figure 3.3: Inverse correlation between security strength and performance using keys

But this benefit comes at the expense of performance; longer keys involve greater resource consumption. In resource-constrained environments, this is a major consideration. Based on the security goals of a specific use case, it is recommended to determine the cost per key (cost/key) of the encryption algorithm in addition to its encryption/decryption speed, memory, CPU, and power usage.

Another point to consider is the type of cryptography to implement. Depending on the usage of keys and key exchange mechanism, there are two main categories of key-based authentication, as discussed in the following sections.

Symmetric keys

In symmetric key cryptography, the sender and receiver share a common secret to encrypt and decrypt messages. Unlike a password, in symmetric-key-based authentication, keys are not required to be sent between the parties at the time of the authentication event. The keys are usually established before a session is initiated using a public key algorithm. The key is sent either out-of-band, or ahead of time to the devices, encrypted using **key encryption keys (KEK)**. *Figure 3.4* shows the workflow involved in symmetric-key-based cryptography:

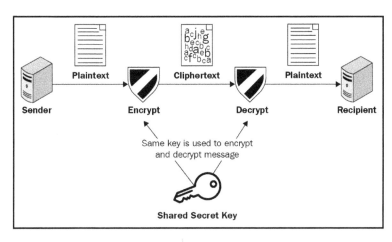

Figure 3.4: Event flow in Symmetric key cryptography

There are multiple symmetric encryption algorithms that use block or stream ciphers. The **Advanced Encryption Standard (AES)**, considered a secured algorithm, is commonly used and offers 128, 192, and 256-bit keys. Blowfish and Twofish are also block cipher symmetric algorithms. RC2 is a stream-cipher-based symmetric key algorithm used in network communications. Wi-Fi, WEP, and TLS standards allow the use of RC2.

The benefits of symmetric key encryption depend on the specific implementation. The following are some of the generic benefits touted by symmetric key solution vendors:

- Simpler to provision and revoke
- Easier to protect while being use
- Faster speed of execution
- Lower power, memory, and CPU usage (compared to RSA and ECC)
- Lower cost/key

A drawback of the symmetric-key-based approach is that the number of keys increases exponentially with the number of parties involved, as shown in the following figure:

Group Size	Symmetric Keys
2	1
3	3
10	45
100	4950
1,000	499,500
10,000	49,995,000

Figure 3.5: The number of keys increases exponentially with the number of parties in a group

Asymmetric keys

Asymmetric cryptography, also known as public key cryptography, solves the scalability problem of symmetric cryptography by issuing a pair of keys—one private and one public—to each participant. As shown in the following figure, in public key cryptography, a key pair is used, one of which is published, the other of which is used by the receiver as a secret and used only for decryption. The robustness of the public key-based approach depends on the degree of computational difficulty in deriving the private key using the public key:

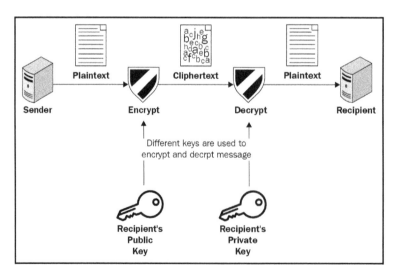

Figure 3.6: Asymmetric key exchange between two parties

One of the common asymmetric key algorithms in use today is RSA, where a key pair (one public and one private) is generated to initiate communication. RSA utilizes two very large randomly generated prime numbers to calculate the key pair, and uses variable length keys ranging between 1,024 and 4,096 bits. As long as the private key is kept secure, decrypting the message is very unlikely.

Elliptic curve cryptography (**ECC**) is another asymmetric algorithm. Instead of the prime factorization problem, it uses the elliptic curve discrete logarithm problem. ECC is more resource-efficient and hence more applicable to resource-constrained edge devices.

All public key, or asymmetric cryptography is based upon the difficulty of solving complex mathematical problems. In the case of the RSA algorithm, the security of the algorithm depends upon the difficulty of factoring the product of two large prime numbers. For the same reason, they provide higher confidentiality of the encrypted message. Also, non-repudiation is possible only with asymmetric cryptography, as discussed in the section on trust models. These benefits, however, come at the cost of slower speed and intensive use of power and computational resources.

Zero-knowledge keys

In IEEE P1363.2, the term **zero-knowledge password proof** (**ZKPP**) is used to explain the concept wherein party-1 (the prover) proves to party-2 (the verifier) that it knows a value of a password, without revealing the password itself to the verifier. This scheme is mainly designed to protect against dictionary attacks. The concept of zero-knowledge keys is similar, but not limited to passwords only.

The concept of proving the knowledge of an assertion without revealing any information about the assertion itself offers benefits over existing options such as shared key and public key cryptography.

In shared key cryptography, two parties agree on a common secret before they begin any communication. As we discussed in the *Password-based authentication* section, this approach is vulnerable to eavesdropping, spoofing, and dictionary attacks. In public key cryptography, a key pair is used, one of which is published and the other is used by the receiver as a secret and used only for decryption. The robustness of the public key approach depends on the degree of computational difficulty of deriving the private key using the public key.

In zero-knowledge cryptography, the prover is able to prove its knowledge of the secret to the authenticator without having to reveal the secret itself at any time during the operations. The authenticator can ask questions to confirm the prover indeed knows the secret, but it is impossible for the authenticator or any third party to discover information about the secret. As long as the authentication messages are handled securely, an eavesdropper is not able to learn anything about the secret or convince any party that they know the secret. A good zero-knowledge-based protocol should also be resilient against a malicious man-in-the middle who might try send, modify, or destroy the message (SANS-1).

Scalability and cryptographic resilience of zero-knowledge keys make them relevant in IIoT IAM considerations. This approach is particularly attractive in proving mutual identity, or during the key-exchange step of a cryptographic application.

Some IIoT identity vendors are already using zero-knowledge key-based authentication services, wherein an IoT device uses the zero-knowledge key as proof of identity, without knowing the actual value of the key.

While using zero-knowledge key-based authentication, it is recommended to evaluate the complexity of the infrastructure matrix providing the service, resource requirements, ease of maintenance, and cost-effectiveness.

Certificate-based authentication

Certificate-based authentication goes a step further. It uses the public key cryptography framework, where the public key is signed by a trusted **certificate authority** (**CA**). The CA uses its private key to sign the requester's public key. This gives the remote endpoint assurance that the originating endpoint has the private key and also serves as the proof of identity. Certificate-based authentication may be used for mutual authentication of server-to-server or device-to-server connections.

From automation and scalability standpoints, public-key-based digital certificates are a promising authentication method in IIoT use cases. Considering the resource-intensive nature of certificate-based authentication, in resource-constrained environments, using this technique can be particularly challenging. However, with industry efforts focused to overcome these challenges, we can expect improvements. Certificate-based authentication provides non-repudiation, and will be elaborated on further when we discuss digital certificates.

Trust models – public key infrastructures and digital certificates

Public key infrastructures (**PKI**) are designed to provision public key certificates to devices and applications. PKI is designed to work exclusively with asymmetric cryptography, and relies upon the trust that the participants have in highly trusted centralized service providers. These providers, known as CA, serve as the root of trust, verify the identity of participants, and issue public key digital certificates.

In the web-based economy, PKI has been providing verifiable roots while conforming to a wide variety of architectures, and finding applicability in IIoT architectures as well. In some architectures, the end entity, which can be an IoT device, may be directly interfacing with the CA. In other cases, there may be deep trust chains, with many levels between the end entity and the root CA.

In the case of endpoints in an IIoT architecture, the devices are not inherently trustworthy. Besides, the main value proposition of IIoT centers on deriving insights from this device-generated data. This makes the trustworthiness of IoT endpoints all the more important.

PKI as a trust model is applicable to IIoT use cases, as it can build on the standards that already exist in the internet-based world. To provide an IoT device with a cryptographically strong identity, a trusted PKI CA or trust anchor can be used to verify the identity, and in some cases the trust level, of the device. To assert an identity, a digital certificate can be used to sign messages in an application, or to sign data as part of an authenticated key exchange protocol such as TLS (IOT-SEC).

In this scheme, devices can self-generate public and private key pairs using a key-pair generation function (FIPS-180). The key-pair may also be centrally generated. When self-generated, the end IoT device requiring the digital certificate performs a key-pair generation function (as described in FIPS PUB 180-4).

Figure 3.7 illustrates the event-flow in a multi-level trust chain from the root of trust CA to the IoT endpoints. The optional **registration authority** (**RA**) often acts as an intermediary that receives **certificate signing requests** (**CSR**) from endpoints and runs some basic validations before forwarding the request to the CA. The CA sends the certificate response using a suitable signature algorithm, such as RSA, DSA, or ECDSA. The certificate response message contains the public key (which could be self-generated and part of the request message) and the CA's digital signature. In all subsequent identity and authentication-related workflows, the IoT device can present this certificate as a proof of trust. Other devices and trust authorities can validate the signature of the CA and can trust each other if they have the CA key that provides them with the chain of trust:

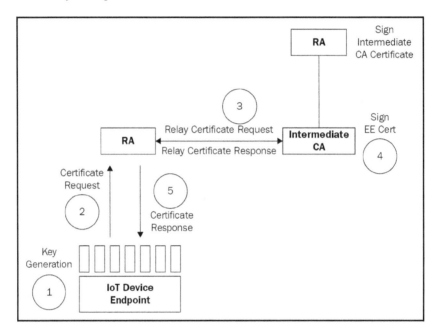

Figure 3.7: PKI-based trust chain workflow in IIoT applications; Source: Adapted from (IOT-SEC)

In IIoT use cases such as verified boot and firmware updates, the trust anchor is usually a hardware component in the device, like TPM, which serves as the root of trust in the digital signature-based validations, measurements, and attestation. This is further elaborated on in `Chapter 4`, *Endpoint Security and Trustworthiness*.

PKI certificate standards for IIoT

PKI-based access control has traditionally relied on ITU-T X.509 certificate standards. In this section, we shall evaluate X.509 and also the emerging IEEE 1609.2 standard, specifically in the context of IIoT use cases.

ITU-T X.509

ISO/IEC/ITU-T X.509 is a digital certificate standard widely used in PKI. In 2008, IETF profiled X-509 Version 3 for internet usage in RFC 5280 (RFC2), also referred to as a PKIX certificate. Today, many IIoT trust implementations use the X.509 digital certificate format (see *Figure 3.8*). It is a highly organized and hierarchical format used to certify the identity of the entity the certificate has been issued to, a validity period, and the associated public key. In many next-generation IIoT devices, the device manufacturer installs the public/private key pair, which is certified and signed by the manufacturer.

The following figure shows the various fields of X.509 certificates:

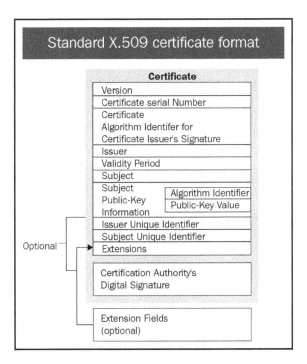

Figure 3.8: X.509 Certificate layout

Although X.509 certificates provide robust identity and access control, they are suitable only for device endpoints with sufficient storage and computational power. Devices with low memory and CPU footprint may not have the storage nor computational power required to validate and participate in public key cryptography. The IEEE 1609.2 certificate format has approximately half the size of a typical X.509 certificate while still using strong, elliptic curve cryptographic algorithms (ECDSA and ECDH), and that's what we'll discuss next.

IEEE 1609.2

The IEEE 1609.2 standard defines secure message formats and trust infrastructure for **wireless access in vehicular environments** (**WAVE**) devices (WAVE-1609). Currently, this standard mainly relates to the connected vehicle program led by USDOT, but can be extended to trust models involving mobile devices, or congested and bandwidth-constrained radio environments. This can find applicability well beyond the connected transportation industry to include other industry verticals.

The main purpose of 1609.2 is to secure WAVE management and application messages and other administrative methods to support security.

The certificate format supports:

- Signing pseudonymous application **protocol data units** (**PDUs**), which excludes sender information
- Certificates for certificate authorities

The signed PDU (*Figure 3.9*) contains either the payload or hash of the external payload. It also contains the following fields:

1. Provider service ID to indicate permissions
2. Optional header fields containing generation time, expiry time, generation location, security management fields, and reference to the signing certificate (which could be the certificate itself or a hash of the certificate and associated signature):

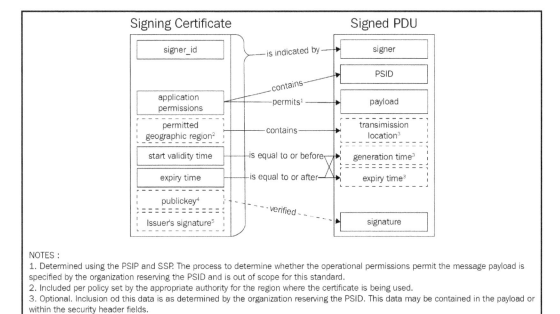

Figure 3.9: IEEE1609.2 Event Sequence; Source: IEEE 1609.2 Working Group

Considering V2X (which includes V2V, V2I, and more) communication requirements, this standard supports certificate trust chaining and peer-to-peer certificate distribution, wherein:

- A trust chain is constructed starting from message signing certificate to a known root by the receiver
- Any unknown certs received from peering senders can be requested by the receivers by using a field in their own outgoing signed messages

These certificates are suitable for M2M communications in general, in scenarios where one sender sends to many receivers and one receiver receives from many senders. They are not suited to scenarios requiring persistent security sessions.

One drawback of this standard is that an eavesdropper with widespread eavesdropping capabilities can track vehicles. Since the messages sent by vehicles contain multiple identifiers such as the 1609.2 certificate, source address, application-level ID field, when an eavesdropper detects two messages in two locations with the same identifier, the same vehicle can be inferred. Although at this time adequate privacy and repudiation are of concern, considering this is an evolving standard, we can expect these to be addressed in future versions.

Certificate management in IIoT deployments

The public key infrastructure heavily relies on certificate management, which includes distribution of certification, maintaining certificate validity, revocation, and so on. In the context of the hyper scale and hyper automation attributes of IIoT deployments, this may be an area of concern.

Certificates play a crucial role in PKI to enable encryption and authentication. The confidentiality and integrity of IIoT data as well as the authenticity of identity of users, devices, services and other participants in communications are ensured by certificates. However, the PKI process is fairly involved and includes a number of steps that must be performed by at least one external organizations (to attain full trust) and may be costly in terms of both time and money.

The PKI applications include access control and endpoint integrity, including the integrity for roots of trust, integrity of endpoint identity, hardware and software integrity, runtime integrity, and integrity of data-at-rest. In addition, PKI is commonly applied to the confidentiality and integrity of communications as well as mutual authentication between endpoints, and therefore can be applied to management and monitoring operations as well as any other data-in-motion operations.

The networking setup takes a significant amount of the time during system installs. Much of that may involve getting the PKI provisioned correctly. The initial challenge is storage of the keys that are the basis of the certificate. The public key is signed by (and sometimes generated by) a **certificate authority** (**CA**), forming the certificate, but the private key which is the corollary of the public key must be securely stored, for example in a TPM, for the certificate to remain trustworthy.

Extending the OAuth 2.0 authorization framework for IoT access control

OAuth is a token-based open standard access control framework. OAuth in conjunction with OpenID Connect protocol provides a federated single-sign-on experience in the web. We see this extensively used by social media sites such as LinkedIn, Facebook, and Twitter. Federated access control holds a lot of promise in IoT applications, and extensions to the OAuth protocol itself to support IoT uses cases are being worked on by IEEE and IETF. At the time of writing, many IoT protocol extensions are also being worked on to fit into the OAuth authentication and authorization framework.

OAuth provides delegated access to resources using Resource Owner (the entity that controls the data being exposed), Authorization Server (issues, controls, and revokes OAuth tokens), Client (the application, website, or other system that requests data on behalf of the resource owner), and a Resource Server (typically an API that exposes/stores and sends the data).

To demand access to protected resources in resource servers, OAuth 2.0 (RFC-6749) uses access tokens requested by clients. OAuth2.0 was primarily designed to provide federated access to protected resources in the HTTP-based web infrastructure. IIoT deployments require special considerations for resource-constrained devices. OAuth 2.0 extensions for use with SASL (SASL-OAUTH) and CoAP (Tschofenig-ace) are recent developments along those lines.

The IETF Draft (Tschofenig-ace) defines extensions to OAuth 2.0 for use with Constrained Application Protocol (CoAP) (RFC-7252)-based transport profiles. The benefits of this extension are discussed in the following (Tschofenig-ace).

Instead of HTTP, the use of CoAP to encode requests and responses leads to smaller and fewer message exchanges since CoAP uses a binary format and relies on connectionless UDP (instead of TCP).

The use of **Datagram Transport Layer Security** (**DTLS**) (RFC-6347) (instead of **Transport Layer Security** (**TLS**) for authentication) for establishment of an integrity-protected and confidential communication channel between the client and the authorization server follows the spirit of TLS, but is tailored to the **unreliable transport protocol** (**UDP**) used by CoAP.

The use of DTLS also allows reusing proven security functionality without the need to redesign the same features at the application layer.

The MQTT specification mentions using OAuth-based tokens in the **connect** packet (currently, it has only username and password fields). So, in the near future, we can expect to see wider adoption of the OAuth framework in IoT protocols. However, being an open security framework, OAuth leaves room for flexible implementation and associated vulnerabilities. Application developers are encouraged to adhere to risk and threat modeling scenarios, covered in RFC 6819.

IEEE 802.1x

The edge layer of an IIoT architecture may need to support a variety of wired and wireless protocols such as Zigbee, IEEE 802.11, 3/4/5G, and so on. To manage trust for devices connected over Wi-Fi, authentication protocols as defined by IEEE 802.1X can be leveraged.

IEEE 802.1x provides strong authentication and authorization support. The 802.1X standard supports a variety of advanced **extensible authentication protocol** (**EAP**) types (TLS, TTLS, LEAP, and PEAP) for mutual authentication and for setting up encrypted tunnels to avoid man-in-the middle attacks.

Enabling 802.1x authentication requires an access device, which is usually a Wi-Fi access point, and an authentication server that supports RADIUS or some **authentication, authorization, and accounting** (**AAA**) protocol such as TACACS+.

The devices participating in 802.1X should both be able to manage the CPU load and have the memory to store strong credentials. 802.1x authentication supports devices with IP addresses. As not all IoT devices have an IP address, this adds a further limitation to the type of devices that can utilize 802.1X-based authentication.

Identity support in messaging protocols

To implement end-to-end trust, it is important that IoT messaging protocols support identity and access controls. In this section, identity controls in the most commonly used IoT messaging protocols are briefly described. Chapter 5, *Securing Connectivity and Communications*, provides a more in-depth assessment of the security capabilities of the protocols at various layers of the IIoT connectivity stack.

MQTT

MQTT allows sending a username and password. Until recently, the specification recommended that passwords be no longer than 12 characters. The username and password are sent in the clear as part of the CONNECT message. As such, it is critical that TLS be employed when using MQTT to prevent man-in-the-middle attacks on the password. Ideally, end-to-end TLS connectivity between the two endpoints (or gateway-to-gateway), along with certificates to mutually authenticate the TLS connection, are advisable controls.

Note that there is an open source variant of MQTT called **Data Exchange Layer** (**DXL**) from McAfee (MC-DXL). It is MQTT with an encrypted payload, which helps to protect the credentials. DXL communication includes TLS 1.2 with mutual authentication; as such, it doesn't require a separate TLS deployment. However, it requires PKI to be implemented first, which adds a degree of complexity.

CoAP

CoAP supports multiple authentication options for device-to-device communication. This can be paired with **Datagram TLS** (**DTLS**) for higher-level confidentiality and authentication services.

DDS

The Object Management Group's **Data Distribution Standard** (**DDS**) security specification supports mutual authentication participating in a distributed system. Both digital certificates and various identity/authorization token types are supported.

REST

HTTP/REST typically requires the support of the TLS protocol for authentication and confidentiality services. Although basic authentication (where credentials are passed in the clear) can be used under the cover of TLS, this is not a recommended practice. Instead, attempting to stand up a token-based authentication (and authorization, if needed) approach such as OpenID identity layer on top of OAuth2 (OAUTH-SEC) can be considered. When using OAuth, additional security controls need to be carefully considered (OAUTH-SANS).

Monitoring and management capabilities

An IAM strategy is incomplete unless it includes controls to support the entire identity lifecycle. The identity lifecycle begins with a device bootstrapping to join a trust relationship with other elements of the infrastructure. It ends with device decommission and associated account deactivation and deletion. Along this lifecycle, there are many events and activities that demands adequate visibility and control paradigms from a security standpoint. Two important device management capabilities are discussed in this section.

Activity logging support

In industrial OT, network log histories are maintained to track control operations and commands. Events and access control-related logs are important to have sufficient visibility on the dynamics of an IoT deployment.

Some IIoT platforms generate event and activity logs. Any anomaly or rogue activity detected is forwarded upstream for further analytics and reporting. But the logs are vulnerable to unintended alteration. Either the logs must be signed (which has its own challenges and weaknesses), or the logs/events should be moved off the device to a more secure environment where the integrity of the log data can be monitored. Logging is commonly implemented with syslog (on Unix systems), and can be accompanied by rsyslog for the "remote" aspect to get the events off the device. The rsyslog connection is the next vulnerable element in the chain, so that needs to be protected as well.

Revocation support and OCSP

Generally speaking, a revocation mechanism should be able to flag to administrative authorities when it is time to terminate a trust relationship and any accounts associated with that device. When authenticating in a system, devices need to know when other devices' credentials are no longer valid, aside from expiration.

When using PKI-based trust models, certificate revocation is part of the overall workflow. PKIs routinely revoke credentials for various reasons, such as a device being compromised or malfunctioning, or simply that it is retired. This is achieved through cryptographically signed **certificate revocation lists** (**CRLs**), which CAs generate periodically. The process involves latency, as it depends how frequently a CA would generate CRLs and also when the devices would detect a new CRL and update their lists. This latency exposes an interval during which an untrusted device may go unnoticed. The **Online Certificate Status Protocol** (**OCSP**) helps to alleviate this risk somewhat as it allows devices to crosscheck with the CA to find out if a public key credential is still valid.

Building an IAM strategy for IIoT deployment

So far in this chapter, we have discussed the various concepts related to IIoT identity and access management. To put this concept into practice, certain key considerations and tools are presented in this section; they can be used to define an IAM strategy for a specific use case.

Risk-based policy management

Managing identity and access control is costly and resource-intensive. Due to the heterogeneity and complexity of the associated technologies and platforms, an efficient and cost-effective IAM strategy must always be risk-based. In this section, the reader will find a few actionable steps to define IAM approaches for their IIoT use case:

- Identify the identity and access-related threats specific to the use case. The threat modeling and risk analysis methods described in `Chapter 2`, *Industrial IoT Dataflow and Security Architecture*, can be used for this purpose. The risk analysis needs to factor in threat scenarios in both OT and enterprise IT environments. This provides a comprehensive basis to determine the level and extent of access control policies required to protect the deployment.
- Prioritize the threats and also the sections of the overall architecture that are more prone to identity risks.

- Evaluate existing access control capabilities and policies before devising new ones. Protocols used in IIoT infrastructure often contain native cryptographic controls. Access control mechanisms are often built into the vendor-specific platforms. Most enterprises already have an IAM framework managed by the IT team. These existing IAM capabilities must be factored in while architecting the overarching IAM strategy for the IIoT use case.
- Ensure identity-based access control is considered for the entire use case, from the device to the cloud. To manage trust beyond the industrial edge, evaluate the identity and access controls integrated in the WAN and cloud infrastructure, or identify the lack of it.

The preceding steps are integral to defining a risk-based IAM strategy that is well-aligned with the available organizational resources and the use-case-specific threat landscape. *Figure 3.10* shows the various technologies in an IIoT IAM stack:

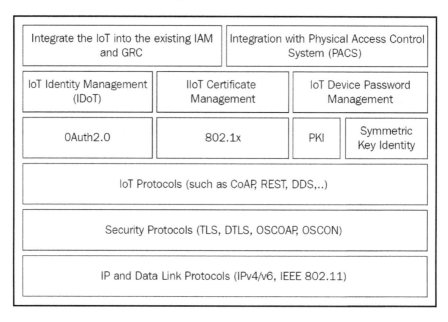

Figure 3.10: IIoT IAM technology stack

Table 3.1 shows a list of security capabilities associated with an IAM framework. The reader can use this table to score these capabilities in their IAM strategy and thus assess the overall strength of the IAM framework:

Capability	Yes/No; OR Assign Value
Confidentiality Authorized Access Only	
Integrity No Unauthorized Changes	
Authentication Proof of identity claims	
Nonrepudiation Verifiable Originator/Actor	
Cost/Key Crypto price performance	
Energy Consumption Battery/Power performance	
Memory Runtime memory consumption	
Processor Requirement CPU/Processor performance	

Table 3.1: List of security capabilities associated with an IAM framework

Summary

In this chapter, we discussed the fundamental tenets of an IAM strategy and evaluated the various distinguishing aspects of an IIoT deployment in terms of IAM requirements. The reader was introduced to the relevant concepts and technologies associated with IAM, and their corresponding benefits and limitations.

This chapter was designed to provide the reader with a holistic baseline and actionable steps to develop a risk-based and cost-effective IAM strategy for a specific IIoT deployment use case.

Chapter 4, *Endpoint Security and Trustworthiness*, takes the discussion of IIoT device security to the next level by providing a comprehensive analysis of IIoT endpoint security and trustworthiness.

Endpoint Security and Trustworthiness

4

"Without security, there is no safety."
- Steve Hanna, Senior Principal, Infineon Technologies

The trustworthiness of an IIoT implementation is rooted in endpoint protection. In `Chapter 1`, *An Unprecedented Opportunity at Stake*, the tremendous business and social opportunities tied to the industrial internet were discussed at length. Inadequate trustworthiness at any point in the value chain poses a major threat to those optimistic claims. This further highlights the importance of securing IIoT endpoints.

An endpoint can be any node in the IIoT architecture that generates or receives data and/or control signals. An endpoint may also route data packets, or can be a storage device. As such, we need measurable and verifiable techniques to protect data at rest, data in use, and data in motion. Even in scenarios where the chances of a compromise are low, the importance of endpoint security cannot be underestimated; since in hyperconnected environments, an unprotected device can be compromised and used to launch coordinated botnet-style attacks on other systems belonging to the same, or a different, organizational domain.

This chapter will dive deeper into the imperative and various practical tools and techniques to design and deploy secured IIoT endpoints. The sections of this chapter will include:

- Defining an IIoT endpoint
- Endpoint security enabler technologies
- IIoT endpoint vulnerabilities
- Establishing trust in hardware
- Endpoint identity and access control

- Initialization and boot process integrity
- Establishing endpoint trust during operations
- Endpoint security using isolation techniques
- Endpoint physical security
- Machine learning enabled endpoint security
- Endpoint security testing and certification
- Endpoint protection industry standards

Defining an IIoT endpoint

IIoT endpoints are often equated to the next generation of machines and IoT devices capable of network connectivity. These devices, however, are a subset of the endpoint universe in the context of security and trustworthiness. An IIoT endpoint can be any device or system in an IIoT implementation that generates, processes, routes, or stores data.

The IIC Vocabulary defines an endpoint as a *"component that has computational capabilities and network connectivity."* Thus, IIoT endpoints are not limited only to connected field devices, such as sensors, actuators, and plant equipment (turbines and so on), but include other nodes of an ICS/SCADA system (such as PLCs, RTUs, and DCS) and intermediator systems (such as industrial routers, firewalls, gateways, and edge devices), spanning all the way to cloud-based appliances and servers. Physical endpoints may have independent hardware and dedicated silicon fabric, or may run as virtual instances in virtualized environments. Some of these endpoints are resource-constrained, with low-end microcontrollers, while others are high-end computing platforms, with high-end computing resources. Given the average lifespan of industrial machines (where decades are normal), brownfield IIoT deployments are common. In brownfield deployments, both legacy and next-gen IoT systems are considered as endpoints.

Protection of this wide diversity of endpoints, though apparently daunting, can be less complicated than it sounds. As this chapter unfolds, the reader will find mechanisms that can be applied as general trust frameworks, both horizontally (across any one layer) and vertically (across the architectural hierarchy), as shown in *Figure 4.1*:

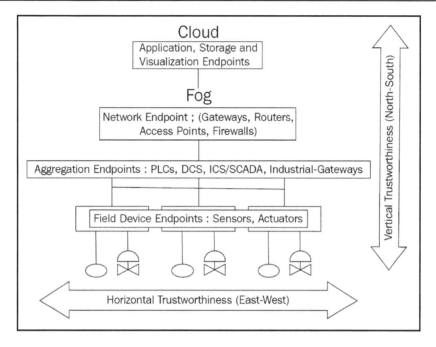

Figure 4.1: Trustworthiness of device endpoint in an IIoT deployment

Motivation and risk-based endpoint protection

Endpoint protection involves two important tenets: motivation and risk analysis.

The most common motivations for endpoint protection include:

- Protecting the safety, reliability, security, resilience, and privacy of the device, equipment, or system
- Ensuring system integrity and availability
- Ensuring data integrity and confidentiality
- Hardening to prevent exploits, using IoT devices (bots) as attack vectors

The motivation closely ties in to the use case. In the case of transportation and connected vehicles, safety is the top priority. In healthcare, patient safety and confidentiality of patient data take the prime seat. In manufacturing and industrial use cases, such as smart grids, the safety and reduction of plant downtime are paramount.

Security involves costs, and can be resource-intensive. That's why to devise a cost-effective endpoint protection strategy, proper risk assessment and threat modeling are essential.

Figure 4.2 shows multiple checkpoints in the endpoint protection life cycle, where trust needs to be explicitly integrated:

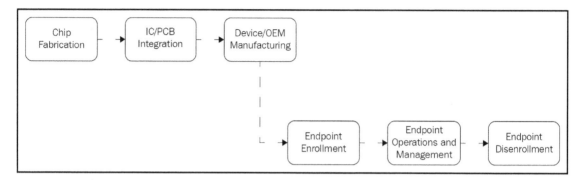

Figure 4.2: Establishing trust across the endpoint life cycle

Resource-constrained endpoint protection

Low-end and remotely positioned field devices might be resource-constrained, with respect to the following:

- Processing capacity
- Non-volatile and runtime memory
- Power availability
- Connection bandwidth

However, these constraints do not lower their security necessities in terms of secure bootstrapping, secure firmware updates, identity, secured access, and connectivity. To ensure adequate trustworthiness in these resource-constrained scenarios, the following are some security considerations (IIC-IISF):

1. Crypto accelerators and coprocessors, such as TPM, are separate hardware modules dedicated to security and cryptographic processing. They have a small footprint, consisting of a single integrated circuit using the **System on Chip (SoC)** design. These modules relieve the main CPU from security operations and can be used to improve the endpoint's processing capacity and battery life.

2. **Field-programmable gate arrays** (**FPGA**) are included in many new devices. FPGAs are reprogrammable in the field, which is a major consideration for long-lived IIoT devices.

3. The choice of cryptographic algorithm, offering comparable strength for a smaller key size (strength/key), is another factor to be considered for resource-constrained devices. For example, a 283-bit ECC key is equivalent to an RSA 3072-bit key (SYM-ECC). This is, however, just an example, and in the choice of elliptic curve algorithms, several other factors should be considered (RFC-6090).

4. For resource-constrained endpoints, security functions can be delegated to a security gateway.

5. Virtualization is an option to instantiate multiple endpoints on the same physical platform. In virtualized environments, a dedicated **virtual machine** (**VM**) can be used as the security agent for all other endpoints in that platform (this concept has been elaborated on in the *Endpoint Security Using Isolation Techniques* section).

6. Limitations in bandwidth and the availability of communication channels, power, and plant maintenance windows make it harder to apply patches and updates in resource-constrained environments. Using incremental updates instead of pushing a monolith is a viable option to address these challenges. In PKI-based scenarios, the OCSP, or OCSP stapling, **Short Lived Certificates** (**SLC**), or evergreen certificates can be considered in place of a CRL.

7. In ICS/SCADA networks, endpoints include resource-constrained legacy devices with less computing power and with static configurations, which are not upgradeable at all.

The next section will address challenges related to legacy devices and equipment.

Brownfield scenario considerations

Every industrial system has legacy systems—motors, pumps, turbines—which last for decades. While performing risk assessment, we must account for the vulnerabilities in these systems. Some of these devices often run outdated and unsupported software and hardware versions. One important consideration in brownfield scenarios is loosely coupling cybersecurity policies, so as to minimally impact the industrial processes.

For industrial systems, IEC/ISA-62443-3-2 defines security assurance levels, using the concepts of zones and conduits. Using this specification, a set of endpoints can be provisioned into zone A, and another set in zone B. Secured conduits connect zone A with zone B. Security policies can be enforced, so that zone A endpoints can only interact with those in zone B, but not with any other zone. The policies may also be configured at a device-level granularity, to specify which device communicates with which other device in that zone, and with what messages. This scheme provides isolation from various other connected domains in general, protecting these devices from malicious code or files.

Security gateways are commonly used to protect legacy devices. The gateway provides protection in terms of mutual authentication, identity management and storage, and network whitelisting to allow only explicitly defined flows between two devices. Gateways also resolve interoperability problems due to vendor-specific management inconsistencies between the devices. This makes security agnostic to vendor-specific platforms. However, the gateway itself needs to be a trusted endpoint. It is a sensitive endpoint, since a compromised gateway will compromise other devices behind it, and it must be configured with a high level of security.

It is a hard game to future-proof security, considering the longevity of industrial systems. At a minimum, however, endpoints should include secure update capabilities. Inevitably, as endpoints age, they will eventually become legacy endpoints. For legacy endpoints with inadequate security, countermeasures (such as perimeter defenses) can be considered.

Endpoint security enabling technologies

Endpoint security needs to span across hardware, firmware, and software, including network and application interfaces. To implement a trusted and resilient ecosystem of IIoT endpoints and subsystems, a variety of technologies come into play, as shown in the following diagram, which stacks the security technologies into hardware, intermediate, enhanced, and intelligent security layers. The main purpose of this classification is to give the reader an idea of the relative role and importance of each of these technologies that are available to protect endpoints:

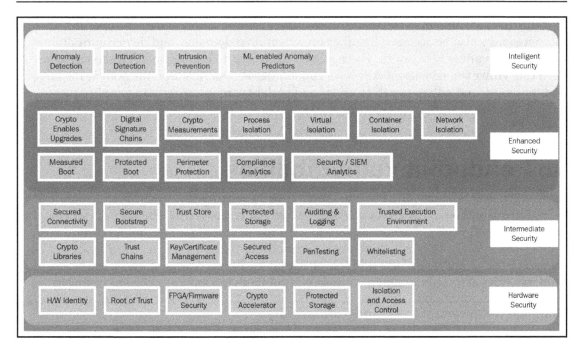

Figure 4.3: Endpoint protection technologies

Subsequent sections of this chapter will further elaborate on some of these techniques.

This technology stack is not designed to correlate with the levels of assurance presented in IEC 62443 3-3 and NIST SP 800-53r4. The best practices to implement assurance level based security for IIoT endpoints have been treated in IIC's **Endpoint Security Best Practices** (**ESec-BP**) specification.

Integrating trust at the silicon or hardware level is a foundational principle of endpoint resilience. Cryptography, secured protocols and storage, and isolation techniques are key to creating an end-to-end trust environment. Although it is recommended to consider all of these technologies, actual security implementation should always be based on use case specific risk assessment. Depending on the security risks associated with a given implementation, the reader can customize this stack, aligning to their corresponding risk profile.

In industrial IoT, data may traverse multiple organizational boundaries. Endpoint interfaces may also be accessed by other organizational domains; and device endpoints come from a variety of vendors. These factors make end-to-end technological consistency a hard call. However, consistent API-level capabilities across all endpoints both at the edge and the cloud; and adherence to modular and scalable architectures, can simplify the overall security design.

IIoT endpoint vulnerabilities

Endpoint risk assessment and the implementation of security countermeasures require a thorough evaluation of the attack surfaces and attack vectors applicable to IIoT-specific use cases. Interested readers are encouraged to refer to the Industrial Internet Security Framework specification, which presents an elaborate analysis on *"Security Threats and Vulnerabilities on Endpoints"* (IIC-IISF). In this section, a few common threats and vulnerabilities associated with the various endpoint components are cited as examples:

Endpoint component	Threats and Vulnerability
Hardware	• Unauthorized seizure of system resources, such as memory, processing cycles, and privileged access modes (privilege escalation exploit) • Improper endpoint initialization by corrupting UEFI/BIOS and corrupting the boot process
Firmware	• Steal code signing key or inject corrupted firmware through tampering • Exploit vulnerabilities in code signing and firmware update process • Rewrite firmware through privilege escalation • Exploit firmware distribution vulnerabilities to replace a good firmware copy with a malware-infected copy
Virtualized platforms	• Exploit access control vulnerabilities in hypervisor, guest OS, or separation kernels, to alter their functions (including security controls) and escalate privilege to corrupt other system resources and virtual instances running in the endpoint
Native OS/Apps/APIs	• Inject malware in executables, execute malicious applications, or access exposed APIs to launch denial of service attacks
Runtime environment	• Execute malicious installation scripts during endpoint deployment, replacement of firmware files in update server
Monitoring, configuration, and management	• Gain visibility and unauthorized access to the endpoint through the management server to alter configuration files or code, corrupt event logs, intercept and override data in motion, or send malicious commands to the endpoint • Always-on nature of IIoT endpoints is a vulnerability to develop coordinated attacks impacting larger IIoT systems

Table 4.1: Common threats and vulnerabilities

Case study – White hack exposes smart grid meter vulnerability

This case study is included in a published research paper, titled *"Security Analysis on Consumer and Industrial IoT Devices (SEC-IIoT)"*. The authors of the paper highlight the deficiencies in security integration in the device manufacturing process, often due to short time-to-market cycles. The paper points to trusted computing best practices e.g. secure firmware updates. It demonstrates that IIoT endpoints may have vulnerabilities that could be exploited, unless augmented with additional controls. Since the authors of this paper conducted the white hack scenario, in this case study, we will refer to them as white-hack analysts, or simply analysts.

This case study analyzes the various endpoint component-level vulnerabilities of an Itron Centron Smart Meter. *Figure 4.4* shows the smart meter:

Figure 4.4: Itron Centron CL200 Smart Meter

Use case

The Itron Centron CL200 Smart Meter is deployed on customer premises. Its main function is to measure and report the energy usage data of a given customer. The meter utilizes an RF channel to communicate the usage data to a nearby meter reader or to a local substation. This data is used to bill the customers for their energy usage, and may also be used to generate analytics on overall energy usage patterns of the community.

Developing the exploit

The device contains a heavy-duty plastic cover, guarding the main hardware platform. The hardware platform measures line voltage and reference voltages. It also checks the energy flow direction, energy, pulse data, and line frequency:

Figure 4.5: CL200 Smart Meter daughterboard

Attached to the main hardware platform is a daughterboard (*Figure 4.5*). In this case, it is used to collect energy usage information, along with tamper data and the ID of the board itself. The daughterboard includes an ATMega microcontroller, a tamper sensor, and a 1 KB EEPROM. By tampering with the microcontroller, the white-hack analysts were able to re-enable JTAG and re-enable write access for on-chip memories.

Their objective was to modify the smart meter ID, so that a meter reader would read the incorrect ID for the device. This ID was stored in the external EEPROM. After noting down the actual ID of the meter (printed on the front of the device, underneath the grey cover), and by analyzing the EEPROM dump, they were able to find where the ID was stored. Subsequently, they were able to overwrite the stored ID to any arbitrary value.

Demonstration

After modifying the meter ID on the meter itself, the analysts wanted to demonstrate that a smart meter reader would pick up the wrong ID of the compromised meter when communicating with it remotely. Utilizing a **software-defined radio** (**SDR**), the analysts executed a TCP server on the SDR and connected it to another program, which parses wireless information and displays the ID, the tamper bit status, and the energy usage for the meter. Using this experimental platform, it was demonstrated that, due to the lack of proper cryptographic protection, one compromised smart meter can "represent" itself as any other smart meter. Thus, two smart meters will share the same ID, but different power consumption values. Through this vector, energy theft can be carried out.

This case study showcases the hardware and firmware vulnerabilities of an industrial field device; in this case, a smart energy meter for residential customers.

The subsequent sections in this chapter focus on various countermeasures to build more resilient industrial endpoints. Device implementations that were assumed to be safe for air-gapped systems can no longer be considered as secure when the devices are connected. Adequate security controls must be built into the entire supply chain of connected endpoints, to protect them across their life cycles, and also across the industrial internet ecosystems.

Establishing trust in hardware

A trust anchor can be implemented in either software or hardware; the choice calls for a trade-off between the complexity and level of assurance. Compared to software-based trust, tamper-resistant hardware provides better trust performance, as it provides a RoT with the secured storage of secrets. Hardware-based trust consumes less power (IIC-IISF), which is an important consideration for resource-constrained environments. These benefits, however, come at the cost of complexities in managing firmware and crypto library updates. Hardware-based security is more rigid, and often involves static implementation. In some instances, due to a lack of update capability, hardware vulnerabilities may last throughout the life of the device. In recent years, innovations in trusted computing have significantly addressed some of these limitations.

Software-based trust is used in many IT systems. It provides a lower level of assurance, and as such, it should be carefully considered for cyber-physical systems. The following table can serve as a quick comparison for hardware- and software-based security:

	Hardware	Software
Level of Trust	High (IEC 62433 Level 3 and 4)	Low (IEC 62433 Level 1, 2, and 3)
Battery Performance	More efficient	Less efficient
Management complexity	High	Low
Crypto Algorithm Reprogramming Complexity	High	Low
Security Updates	More complex when supported	Less complex
Computational Cost	Less burden on CPU	CPU- and memory-intensive
Storing of Secrets	More secure	Less secure

Table 4.2: Comparison of hardware- and software-based security solutions

Hardware security components

For better upgradeability and device performance, newer equipment includes hardware security components integrated in the same board as the main CPU (IIC-IISF). Examples of hardware security components include **field programmable gate arrays** (**FPGAs**), crypto accelerators, **Hardware Security Modules** (**HSM**), **Trusted Platform Modules** (**TPMs**), and hardware-based **Trusted Execution Environments** (**TEEs**).

FPGAs are reprogrammable and support firmware updates. FPGA units may also include a CPU coprocessor, to perform housekeeping operations for the security functions. Crypto-accelerator processing units occupy a small real estate on the chip, where cryptographic capabilities can be embedded.

HSMs are designed and integrated to provide physical isolation of security functions in the same physical device platform.

A TPM (defined in ISO and TCG standards) is usually a chip embedded in the motherboard. HSMs and TPMs are designed to provide strong tamper resistance, cryptographic key storage, key generation using hardware **random number generators** (**RNGs**), strong authentication, boot integrity protection, and so on.

A TEE, as the name suggests, provides a trusted execution environment on a larger chip/SoC. Typically, it does not provide physical isolation.

Root of trust – TPM, TEE, and UEFI

In `Chapter 3`, *IIoT Identity and Access Management*, we discussed the concept of **root of trust** (**RoT**) in PKI, which involves a hierarchy of CA. In PKI, the root CA (or the trust anchor) is absolutely trusted, and can vouch for the identity of other entities. However, for endpoints, the RoTs have a slightly different connotation.

In a device endpoint, the RoTs are components, or computing engines, that constitute a set of unconditionally trusted functions that **always** behave in an expected manner, because their misbehavior cannot be detected (NIST 800-150). In other words, the RoT determines the highest level of trust attainable by a device, and a compromise on the RoT compromises trust for the entire system.

The RoT should be as small and as secure as possible. The RoT can be implemented in software, hardware, or firmware, or in a hybrid of these. A hardware RoT is preferred over a software RoT, since it can be demonstrated to behave in an expected manner in a significantly higher percentage of attack scenarios. A software RoT is usually less expensive, and is only implemented in certain devices. However, nowadays, in most endpoints, regardless of the cost and available resources (that is, whether the endpoint is an industrial PC or a sensor), there is a trend to implement the RoT in hardware, such as a TPM.

In an endpoint, the RoTs are particularly critical for firmware integrity measurement, since the firmware is generally responsible for the configuration of the software execution environment, including the mapping of physical memory and devices.

The RoT includes a public and private key pair, where the private key cannot be extracted from the TPM, but the public key can be accessed via APIs. In the case of a hardware RoT, this key pair is generated, certified, and installed by the chip or device manufacturer. The private key is never exposed; some cryptographic operations are performed inside the TPM as a blackbox, with no external access to the components, other than the input and the output. For some endpoints, digital certificates may be installed by the device or OEM manufacturer and the asset owner, thereby forming a chain of trust.

Securing secrets, or sealing

An endpoint may have a number of secrets, such as passwords, shared secrets, and data encryption keys. The disclosure of these keys to unauthorized parties could compromise the endpoint, and subsequently, the broader ecosystem of devices.

Secrets stored in the TPM can provide substantial protection against loss through physical, network, or software interfaces. However, the limited power of the TPM's crypto engine may impact signing throughput in scaled environments, especially for high-end endpoints, such as gateways, routers, and servers. A possible solution is to hold the keys at rest in the TPM's encrypted storage, but, when in use, release them for access to platform software, or perhaps a high-throughput crypto engine (TCGG-29). This mechanism of storing secrets in the TPM is called **sealing**, where keys (or other secrets) are stored in the device's filesystem, in an encrypted file that can only be decrypted with keys released from the TPM when a predefined set of criteria are met.

Endpoint identity and access control

Endpoint or device identity is a foundational building block in any trust model. Identity is a prerequisite for performing authentication, authorization, secured asset management, remote monitoring, management, and maintenance. **Identification and Authentication Control** is one of the seven foundational requirements in IEC 62443, and associates four assurance levels to it. These assurance levels correlate to the risk profiles of endpoints in a given IIoT use case:

> *"If no threat exists against the endpoint, clear text credential, such as identification numbers may be used. In some rare instances, it may not be required for all endpoints to support identity, but the risks should be well understood and documented. ISO/IEC 24760-1 defines three levels of trust for identities: identity, unique identity and secure identity. Industrie 4.0 provides information on what a secure identity technology consists of, and in the case of digital identity a secure identity is a certificate protected by a HRoT such as a TPM."*
>
> *– Excerpted from (IIC-IISF)*

Endpoint access control includes authentication and authorization functions. An endpoint is authenticated based on its identity credentials. The secret portion (passwords, keys, and so on) of the credential must be securely stored in **trust stores**. Trust stores are implemented in hardware for higher levels of assurance, and can be part of software for lower-risk scenarios. Mutual, or two-way authentication can prevent impersonation of the unauthenticated endpoint. Establishing a secure TLS session (IETF-RFC5246) as a tunnel is a common technique for avoiding transmitting passwords in the clear. Multi-factor authentication is recommended wherever possible.

A separation of duty, least privilege, and role-based access control form the fundamentals of authorization. Endpoint authentication and access control technologies, and recommendations for IIoT use cases, were discussed at length in `Chapter 3`, *IIoT Identity and Access Management*.

For use cases requiring an IEC 62443 assurance level of 3 or 4, asymmetric cryptography is recommended. PKI is the strongest device security scheme known today, although it may someday be superseded by a mechanism that is better suited for device-driven communication and its ever-evolving attack vectors. Most newly fabricated IIoT devices that are expected to last for at least a decade come with one or more digitally signed X.509 certificates, associated with the chip manufacturer, device manufacturer, system integrator, and oftentimes, the asset owner.

Crypto key generation, exchange, and digital signature verification can be too resource-intensive for low-end processors and microcontrollers. Coprocessors and dedicated crypto-accelerators are now widely used to relieve the main CPU from these operations.

As devices need to establish authenticity in a trusted ecosystem, asymmetric cryptography eliminates the need for human assistance every time the device authenticates itself. One-way symmetric keys and zero-knowledge proof can be used to circumvent resource limitations in use cases that require lower assurance levels.

Initialization and boot process integrity

The consequences of an infection in firmware or the boot process can be drastic, and often times, hardware replacement is the only option for failure recovery.

Measuring the device boot process enables the validation of its integrity and asserts that a device has powered up in a known good state. Given that devices may not be rebooted for long periods of time in OT environments, both static and dynamic integrity assurance of the runtime need to be implemented. The boot process initializes the main hardware components and starts the operating system.

Trust must be established in the boot environment before trust in any other software or executable program can be claimed. So, the booted environment must be verified and determined to be in an uncompromised state.

The primary firmware used to initialize the system is called the **Basic Input/Output System** (**BIOS**). (*Author's note: Although the term BIOS is prevalent in the "computer world", to specify firmware functionality, we shall use it here for embedded IIoT systems as well*). If a BIOS is altered from its intended state, either maliciously or accidentally, the device on which it was altered may have a negative impact on the organization, because the device is not necessarily operating in its intended state. Possible consequences include system instability, system failure, information leakage, and other losses of confidentiality, integrity, and availability.

The following are key requirements and recommendations for vendors supporting BIOS integrity measurement (NIST 800-155):

- Provide the hardware support necessary to implement credible RoT for BIOS integrity measurements
- Enable endpoints to measure the integrity of all BIOS-executable components and configuration data components at boot time
- Securely transmit measurements of BIOS integrity from endpoints to the **Measurement Assessment Authority** (**MAA**)

BIOS measurements and hashing can be performed by both TPMs (in hardware) or by using crypto libraries to provide software RoT.

Boot process integrity includes the following boot mechanisms applicable to endpoint installation, and subsequent OS and firmware updates.

Secured boot is sometimes referred to as verified or authenticated boot. In this process, each component in the boot sequence cryptographically validates the authenticity of the subsequent component in the boot sequence, before allowing it to load in the runtime memory space. If an improper or unsigned component is detected, the boot process is interrupted (halted). Since no measurement is done, if a hacker can somehow defeat the RoT, then it is not possible to detect whether the system has been compromised:

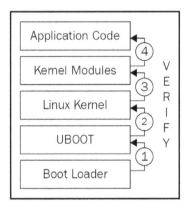

Figure 4.6: Secured boot sequence

In **measured boot**, every entity in the booting sequence not only validates, but also measures, the next entity in the execution chain, by generating a hash. The hashes for each entity are sent to the RoT (TPM or software RoT). The RoT keeps a running hash of the measured hashes so that, at the end of the boot process, if the hash doesn't match the expected value, it can indicate that something changed in the boot sequence (a bad sign). The measurements may be remotely attested to in a server, or locally in a TEE, and used to evaluate the boot integrity at the endpoint:

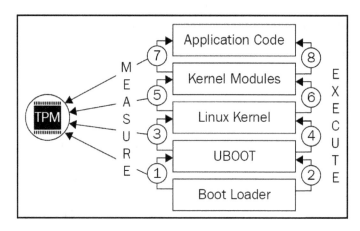

Figure 4.7: Measured boot sequence

In verified boot the system is halted in the event of an integrity failure. However, in the case of a measured boot a system completes the boot sequence even if it is maliciously corrupted and subsequently fails the remote attestation. The measured boot attestation outcome allows the system to be fixed. Thus, these two boot integrity mechanisms address two different risk profiles, where one may be more appropriate than the other depending on the use case. Secure boot can convert an innocent mistake, such as a key mismatch, into a network outage, by terminating the boot sequence. Measured boot wouldn't cause such drastic consequences, but it might allow a corrupted network component to continue running, risking further damage (TCG).

While boot-process integrity in itself is not a complex process, remote attestation and management of the integrity metrics or measurements can pose a sizable problem in IIoT environments. In the case of OT deployments involving several endpoints geographically dispersed, if the endpoint needs to be field upgraded, the software and firmware integrity metrics need to be updated in a secure way. This management mechanism calls for additional resources across the endpoint life cycle. This complexity is an integral part of remote attestation protocols and is usually handled by external management services.

Establishing endpoint trust during operations

Integrating robust trust mechanisms during the operations phase is crucial for industrial endpoints, which are expected to run uninterrupted for extended periods. Firmware is the most fundamental piece of code that runs on any device and interfaces directly with the hardware. It is important to ensure that the firmware and software are updated on a regular basis, to incorporate security bug fixes.

Although the consequences of loading an infected firmware are typically irreversible, it is important to secure the update process for both software and firmware. In this section, we shall delve into secure update processes, and the mechanisms to establish endpoint trust during the operations phase.

Secure updates

Software and firmware are never fully devoid of vulnerabilities and defects; thus, regular upgrades to incorporate bug fixes and security updates are required.

Attackers can exploit vulnerabilities in the update or in the update process, or can gain backdoor access to the endpoint through application software vulnerabilities and privilege escalation. Software and firmware infections can potentially infect the entire device; it can also lead to coordinated attacks across an IIoT system, and in many instances, recovery can be extremely difficult. That's what makes secure updating so crucial for endpoints.

Digital signature verification and hashing are currently common mechanisms to secure firmware updates. Secure or verified boot and measured boot (already elaborated on in the *Boot process integrity* section) use signature verification and crypto measurements to secure the firmware. Verified boot prevents the execution of unauthorized firmware, which, when detected, halts the entire boot sequence.

Measured boot can detect malicious code in the firmware, and can detect firmware vulnerabilities and obsolete versions to trigger a firmware update.

An added security measure for the update process is to cryptographically protect the firmware update transport. Certain IIoT trust vendors provide a tunneling mechanism (using a PKCS envelope) to securely transport updates **over the air** (**OTA**), or wire or web (MOC-NAN).

It is a good practice to sign the firmware update, not only by the manufacturer (which must be done at a minimum), but also by other participants in the supply chain, to create a trust chain. Consider the example of a TPM firmware update. The TPM firmware is signed by the TPM manufacturer, the chip vendor where it is integrated, the equipment maker that uses the chip, and finally, the operator. When an update is protected by multi-level signatures (four levels, in our example), and their verification is enforced by policy before the update process locally initiates, such a chain of trust significantly enhances the assurance level of the firmware upgrade.

A trustworthy execution ecosystem

In addition to establishing trust locally in an endpoint, trust must be established horizontally across the OT environment, and also vertically, from device to cloud, to ensure trusted communication and data exchange. Identity enables basic trustworthiness in endpoint transactions. For a high level of assurance, PKI and digital certificates can be used to implement trust measurements.

In IT environments, there is a PKI-based identity service provided by certificate authorities and the CA chain of trust. However, in M2M domains, involving peer-to-peer communications, PKI-based certificate distribution and life cycle management has been slow to penetrate OT environments, due to its inherent complexity. Although there are some instances of proprietary certificates, cross-vendor interoperability between subsystems needs open standards, such as PKI and X.509 certificates. As of the time of writing, there is an evolving ecosystem of vendors (DigiCert, GlobalSign, and so on) that are fulfilling this need by acting as root CAs and generating X.509 certificates.

Managing the certificate life cycle (install, manage, update, and revoke) in scaled IIoT deployments is still a challenge. One option to distribute X.509 certificates is by using EST (EST-CERT), which allows for RFC 7030 (RFC-7030)-based certificate provisioning over secure wired or wireless channels. To future-proof installations, policy-based updates allow for reprogramming the strength of the cryptographic algorithms and key lengths, when necessary.

Cryptographic controls can be optimized, as not every endpoint needs them. For example, for endpoints handling data that exists in the public domain, data confidentiality is not a high priority. When there are redundant sensors behind a gateway, the cryptographic operations can be performed at the gateway, instead of at the sensors.

Endpoint data integrity

The integrity of data is the very basis of data-driven business operations. Any compromise in the integrity of context-sensitive data can potentially compromise the entire IIoT value chain. Common examples of endpoint data include raw data, configuration and log files, secrets, software libraries, and binary executables. These can be classified into:

- **Data at rest** (**DAR**), or stored data
- **Data in use** (**DIU**); that is, files and data resources used at runtime
- **Data in motion** (**DIM**); that is, data leaving the device

Integrity verifications enable the detection of any intended and malicious or unintended alterations in the data. The CRC checksum has traditionally been used to verify data integrity; however, the modern threat environment demands more advanced integrity controls, because an attacker can modify the checksum to match their changes to the data.

DAR integrity can be achieved by securely storing the secrets in hardware/TPM, or by using specialized software-enabled stores which employ symmetric key encryption. The symmetric key can be dynamically generated with protected primary seed-based key derivation function (MOC- TRUST).

For the runtime integrity of executables, some of the controls are: policy-based blacklisting or whitelisting of files; controlling memory rights access by protecting memory regions from unauthorized access; and runtime process integrity attestation.

Proper coding techniques, such as assessing the suitability of programming language, buffer overflow protection, and input/output checks are some techniques to ensure DIU integrity. More advanced techniques include secure processors with onboard storage, to ensure that data never leaves the processor without proper protection.

Compared to checksums and hashes, a more reliable technique is to cryptographically ensure data integrity by using digital signatures. Private key based cryptographic signatures can attest to the actual data at the time of signing. At any point in the workflow, the integrity of signed data can be validated, thereby ensuring the integrity prior to applying software and firmware updates. The same applies to validating configuration and log files. The signing operation is usually performed in a hardware trust root, such as a TPM, where the signing key can also be securely stored. A downside of cryptographic protection is the need for additional runtime processing resources, to handle the cryptographic operations.

For DIM protection, in addition to providing integrity using signed message digests, session key based encryption and digital certificates can be used to provide data confidentiality and device identity, respectively.

Endpoint configuration and management

In industrial deployments, where the endpoints are often geographically dispersed, the remote management and reconfiguration of endpoints is an important use case. The trustworthy decommission of endpoints is part of the device management as well. For remote management, a secure communication channel between the device and management station needs to be set up to send reconfiguration commands and monitor device status. This secure channel needs to ensure device authentication, data confidentiality (encryption), and integrity protection (TCGG-29).

In some cases (such as when device management or monitoring is outsourced), this communication channel may traverse multiple organization boundaries and data ownership zones.

Control over the configuration and policy changes on the endpoint can be managed by the asset owner or a third-party service provider. In both cases, it is recommended to encrypt and digitally sign configuration files, such that files can only be applied to the intended device, and configurations are not read by unauthorized parties.

Signing and attestation can also ensure the integrity of the configuration file. The prevention of rollback to previous configuration versions can also be a trust control mechanism, in some cases. Attestation can be performed by the remote management station.

Endpoint visibility and control

Proper visibility of cyber-physical systems in large-scale industrial deployments is a practical challenge. In addition to the endpoint inventory during the design and deployment phases, many endpoints can be connected during the operational stage and remain unaccounted for. Connected appliances, such as smart light bulbs and refrigerators, regularly get added to enterprise IT networks, and often evade security monitoring. The compromise of a connected fish tank to steal valuable information from a casino business provides a case in point (DARKT-THREAT). Adequate visibility and policy control of endpoints must be emphasized in the security strategy.

Remote policy management over secured channels is necessary to define or update security controls. Policy orchestration distributes policies across several endpoints (ESec-BP).

Another important aspect of visibility is event log monitoring; regular audits should ensure that the device is at a known good state and allow for responding to incidents effectively.

Event log generation is important for securing endpoints across ICS/SCADA systems. To continually measure and assess risks, event logs are a valuable input. Internal log files or system-wide event logs usually feed into endpoint and security analytics (SIEM, SACM, and so on) systems, to determine operational trustworthiness (TCGG-29). Digital signatures can be used to attest to the origin of the log data, creation time, and endpoint state when the log was created. To avoid an unintended alteration of the log data, it is recommended to move and store log files in secure environments, for upstream processing and analytics.

For continuous incident response and audits, the IIC Endpoint Best Practices Specification (ESEC-BP) recommends the ability to:

- Provision policy-based risk monitoring profiles
- Distribute rules and manage behavioral analysis using open interfaces, data models, or extensible formats (REST APIs, JSON, and so on) across industry sectors
- Trigger rules and feed behavioral analysis with contextual event-related data
- Log the generated events to SIEM services and data historians in extensible formats (CEF, SNMP, and so on)

Endpoint security using isolation techniques

A practical acknowledgement of the information world is that vulnerabilities can be minimized, but their 100% eradication is only as real as catching the horizon. When the probability of an exploit cannot be totally eliminated, a practical prevention technique is to contain the impact of the exploit. Isolation techniques implemented in the hardware, software, and virtualized environments allow for minimizing the impact from an attack by a separation of territories.

To provide the reader with deeper insights into various isolation techniques, some of the common options are discussed in the following sections.

Process isolation

In process isolation, at runtime, the operating system isolates business and operational functional components from security components. Using a privilege-based hierarchy of protection domains, functions and data in more privileged layers are protected from an unintended or malicious failure in a less privileged layer (IIC-IISF). Security agents, dedicated security software libraries, software-based trust stores, and access control lists for files and directories, are some examples of process isolation. However, when any component on the endpoint, including applications and libraries, is compromised, it breaks the integrity of the device, and may become a stepping stone for further attacks exploiting privilege escalation vulnerabilities:

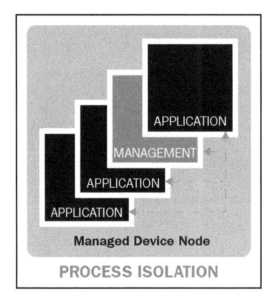

Figure 4.8: Process isolation in a managed device node: Source: (IIC-IISF)

Container isolation

In container isolation techniques, boundaries can be enforced in either software or in hardware. Hybrid containers overlap both approaches.

In the case of software containers, resource isolation boundaries are enforced by the OS. Hardware containers use physically separated computing elements fabricated on the same chip, on the same board, or on a daughterboard in the same physical platform. The security coprocessor not only isolates security processing from the main CPU, but also offloads the security processing load from the main CPU.

The following are some examples of software containers:

- Canonical's Ubuntu Core runs secure Linux application packages, known as snaps, that can be upgraded remotely. Snaps use the same kernel, libraries, and system software as classic Ubuntu.
- Android (Trusty TEE) or Linux containers, such as LXC and Docker.
- Secure memory mapping that provides suitable entry/exit locations, to implement security in very small sensor-type devices.

A common example of a hardware container is a TPM, which is commonly used as a hardware RoT. The TPM is physically isolated from the main CPU, and can be implemented as either a discrete chip or a security coprocessor. The TPM is used to securely store credentials, to ensure trust through cryptographic processing.

Virtual isolation

In a virtual or hypervisor isolation model, a hypervisor implements isolation between the various virtual instances running on a physical platform. One of the instances running on the hypervisor can be a security instance that acts as the trust anchor on the device. This virtual trust anchor can execute various trust functions, such as two-way authentication and PKI-based access control, connection authorization, remote boot and update attestation, firewalling, deep packet inspection, and so on.

During the boot sequence of the physical platform, after the hypervisor integrity is measured and validated, the hypervisor instantiates each of the VMs and measures their integrity. Thus, the chain of trust is extended up to the virtual trust anchor instance, and after it is booted, the runtime integrity of the platform should ensure that the trust anchor maintains its measured state.

Figure 4.8 illustrates the separation or isolation kernel, which provides strong isolation for resources, such as processor time, memory, and I/O devices, provided by the underlying hardware platform. In addition to isolating components from each other, they also enable communication control between components and devices, according to a security policy. In contrast with monolithic hypervisor kernels, separation kernels do not implement certain services commonly associated with operating systems, such as device drivers, filesystems, and network stacks. Separation kernels exist to provide separation between components, and to enable controlled communication among them. By intentionally limiting the functionality of the kernel to isolation and simple IPC primitives, separation kernels can greatly reduce the attack surface and implementation complexity (IIC-IISF):

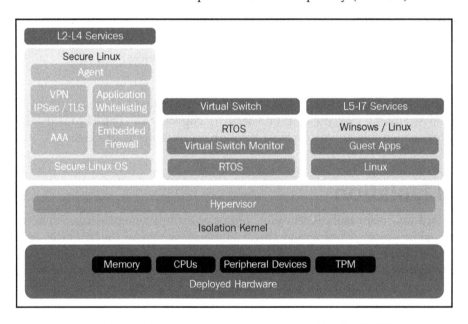

Figure 4.9: Virtual isolation using hypervisors and separation kernels: Source: Adapted from (IIC-IISF)

There are multiple advantages of virtual isolation:

1. The software-based security functions are isolated from each individual VM's guest OS. This is analogous to deploying a security gateway inside the device, rather than in front of it.

2. Multiple endpoint functionalities can be consolidated in the same hardware platform, which has economy of scale advantages similar to cloud models. As an example, **programmable logic controller (PLC)** logic, RTU, Windows HMI, and so on, have separate endpoint functionalities and can be implemented in separate VMs, using the same physical hardware.

3. IIoT deployments have many brownfield use cases. Brownfield deployments do not require changes to the existing guest OS. This model can be secured by using a virtual trust anchor VM that independently runs security functions, such as embedded identity, secure boot attestation, and communication interceptor patterns, to secure the legacy virtual endpoints. However, if real-time constraints must be met, the isolation kernel must ensure this.

4. Another advantage of this model is that asset owners and operators can perform software updates without having to bring down a functioning device. For example, if PLC-1 requires an OS or software update, a separate VM PLC-2 can be instantiated with the new OS and/or software updates and loaded with functionalities identical to PLC-1, which is still operational. Once PLC-2 is booted and attested by the trust anchor, PLC-2 can take over PLC-1 functionality. The need for downtime is thus minimized, if not eliminated. This also facilitates the automation of the update process, which can enable greater efficiency in updates, with minimal downtime.

On the downside, in this scheme, a vulnerability in the firmware, hypervisor, isolation kernel, or the security instance software can lead to the compromise of the entire system. As such it is not quite a silver bullet, as we need to employ additional security controls specific to virtualized environments.

Physical isolation

Physical isolation is particularly relevant to brownfield use cases. The use of security gateways (discussed in the *Brownfield scenario considerations* section) to protect legacy systems behind it, is the most common example of physical isolation in IIoT use cases.

Endpoint physical security

IIoT endpoints deployed as field devices can be exposed to extreme weather conditions, and are vulnerable to theft, hardware tampering, vandalism, and so on. Physical security mechanisms are discussed in greater detail in `Chapter 5`, *Securing Connectivity and Communications*. The interested reader may also refer to existing guidelines on endpoint physical security. **Physical and Environmental Protection** of NIST SP 800-53 (NIST-PE) provides information on methods for physical protection, access control, and monitoring. The Industrial Internet Security Framework (IIC-IISF) can also be referred to, to obtain detailed guidance on this topic.

Machine learning enabled endpoint security

Cybersecurity countermeasures have traditionally been reactive; in other words, the vaccine comes only after the virus has infected the system. The countermeasure typically follows the evaluation and remedy of a security incident. Cryptographic measurements and controls (to create trusted IIoT ecosystems) and anomaly detection functions address this reactive behavior. **Host intrusion detection** (**HID**) and **host intrusion protection** (**HIP**) are examples of dynamic integrity attestation controls to proactively secure an endpoint.

In IT environments, network and application blacklisting policies are commonly used. Whitelisting is more common in OT environments. But, when new exploits of zero-day vulnerabilities are detected, these policies are updated **after the fact**. AI/machine learning allows us to dynamically update blacklisting and whitelisting policies, based on anomalous behavior.

Machine learning extensively uses mathematical models based on historic data to build predictors. These technologies have a lot of potential in security intelligence-based endpoint protection.

Machine learning based security intelligence uses ML algorithms (such as pattern recognition) and predictive analytics. Large volumes of training data are extracted, transformed, and vectored to train the models, in order to cluster and classify connections or files as either malicious or benign. This intelligence can be deployed in IIoT endpoints.

A few challenges with machine learning are as follows:

- Accuracy of a prediction is uncertain
- Needs a vast quantity of training data
- Requires a sacrificial lamb, or a training dataset that includes data related to a similar breach

Cylance (`www.cylance.com`) is one of many vendors in ML-based endpoint security that are trying to overcome these challenges by using techniques to detect zero-day threats yet to be developed.

A few selection criteria for ML-based endpoint security solutions are as follows(CYDATA):

1. Proven capability to detect zero-day threats without the need of pre-existing exploits; that is, patient zero or sacrificial lamb
2. How extensively (number of years) the mathematical model has been tested in the real world
3. Ability of the solution to prevent threats from executing

4. Threat prevention in both connected and offline environments
5. Threat prevention resolution of milliseconds, without significant impact on CPU usage

Endpoint security testing and certification

For IIoT end users, equipment owners, and operators, it is crucial to ensure that the endpoint is adequately tested for security conformance. For device manufactures and OEMs, it is crucial to ensure that their equipment is trustworthy, in terms of both hardware and software. Often, time-to-market pressures and accelerated development cycles compete with adequate security testing. However, security verifications should be integral to the product development life cycle. While some vulnerabilities may still escape, proper security testing can significantly reduce their number. The sooner a vulnerability is detected in the product life cycle, the lower the cost of its repair, which also improves operational savings and brand reputation.

Some of the security test approaches for embedded systems include:

- Common Criteria (ISO (https://en.wikipedia.org/wiki/International_ Organization_for_Standardization) and IEC (https://en.wikipedia.org/ wiki/International_Electrotechnical_Commission) 15408) based testing at the component level
- System-level testing using ISASecure methodologies
- Test automation to detect and mitigate security regressions
- Simulation-based testing
- Black-box and white-box testing (using the Common Weakness Enumeration specification) accompanied by static analysis and code coverage analysis
- Assurance of software tagging to confirm that the software came from authenticated and authorized sources (ISO/IEC 197702)
- White-hat or penetration testing

The **ISA Security Compliance Institute** (**ISCI**) (www.isasecure.org) operates the first conformity assessment scheme for IEC 62443 IACS cybersecurity standards. This program certifies **Commercial Off-The-Shelf** (**COTS**) IACS products and systems (ISA-SECURE).

Penetration testing goes beyond the endpoint, and includes the processing and people who are involved. The greatest industrial vulnerabilities are often non-technical, and are related to processes and people. For example, social engineering or phishing attacks can convince an insider to disclose their passwords. Penetration testing is a recommended user-acceptance criteria.

For IIoT endpoints, the following certifications can be considered for security compliance:

- ISASecure **Embedded Device Security Assurance (EDSA)**, certifying IACS products to the IEC 62443-4-2 IACS cybersecurity standard
- ISASecure **System Security Assurance (SSA)**, certifying IACS systems to the IEC 62443-3-3 IACS cybersecurity standard
- ISASecure **Secure Development Life cycle Assurance (SDLA)**, which certifies IACS development organizations to the IEC 62443-4-1 cybersecurity standard, providing assurances that a supplier organization has institutionalized cybersecurity into their product development practices
- Common Criteria (ISO/IEC 15408) based test certification

To ensure the safety and reliability of a **real-time operating system** (**RTOS**), the following certifications can be considered:

- DO-178B, for avionics systems
- IEC 61508, for industrial control systems
- ISO 62304, for medical devices
- SIL3/SIL4, IEC for transportation and nuclear systems

Endpoint protection industry standards

The various industry standards and references relevant to industrial endpoint security are provided in *Table 4.3*:

SECURITY CAPABILITY	INDUSTRY STANDARD
BOOT PROCESS INTEGRITY MEASUREMENT	NIST SP 800-155
ICS CYBERSECURITY STANDARDS	IEC 62443
SECURITY AND PRIVACY CONTROLS FOR FEDERAL INFORMATION SYSTEMS AND ORGANIZATIONS	NIST SP 800-53
INDUSTRIAL INTERNET SECURITY FRAMEWORK	IIC:PUB:G4:V1.0:PB:20160926
INDUSTRIE 4.0 STANDARD	Industries 4.0
IIC ENDPOINT SECURITY BEST PRACTICES	IIC:WHT:IN17:V1.6.3:ID:20180129
COMMON WEAKNESS ENUMERATION	CWE
SPECIFICATION ON SOFTWARE TAGGING	ISO/IEC 197702

Table 4.3: Standards and references related to industrial endpoint security

Summary

This chapter covers the essential dimensions of IIoT endpoint security. It establishes an working definition of IIoT endpoints and discusses various use-case specific considerations for securing them. A real-world case study is cited to illustrate the vulnerabilities of typical industrial device endpoints. In this chapter the reader also finds an elaborate treatment of the endpoint security enabler technologies which spans the silicon, software and processes. The increasing use of machine learning and the importance of testing and certifications using industry standards have also been discussed in this chapter.

Chapter 5, *Securing Connectivity and Communications*, focuses on the next level of the 4-tier IIoT security model.

Securing Connectivity and Communications

5

"Once a new technology rolls over you, if you are not part of the steamroller, you are part of the road."

– Stewart Brand

Secured connectivity underpins the success of the industrial internet. The internet and cloud connectivity have already enabled many industrial enterprises to streamline operations and profitability. In addition to cloud connectivity, IIoT use cases such as smart cities and connected cars also require horizontal interconnectivity and interoperability across vertical technologies and systems.

However, interconnectivity exposes industrial systems to newer threats and attack surfaces. For example, the adoption of cloud-connected ICS systems, SCADA-as-a-service, and so on has been accompanied by a steady rise in security incidents. Attacks targeting industrial control systems were reported to have increased by 110 percent in 2015-2016 (IBM-MSS).

In SCADA systems, common attack types include gaining unauthorized access to network and system resources, intercepting data transfer, and injecting malicious frames to gain control over SCADA systems. Ranging from simple spear phishing to **advanced persistent threats** (**APT**), not only do modern industrial attacks damage equipment and company reputations, they also disrupt production, inflict outages, demand ransoms, trigger environmental incidents, or even target human lives.

Back in 2013, using remote access over a cellular modem, attackers were able to compromise the command and control systems of a dam in New York State. In June 2016, Windows-based SFG malware was injected into the communication networks of a European power company to maliciously extract data and potentially shut down its energy grid. In December 2015, the BlackEnergy malware was injected through spear phishing into three Ukrainian power grids, leading to large-scale power outages. According to SEC 10-Q statements and European financial releases, there have been at least 1 billion USD in losses due to infections in industrials (CSC-FAC). In the worst cases, workers' health and safety are put at risk.

Fears of security threats inflicted by connectivity is a major deterrent to IIoT adoption. However, in this digital era, the cost of denying connectivity could be far greater in terms of competitiveness and profitability. The right balance would be to implement a threat-based defense-in-depth strategy to secure the IIoT connectivity framework.

In this chapter, the reader will find a detailed assessment of IIoT connectivity standards, technologies, and security methodologies to build a reliable industrial connectivity infrastructure. The topics covered in this chapter are the following:

- Definitions – networking, communications, and connectivity
- Distinguishing features of IIoT connectivity
- IIoT connectivity architectures
- Controls for IIoT connectivity protection
- Security assessment of IIoT connectivity standards and protocols
- Fieldbus protocols
- Connectivity framework standards
- Connectivity transport standards
- Connectivity network standards
- Data link and physical access standards

Definitions – networking, communications, and connectivity

The terms **networking**, **communications**, and **connectivity** are often used interchangeably, although these terms do have context-specific differences. For the sake of clarity, in this section, we shall define these terms and adhere to those definitions for the remainder of this book.

To arrive at the definitions, let's take recourse to the three prevalent standard-based information technology stack models:

- Seven-layer OSI model (ISO/IEC 7498)
- Four-layer TCP/IP stack
- IIoT connectivity stack model (IIC-IICF)

Figure 5.1 shows the relative mapping of the various layers in each of the stack models:

	IIoT Connectivity	OSI Model	Internet (TCP/IP)		
Network	Framework	Application	Application	Common Protocol used to share structured data between endpoints	Connectivity
		Presentation			
		Session			
	Transport	Transport	Transport	Messages and information shared between endpoints	
	Network	Network	Internet (IP)	Data shared (routed) across diverse datalink and physical access domains	
	Link	Data Link	Link	Shared/Dedicated Media Access layer for Data Packets	
	Physical	Physical		Physical Media (Wired/Wireless/RF)	

Figure 5.1: Relative mapping of the communication stack models

As shown in *Figure 5.1*, the **Network** section of the stack deals with the infrastructure, technologies, and protocols for routing and forwarding packets between any two devices. The **Connectivity** section involves infrastructure, technologies, and protocols that encompass the entire stack, including transport and applications. Using this reference illustration, we can define the terms as follows:

- **Networking**: It involves technologies and protocols encompassing the **physical infrastructure** (optical, electric, RF over wired/wireless media), **media access link layer infrastructure**, and **the network or internet (IP) layer infrastructure**. Networking enables packet exchange between adjacent and non-adjacent endpoints, which are interoperable at each of these layers.
- **Connectivity**: It provides the infrastructure for data exchange between endpoints and determines how devices and applications can communicate by utilizing technologies and protocols at the networking, transport, and framework layers.

- **Communication**: It refers to the process of information exchange between interoperable participants in a connectivity framework. The participants can be adjacent or non-adjacent and may belong to separate organizational domains. **Connectivity enables communications**.

In the subsequent sections, the scope of securing connectivity and communication will encompass the protection of the layers of the IIoT connectivity stack model, from the physical layer to the framework layer, in order to protect data in motion and data in use:

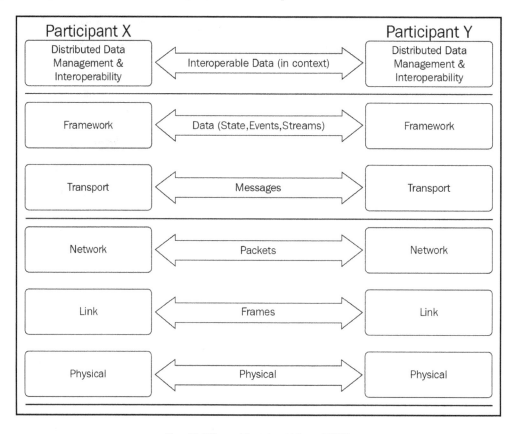

Figure 5.2: IIoT connectivity stack model; Source: IIC-IISF

Distinguishing features of IIoT connectivity

The industrial internet and Industrie 4.0 are driving the transformation of industrial assets into cyber-physical entities. The erstwhile air-gapped devices and operational domains are now being connected to business application systems over IP-based network infrastructure (*Figure 5.3*):

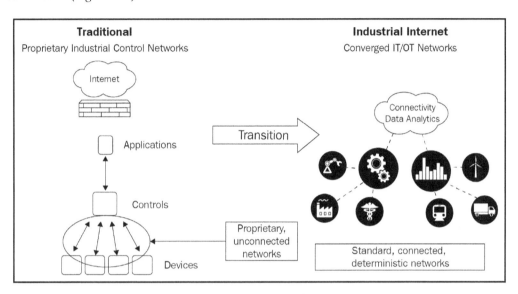

Figure 5.3: Transition of industrial systems from unconnected to converged IT/OT model

Ubiquitous connectivity introduces new operational dynamics in OT environments. To adequately protect OT connectivity, we need to consider its key distinguishing aspects, as discussed in this section.

Deterministic behavior

Traditionally, in industrial systems, field devices such as sensors communicate with control and actuation devices such as PLCs in highly deterministic modes. Consider the example of an oil and gas plant where the field sensors send out data in deterministic timeframes. The control devices receive, process, and analyze this data to send out control and actuation commands in strict deterministic timeframes as well. This calls for precise time synchronization and priority-based traffic scheduling.

The defining requirements of this deterministic behavior are use case specific and vary across industry verticals. As a result, the connectivity technologies and protocols used in these control networks are bespoke, proprietary, and often unconnected.

With the introduction of IIoT and Industie 4.0, there is, however, a shift in context for field-generated data. In a manufacturing plant, for example, the data generated by a sensor can pertain to control and actuation, and it may contain telemetry and diagnostics data. The latter may not be immediately consumed by the control-level devices, but it needs to be communicated to higher business application functions, where the telemetry and diagnostics data is analyzed for optimization, anomaly detection, predictive maintenance, and so on. To enable these new forms of communication, new standards-based connectivity technologies come into play, while still maintaining compliance with the deterministic requirements of control networks.

The deterministic control signals are also mission-critical for a given use case. Consider the example of operating the water level in a dam in a smart power generation plant, where a security breach can have costly safety and reliability implications.

Interoperability – proprietary versus open standards

As shown in *Figure 5.3*, in traditional industrial systems, the control networks commonly connect with field devices using proprietary protocols. For plant information systems (data historian, asset manager, manufacturing execution systems, and so on), these protocols have evolved into Ethernet- and standard IP-based variants, typically to satisfy the needs of a specific industry vertical. Being nonstandard with bespoke design, these fieldbus technologies were considered less vulnerable to intrusion and attacks. Even though it may sound like a myth in the post-Stuxnet era, these protocols are still running in traditional industrial networks with hardly any built-in security controls.

In IIoT deployments, sensor data needs to be communicated for higher levels of processing and analysis. As such, IIoT involves the interconnectivity of diverse network segments in the plant, and often interconnecting systems in different functionally vertical domains. This is possible only when systems can interoperate at the network, transport, and framework layers by using open, standard-based, interoperable technologies.

Connecting vertical technologies horizontally adds to technical, operational, and multi-vendor complexities, which again may increase the attack surface due to misconfiguration and zero-day vulnerabilities.

Performance characteristics – latency, jitter, and throughput

In IIoT systems, especially with sub-millisecond control loops, the connectivity infrastructure must be capable of near-real-time performance. The performance-defining parameters are:

- **Latency**: The travel time for data from source to destination
- **Jitter**: The variation in latency
- **Throughput**: The volume of data flow per unit of time
- **Bandwidth**: The channel capacity of a connectivity technology

In industrial automation and control systems, for effective process operations, short reaction times or tight coordination is needed. Short bursts of data produced by industrial devices in the plant networks usually do not need much bandwidth. However, this data is produced in short time intervals for tight control loops, and as such must be communicated quickly, consistently, and correctly. In such scenarios, low latency and low jitter are more important performance criteria than throughput and bandwidth.

Legacy networks with disappearing air gaps

IIoT adoption presupposes the coexistence of newer devices and technology with legacy systems and networks. Industrial automation systems have existed for decades. Over the last decade, as the adoption of web- and IP-based business information systems grew, these legacy networks and protocols evolved to use routable technologies. However, due to the physical and electronic air-gapped design of control networks, safety and reliability took precedence over information security, and the integration of security controls was left out of the protocol design. With the increasing use of information technologies, computing platforms, and portable media disks such as USB drives and CDs, today there are practically very few air gaps in industrial systems (INS). This calls for more emphasis and OT awareness on the importance of implementing network security controls.

Access to resource-constrained networks

Industrial sensors are often geographically dispersed and situated in remote locations. Along with low power availability, this has led to predominantly wireless (cellular, Wi-Fi, and satellite) and RF-based sensor networks. For the monitoring and management of distributed services such as heat, water, and electricity in large-scale SCADA systems, GPRS/3G modem connections are used (**wireless sensor networks (WSN)**) for transport, which makes these WSN vulnerable to unauthorized public access.

The methods and extent of protection in any network infrastructure depend on both the device endpoints and the data transmission capabilities in the underlying media. Wireless media are more vulnerable to eavesdropping, interception, code injection, and other channels of attack. The limited computational and power resources of these transmission networks deters the use of resource-intensive information security measures such as sophisticated encryption algorithms, multi-factor authentication, antivirus and patching tools, or firewalls. In predominantly proprietary deployments, the use of standard-based protocols, for example, IPSec (DEF-IPSEC), and TLS/SSL-based security controls are also challenging.

Massive transition by connecting the unconnected

Digital transformation in industries is rooted in machine and plant equipment connectivity to external networks. By some recent estimates, there are 60 million machines in factories throughout the world, and 90 percent are not connected (CSC-FAC). As industries prioritize connecting the unconnected machinery for improved **overall operations effectiveness (OOE)**, **total effective equipment performance (TEEP)**, predictive maintenance, process optimization, and so on, the number of connections is expected to grow very rapidly. The operations and control domains of various industries traditionally use fieldbus protocols that cater to specific verticals (ProfiNet, Modbus, Common Industrial Protocol, and so on). Connecting this wide variety of proprietary technology domains to the open standard-based IP is a significant transition.

Even though some of these fieldbus protocols have evolved to use the Ethernet/IP stack, these protocols were never built for interoperability and security. This poses a serious challenge to effectively connect machines and an assortment of technologies, without compromising safety, reliability and secure interoperability.

IIoT connectivity architectures

In the industrial world, 100 percent greenfield IIoT use cases are a rarity. As industries embrace digital innovations, they must factor in the unique characteristics of their existing connectivity frameworks, as discussed in the previous section. Due to the convergence of legacy OT infrastructure with IT connectivity frameworks, the cybersecurity envelope must extend to the industrial edge, factory floors, and remote field sites.

Security, however, incurs a cost. Plant downtime has massive cost implications, which plant managers want to avoid under any circumstances. Before introducing secured connectivity to a production environment, the threat landscape for the specific use case needs to be properly assessed, as does how these security technologies would interplay with that operational environment. An architectural understanding of secured industrial connectivity is also a precursor to implementing the appropriate security controls.

To design a secured network architecture, it is recommended to define network segments based on differing functions and purposes. Mechanisms also needs to be in place to control traffic flow across various segments. This would enable the implementation of security measures with greater granularity and avoid the unnecessary flow of information.

Since the 1990s, there have been standards for ICS infrastructure specifying the separation of network domains (INCIBE). The **International Society of Automation** (**ISA**) formulated the ISA-95 standard (ISA-95) on the integration of business and control systems. This standard proposes a model called the **Purdue Enterprise Reference Architecture** (**PRA**). The PRA establishes five logical levels in which elements with different functions in an ICS architecture are to be grouped, as shown in *Figure 5.4*. Each segment (levels 1-4) is separated by firewalls. A **demilitarized zone** (**DMZ**) is defined between the industrial and corporate networks.

This level-based segmentation allows for developing security strategies with the granularity of specific measures on each of the levels, and to establish secure mechanisms for information flows between them:

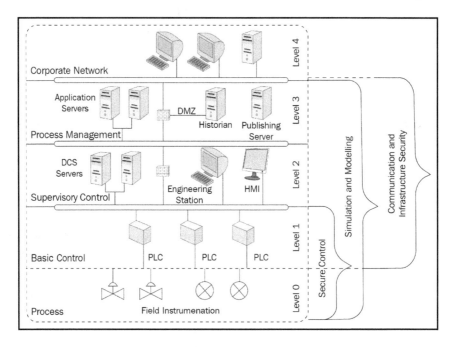

Figure 5.4: ICS reference architecture based on ISA-95

To align with the industrial internet, ISA-95-based connectivity architecture needs to evolve for the following reasons:

- To collect and analyze machine-generated telemetry and diagnostic data by using hosted applications, cloud connectivity is necessary, which implies:
    - Introduction of an edge connectivity layer to connect the industrial site to the cloud
    - Exposure to newer cyberattack vectors
- The industrial internet is about building connected **systems of systems**. To build a smart city or an autonomous vehicle solution, multiple verticals such as manufacturing, automotive, medical, and transportation have to interconnect and interoperate horizontally. The interplay of multiple vertical domains and vendors contribute to a complex ecosystem, thereby opening the doors to unintentional errors and security "holes."

Multi-tier IIoT-secured connectivity architecture

The evolution of the ISA-95-based segmented reference architecture to a multi-tier IIoT connectivity model is shown in *Figure 5.5*:

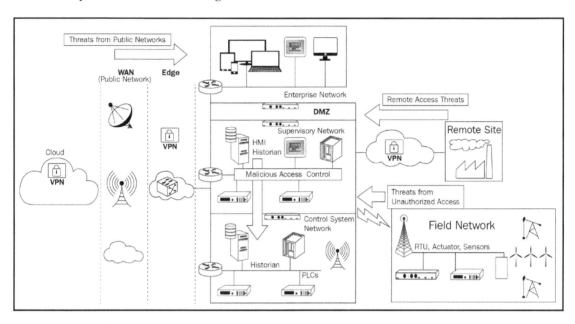

Figure 5.5: Multi-tiered IIoT connectivity architecture (with possible attack vectors)

The multi-tiered IIoT connectivity architecture in *Figure 5.5* is a generalized connectivity model, applicable to many industrial use cases. The field network with RTUs, sensors, and actuators is mostly RF-based. Secured connectivity should be implemented to protect the communication with one or more remote sites. In the industrial network, the control and supervisory networks are segmented with firewalls for traffic inspection and intrusion detection. A DMZ separates the industrial network from the enterprise IT network.

The edge gateway provides secured connectivity between the industrial site and the cloud over the WAN infrastructure, which could be cellular, satellite, or the public internet.

Each of these connectivity gateways and associated connectivity technologies introduces newer threat vectors, and increases the attack surface of industrial systems. To assess the risks associated with a connectivity infrastructure threat modeling for the specific use case is recommended. This risk-managed approach can be used as a basis to build a defense-in-depth strategy to protect the assets, the data, and the overall value chain. The various IIoT connectivity standards and available security controls for an effective strategy are discussed in the subsequent sections.

Layered databus architecture

In industrial IoT **systems of systems**, data plays a central role and needs to be efficiently transported, accessed, and interpreted from the point of origin to various points of consumption. The layered databus architecture is useful in evaluating end-to-end protections at the higher layers (application and middleware) for both **machine-to-machine** (**M2M**) and **machine-to-cloud** (**M2C**) connectivity.

A databus (shown in *Figure 5.6*) runs over existing network and transport layer infrastructure and provides a middleware platform for both north-south and east-west data communications between application endpoints (data):

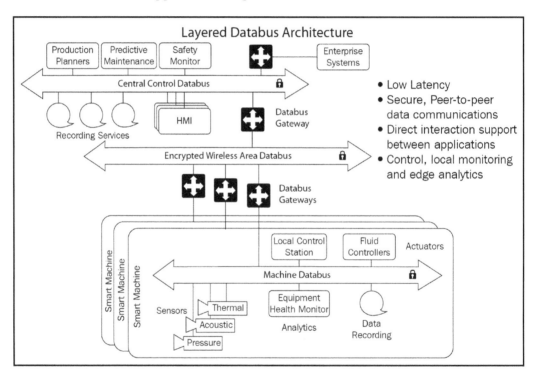

Figure 5.6: Layered databus IIoT architecture; Source: rti.com

Controls for IIoT connectivity protection

Whether it is the factory floor, an autonomous vehicle on the road, a connected surgery room, or a smart energy grid powering up a city, ubiquitous connectivity has exposed these industrial applications to unprecedented cyber threats. We are architecting a connected world where the network itself has been "weaponized." The increasing use of open standards in OT infrastructure, cloud connectivity, and multi-vendor-based highly complex solutions has seized the protection of using "little-known" protocols and technologies in industrial networks. Wireless technologies are providing a fast track to connectivity, but are also easier avenues (compared to wireline) for interception, code injection, and other forms of "man-in-the-middle" attacks (WSN).

Insider attacks and human errors can also cause havoc. The Stuxnet virus, for example, could slip through **automated process control system** (**APCS**) firewalls by taking stealthy routes such as USB drives, CDs, or protocols the firewalls were not configured to detect. Besides, these sophisticated technologies are now operated by personnel who need not be IT experts, and for whom productivity and efficiency are far more critical than patching bug fixes. All these factors demand highly comprehensive and integrated security strategies to protect the connectivity infrastructure, from inception through the production life cycle.

Security controls must be integrated at every layer of the IIoT connectivity stack and also at the procedural, physical, and software levels with appropriate defense-in-depth strategy.

Traditionally, industrial connectivity infrastructure has lacked well-orchestrated security architecture, though certain security implementations may exist in certain pockets of the network. This section presents a comprehensive list of security mitigations to protect connected assets. Readers may utilize these options in security architecture and associated threat models specific to their use case.

Secure tunnels and VPNs

Tunnels provide secured data transport, where the payload remains isolated from the underlying infrastructure. A **virtual private network** (**VPN**) is a prevalent application of tunneling technology. VPNs provide a cost-effective and reliable mechanism to extend a private network across a public network (VPN-DEF) without requiring dedicated transport links. **Virtual Private LAN Service** (**VPLS**), **pseudo-wire** (**PW**), and Ethernet over IP are some other OSI layer 2-based tunneling solutions.

VPNs can be used to connect a single device to a remote network, or securely connect two network domains over a public network. To protect privacy, VPNs typically allow only authenticated remote access using tunneling protocols (for example, MPLS) and encryption (for example, IPSec). Encrypted VPNs provide:

- Data confidentiality—an attacker sniffing network traffic at the packet level only sees encrypted data.
- Access control, by enforcing endpoint authentication to prevent unauthorized access. Remote user authentication may use passwords, biometrics, two-factor authentication, or other cryptographic methods. In the case of M2M or network-to-network authentication, digital certificates and PKI automate tunnel establishment, without any human intervention.
- Message integrity, by providing a mechanism to detect tampering with transmitted messages.

IP-based VPNs can protect several industrial use cases:

- Connecting multiple remote industrial sites to the core ICS infrastructure.
- Providing remote access to users and devices, for example, a connected car communicating to the automobile manufacturer's network or to a cloud-based control center.
- Pushing over-the-air firmware and software
- Connecting the industrial edge to the cloud. As an example, AT&T's NetBond solution allows extending MPLS VPNs to a **cloud service provider** (**CSP**) infrastructure (ATT-NB). This software-defined VPN solution is integrated with many leading CSPs.

Cryptography controls

Encryption protects data integrity and confidentiality. Although encryption can be a costly processing overhead, for IIoT connectivity systems, the price-to-protection ratio of encryption is not all that high. Chapter 3, *IIoT Identity and Access Management*, presents various encryption algorithms used for mutual authentication, to encrypt session keys and data -in motion, -in use, and -at rest.

At the network layer of the IIoT connectivity stack, IPSec (DEF-IPSEC) supports encryption for IPv4 and IPv6 in two encryption modes: **transport mode** and **tunnel mode**. **Transport mode** encrypts only the data portion (payload) of each packet, whereas in the more secured **tunnel mode**, both the payload and the header are encrypted. IPSec was designed to interconnect networks by strengthening protection against many network-level attacks such as spoofing, sniffing, and session hijacking.

Transport layer security protocols, such as TLS/SSL (for TCP) and DTLS (for UDP), provide encryption for application layer payloads. **Data Distribution Service** (**DDS**), a connectivity framework layer standard from OMG, provides encryption services (DDS-SECURE) independent of lower layers of encryption. DDS selectively encrypts only sensitive data, thereby significantly reducing encryption overhead. Resource-constrained environments such as WSN and legacy infrastructures lack encryption capabilities. In such scenarios, data encryption should still be performed at the gateway that connects them to advanced platforms.

Network segmentation

Network segmentation is a foundational security principle in industrial connectivity. Industrial security standards specifications ISA/IEC 62443-1-1, ISA/IEC 62443-3-3, ANSSI, and NIST 800-82 recommend separating networks into segments. These standards define segments as groups of assets that require similar security policies and can be assigned at the same trust level. In the case of an autonomous car, traffic-based segmentation can be done to isolate the telemetry traffic from that of infotainment. In the *IIoT connectivity architectures* section, we also discussed the ISA-95-based Purdue Reference Architecture, which defines function-based levels for separating networks. The segments of an IIoT connectivity reference architecture were illustrated earlier, in *Figure 5.5*.

Segmentation makes a complex network architecture more manageable to implement domain-specific security policies, remote monitoring, and access control rules. It is also an effective threat prevention technique. Segmentation contains the damage of a compromise, such as a malware injection, to only the affected segment, and optimizes incident response and resolution. Traffic between segments is isolated using firewalls, DMZs, and other traffic filtering schemes such as unidirectional filtering.

Industrial demilitarized zones

Until recently, the DMZ was selectively used in industries by defining few broad perimeter networks. However, with the increasing sophistication of cyberattacks, and as traditional factory assets become intelligent and connected, just one line of defense isn't enough. In the case of an intrusion, a countermeasure is critical to prevent lateral movement of the malware. As a result, zoning between IT and OT networks is as important as zoning *within* the corporate IT and OT networks.

An **industrial DMZ** (**IDMZ**) enforces security policies between a trusted network (industrial zone) and an untrusted network (enterprise/IT network). An IDMZ is a subnetwork, or a "neutral zone" placed between the industrial and IT zones. It contains twin firewalls to detect and isolate suspicious traffic before it penetrates trusted networks, servers, and systems (CSC-FAC).

The industrial internet and Industrie 4.0 are leading a massive convergence of IT and OT networks, and the horizontal consolidation of multiple industrial sites and factory zones. In these converged connectivity architectures, IDMZs should be an essential element for protecting assets across disparate network boundaries.

Boundary defense with firewalls and filtering

Intrusion detection and prevention (**IDS/IPS**) using content filters, firewalls, anti-malware, and antivirus gateways are some of the recommended controls to protect network boundaries. Network firewalls are usually deployed in network perimeters to detect and filter malicious traffic, malware, viruses, worms, and so on by using predefined whitelisting and blacklisting rules (based on protocols, ports, IP addresses, and so on) and thresholds.

Network firewalls operate on network layer traffic, which may not be adequate to protect industrial networks. Firewalls used in ICS networks should be equipped to perform deep packet inspection to detect intrusion at a finer granularity. Industrial firewalls need to be equipped to detect anomalies in the application layer or any malicious changes in command and control messages. Bayshore Networks' IT/OT Gateway is an example of an OT firewalls that provides visibility into OT infrastructure, networks, applications, machines, and operational processes (BAYNET).

In the case of the BlackEnergy malware, malicious control traffic hoodwinked traditional boundary defense controls to harm industrial systems (for example, centrifuges in a nuclear power plant). The malware went undetected despite spiking traffic flow by 50-100 times. In such scenarios, device-embedded firewalls can be used. Device-embedded firewalls are designed to provide device-level firewall protection.

Embedded firewalls installed at the device connectivity layer enforce rule-based filtering policies to detect and block attacks before a connection can be established with the target device. Thus, embedded firewalls will provide another level of defense after all other network controls have been defeated and the intruder has reached the target system.

These device firewalls can detect and block packets at the lowest layers of the TCP/IP stack and perform stateful packet inspection to filter packets based on connection state, and filter based on thresholds to block packet floods. Icon Labs' Floodgate Defender is a good example of a device-embedded firewall implementation (ICO-DEF).

User-configurable firewalls allow, for example, selective read/write permission to certain device registers (IIC-IISF). Software-defined adaptive firewalls are capable of learning on the fly to monitor and filter application layer traffic. In the learning mode, they dynamically create filtering rules by observing normal traffic as permitted. After the learning mode, the firewalls can be configured to forward only traffic that agrees with the filters, and to drop all other traffic. A downside of this approach is that they can also learn to accept bad behavior. The combination of fixed rule-based AND behavior-based solutions is usually recommended. The rules eliminate known bad situations, which are **never** okay, and the behavior-based solution picks up all of the combinations where you'd never be able to write enough rules.

Using firewall-on-demand solutions, virtual firewalls can be installed in a hypervisor, which provides instances of zone-based stateful firewall and IPS solutions in a virtualized hosting environment. Virtual firewalls can be used to enforce attack-based policies and dynamic rules (SIF-ODF).

Comprehensive access control

To onboard, manage, and retire an ever-increasing number of IIoT endpoints, the access control technologies need to be robust and highly scalable. These connected endpoints can be fixed or mobile devices, remote assets, onsite or mobile users, or virtual/software entities. Thus, the next generation of access control must be rugged at every layer of the IIoT connectivity stack. Some desired features of an IIoT access control framework are listed here:

- Centralized context-awareness to efficiently control access in both the industrial and enterprise zones. Dynamic discovery, identity-based secured device onboarding, role- and group-based authentication, and authorization to access network resources are necessary capabilities.
- Centralized policy management and dynamic enforcing. Policies using access control lists ("default deny" in industrial zones) or whitelisting (command-level-, application-, or L2/L3/L4 port-based) can be implemented statically or can be dynamically learned and enforced. IP- or URL/URI-based whitelisting to control access to applications.
- Monitoring network data flows to ensure users, devices, and applications are granted access only to resources they are authorized to use, barring access to unauthorized domains and privileges. This also facilitates network usage measurements, anomaly detection, and response to threats such as data exfiltration or anomalous phishing behavior.
- Managed remote access controls to secure sessions. VPNs provide secured remote access in session establishment. However, after the session is established, controls must be in place to prevent the remote user (could be a third-party entity) from performing malicious activity, such as data exfiltration or code injection. Remote sessions are also prone to replay attacks, session hijacking, and so on. These are detrimental in industrial zones. **Managed remote access (MRA)** solutions help to create encrypted, policy protected, bidirectional tunnels on demand between remote users and the industrial connectivity infrastructure (MRA-DOC). In multi-vendor industrial use cases, third-party remote sessions can be managed and monitored from a central **security operations center (SOC)**.
- To provide role-based access control at the higher layers, a databus architecture using the DDS connectivity framework can be used. DDS security provides fine-grained role-based access control for applications communicating over the databus.
- 802.1X provides a robust access control framework for mobile and fixed line endpoints.

Core and edge gateways

The evolution of legacy industrial networks into the industrial internet and Industrie 4.0 connectivity architectures has ushered in a new marketplace for industrial gateways. An industrial gateway acts as a mediator between legacy industrial network segments and modern IP-based IIoT platforms and applications. The gateway performs protocol translation, encapsulation, and so on. A protocol-translation gateway connects network segments by translating legacy, insecure communication protocols into modern, encrypted protocols and vice versa. These functions open up new attack surfaces, and it is recommended to have security engineering teams assess risk using threat modeling on a case-by-case basis.

The security capabilities of a gateway need to align with the trust level of network segments they connect. For example, using unhardened gateways to connect a legacy network of safety and control devices to the corporate network, or to the internet, is not a good idea.

A gateway may also provide advanced processing and security functions such as mutual authentication, trust relationships using digital certificates, encryption, and so on, and act as a proxy for battery-operated, resource-constrained field devices. A gateway may also define additional security by implementing a firewall (hardware- or software-defined) and perform rule-based traffic filtering, whitelisting, and so on. The filtering rules could use L2/L3 addressing or application and middleware layer identifiers:

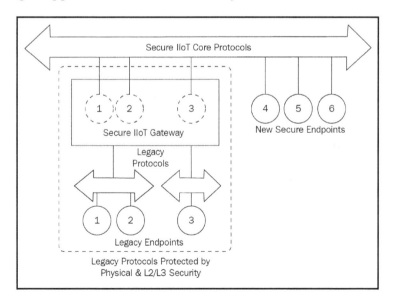

Figure 5.7: Secure IIoT gateways for legacy and modern network interconnectivity; Source: IIC-IISF

Gateways are also needed to support the convergence of industry adjacencies (for example, energy, manufacturing, and industrial services), which depends on the interoperability of disparate vertical-specific technologies. The IIC's **Industrial Internet of Things Connectivity Framework** (**IICF**) defines a set of connectivity core standards (IIC-IICF) to provide syntactic interoperability between verticals by introducing the concept of "core gateways." Core gateways perform protocol translation (for example, DDS to OPC UA) and thus expose new attack surfaces. Security vulnerabilities inherent in each protocol and new exploits associated with the bidirectional translation should be carefully threat modeled when developing core gateways and during use-case-specific deployments.

An edge gateway connects the industrial premises with the internet, a public or private cloud provider, or a fog computing infrastructure. Fog computing and edge gateway security are discussed in `Chapter 6`, *Securing IIoT Edge, Cloud, and Apps*. For secured connectivity, blocking unused ports, enforcing whitelist rules for access control, blocking incoming traffic, and embedded firewalls for application layer protection are some of the security controls recommended in an edge gateway to protect the on-premise industrial assets behind it.

Unidirectional gateway protection

A unidirectional gateway, as mentioned in the IEC 62443-1 and NIST 800-82 standards, is an industrial network perimeter defense technology, brought to market by companies such as Waterfall Security (WATERSEC). These gateways are used in network boundaries between trusted and untrusted network domains. A unidirectional security gateway provides real-time access to information from the industrial sites to support IIoT operations such as IT/OT integration, visibility to enterprise IT systems, real-time monitoring by third-party vendors, industrial cloud services, and so on, using a replication process that physically isolates the industrial environments from external systems and potential attacks (USG-WS).

Figure 5.8 shows a schematic representation of a unidirectional gateway replicating a plant historian server in an external corporate network. Agents are installed on both "sides" of the gateway. The TX (transmit) agent gathers historical data from the plant historian in real time. The RX (receive) agent uses this to create a fully updated, fully functional "mirror copy" of the historian server. To access the historical data, external users and applications query the replica server and not the "real" plant historian. The TX and RX modules can be isolated either optically or through electrical means (IIC-IISF):

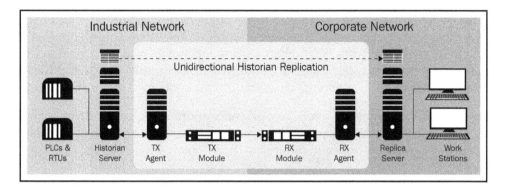

Figure 5.8: Unidirectional security gateway schematic representation; Source: IISF

Unlike firewalls, in this case, messages are not forwarded from source networks to destination networks or vice versa. The gateway software independently communicates on each side. As such, no attack from the corporate network or the replica historian server can propagate into the plant network.

Asset discovery, visibility, and monitoring

The IoT era is driving the addition of disparate connected products in industrial enterprises at the scale of thousands or even millions. Some of these products may not be even directly related to operations, for example, connected lightbulbs, smart fishtanks, and so on. Regardless of their usage, visibility of connected assets in the network is critical. After all, we can protect only what we can "see". The connectivity infrastructure must support automated asset discovery and visibility. To make this process robust, in addition to using automated asset discovery platforms, security policies may also be enforced to trigger notifications to the enterprise IT team (through an online registration process or otherwise) when new assets get connected to the infrastructure. Asset management applications are recommended to maintain an accurate asset inventory. Many cloud-based IoT solution providers also offer these services.

Monitoring network traffic at various levels of granularity is needed to identify anomalies in traffic patterns that could be related to potential threats. By leveraging public and private sources of threat intelligence, it is necessary to establish and maintain a baseline of acceptable behavior. Adaptive learning techniques can be employed to dynamically adjust this adaptive behavior. Technologies such as NetFlow (CSC-FAC) can track both north-south and east-west network traffic, useful for network usage measurements and anomaly detection.

Anomalous traffic behavior may be caused by a variety of factors; it could be an insider threat, consequences of a successful phishing attack, or a stealthy intrusion attempt to penetrate the industrial network. Traffic monitoring technologies, when combined with machine learning and behavioral modeling platforms (for example, Cisco Stealthwatch), provide capabilities to analyze anomalies to identify the root cause and respond to threats.

While shopping for a comprehensive asset and traffic monitoring solution, make sure it provides a historic audit trail data, which, in the case of an incident, enables forensic investigations to determine how and where the threat entered the network.

Physical security – the first line of defense

Physical security controls protect network assets (for example, routing equipment, data centers, computer platforms, remote field devices, and so on) from both natural and human threats such as fire, flood, natural disasters, unauthorized exploitation, and terrorism.

There are multiple ways to provide physical security:

- **Perimeter protection**: This is almost like building a physical "firewall" with blast-resistant glass, fence-mounted surveillance systems (cameras, temperature and touch sensors, alarms, and so on), equipment casings, or enclosures. This is the first line of defense to deter physical intrusion and to protect against natural threats.
- **Controlling physical access**: At various tiers, access to the entire facility can be controlled by employing ID badges, biometrics, manual ID checks, and surveillance cameras. Unauthorized physical access to computers and network ports by insiders is also a major threat. The TIA-942-A ANSI standard further elaborates on physical security at multiple tiers for data centers (TIA).
- **Authorized device-based access**: Before granting access to industrial networks, devices, for example, employee/vendor laptops, mobile devices, and so on. should be authenticated and verified as having adequate security controls installed.
- **Monitor entire site**: A network of IP-based surveillance cameras can be installed at various strategic points to remotely monitor the entire site from a central control station and detect suspicious activities.

Security assessment of IIoT connectivity standards and protocols

As mentioned earlier, for industrial systems, automation and connectivity technologies have evolved mainly to cater to the needs of specific industry verticals. Network security controls were omitted from design for reasons already discussed. Legacy industrial networks using domain-specific proprietary protocols continue to be part of brownfield IIoT deployments. For inter-domain connectivity, such as between field sensors with cloud-based applications, or even for connecting multiple verticals such as a smart grid interfacing with a manufacturing facility, it is important to understand the security dimensions of both legacy protocols and also the interconnecting standard protocols.

Figure 5.9 shows a mapping of some of the connectivity protocols and standards to the IIoT connectivity stack model (IIC-IICF). Each layer of this technology stack needs layer-specific security controls. Enabling exhaustive security controls at every layer may induce unacceptable performance costs. However, selective security implementation at only certain layers may result in unwanted security gaps. Here we need to strike a balance. Using a risk-based approach for specific use cases is a recommended way to implement enough security without tipping over performance or the economies:

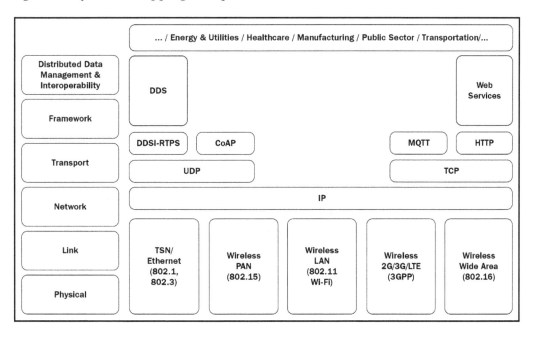

Figure 5.9: Protocols mapped to the IIoT connectivity stack model; Source: IIC-IISF

The subsequent sections analyze the security postures and controls available (or lack thereof) for various connectivity protocols and standards commonly used in IIoT deployments. This assessment can serve the reader with a comprehensive view of the IIoT connectivity security landscape.

Fieldbus protocols

The term **fieldbus** was coined to refer to a family of industrial computer network protocols used for real-time distributed control.

The ecosystem of fieldbus-based protocols is going to remain in deployment for the foreseeable future. Industrial internet platforms and applications have to directly or indirectly interact with fieldbus protocols to acquire data or to communicate actuation signals. In an IIoT context, the security of these protocols becomes all the more important.

Most of the fieldbus protocols facilitate data exchange between field devices, PLCs, and so on. Some common characteristics of fieldbus technologies are as follows:

- Information security mechanisms are typically not built into fieldbus protocols. They are designed for highly controlled, air-gapped operational domains.
- These protocols are not supported by open standard communities.
- Originally developed by a given industrial connectivity vendor, the protocols were adopted in an ecosystem serving vertical-specific operational and management use cases.
- Fieldbus protocols handle messages and services at the framework (OSI: session, presentation, and application) layer of the IIoT connectivity stack model. As industrial control system networks began interconnecting with industrial automation and information systems, these protocols evolved into their respective Ethernet/IP incarnations, mainly based on the underlying transport, network, and physical media infrastructure. Some of these variants run on top of the standard Ethernet/IP/IGMP protocols using TCP or UDP ports, and are exposed to the same vulnerabilities as Ethernet/IP (malicious code injection, spoofing, denial of service, and so on).
- A mix of unicast, multicast, and broadcast messages are used. CIP, for example, uses both implicit producer-consumer multicast and implicit request-response connection patterns.

Table 5.1 presents security assessments for a few prominent fieldbus protocols:

Protocol		IP/Transport	Application	Encryption	Authentication
Common Industrial Protocol (CIP)	DeviceNet	DeviceNet (Proprietary Protocol)	CIP Security	No	No
				No	No
	ControlNet	ControlNet (Proprietary Protocol)		No	No
	CompoNet	CompoNet (Proprietary Protocol)			
	Ethernet/IP	TCP/IP		No	No
MODBUS	Serial Modbus	Not Applicable (Serial)	Modbus (no security)	No	No
	Modbus TCP	TCP/IP	Modbus (no security)	No	No
DNP3		Secure DNP	No built-in security	Secure DNP	Secure DNP
Profibus		Not Applicable (Serial)	No built-in security	No	No
Profinet		TCP/IP, UDP/IP	No built-in security	No	No
PowerLink Ethernet		IP/Ethernet	No built-in security	No	No
EtherCAT		IP/Ethernet	No built-in security	No	No

Table 5.1: Security assessment of fieldbus protocols

Table 5.2 presents security recommendations for the fore-mentioned fieldbus protocols:

Protocol		Security Measures
Common Industrial Protocol (CIP)	DeviceNet	Logical Separation from external networks, Industrial Firewalls with deep packet inspection for intrusion detection and prevention (IDS/IPS)
	ControlNet	
	CompoNet	
	Ethernet/IP	Perimeter defense, network traffic monitoring to detect extraneous control traffic or sources (equipment).
MODBUS	Serial Modbus	Modbus Serial commands are issued as broadcast messages. Being widely used to program control elements like PLCs, RTU's, injection of malicious code can propagate into all elements. Encryption (SSL, VPN) or traffic inspection measures like (Snort), IPS (Tofino) etc. are recommended.
	Modbus TCP	Generic security measures like IDS/industrial firewalls possible for Modbus-Ethernet Actively monitor traffic to allow traffic only from legitimate devices, detect packets with erroneous values etc.
DNP3		Designed to provide high system availability. Less controls for data confidentiality and integrity. Secure DNP3 has challenge-response based authentication framework at application level, which can be used. Alternately use DNP3 encapsulated in TLS tunnels. Monitor DNP3 ports in TCP/UDP to detect any non-DNP3 traffic.
Profibus		Due to lack of authentication/security, perimeter security and network segregation are recommended.
Profinet		Profinet uses Ethernet/TCP/IP in lower layers and all IT security best practices namely network segmentation, Industrial DMZ and perimeter security using deep packet inspection are recommended.
PowerLink Ethernet		Even though communication happens in fixed time intervals, lack of authentication opens the door to device spoofing and denial of service traffic. Traffic monitoring to verify authenticity of traffic source, perimeter security and network segmentation to block intrusion and code injection attacks.
EtherCAT		Has all the vulnerabilities of Ethernet such as malicious packet/ code injection. Security measures include Deep packet inspection, source authenticity verification, network separation.

Table 5.2: Measures to secure fieldbus protocols

Connectivity framework standards

IIoT connectivity framework standards facilitate logical data exchange services among participating devices in real time. Connectivity framework standards need to support secure data exchange with low latency and jitter, hardware and transport layer agnostic performance, efficient device discovery and authentication, and interoperability with legacy fieldbus and other open standards.

Two predominant data exchange patterns in IIoT data communication are **publish-subscribe** and **request-response**. In publish-subscribe mode, an application publishes data on well-known topics, independent of its consumers or subscribers, while applications that subscribe to the well-known topic are agnostic of publishers. This provides loose coupling between participating endpoints, where an endpoint may operate as a publisher, a subscriber, or both. In the request-response data exchange pattern (also known as the **client-server** pattern), requestors (clients) initiate a service request, which is fulfilled by an endpoint in the replier role.

The connectivity framework layer needs to ensure integrity, confidentiality, authenticity, and non-repudiation of the data exchange. To achieve these and also to minimize the consequences of a security breach, guidelines for the framework layer standards are as follows (IIC-IICF):

- After a new endpoint is discovered, it needs to be first authenticated and only then added to the connectivity infrastructure
- Access control policies need to adhere to the principle of least privilege and be granular enough to grant read/write permissions only for resources which are absolutely required
- To protect data at rest and data in motion from tampering, data integrity controls should be built-in
- To avoid excess performance overhead in data encryption and decryption, encryption can be done selectively for sensitive data flows
- To detect and assess the impact of security attacks, the framework supports secure logging and auditing capabilities

Data Distribution Service

DDS is an open connectivity framework standard maintained by the **Object Management Group** (**OMG**). DDS is widely used in mission- and business-critical IIoT applications for reliable, real time performance characteristics at scale. DDS provides a data-centric software abstraction layer, known as a databus, where unlike point-to-point message exchange, the participants maintain distributed local data caches. These caches are kept up to date in real time using a decentralized peer-to-peer protocol (without requiring any brokers or servers):

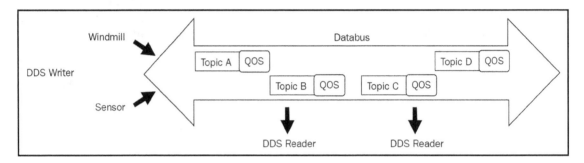

Figure 5.10: Publish-subscribe data exchange using DDS databus

As shown in figure 5.10, DDS DataReader's local data cache is automatically kept up to date in real time as data objects are updated by DDS DataWriters anywhere on the network.

In IIoT systems, data is shared across devices and network domains. The sheer volume of data and additional safety, security, and management traffic can often overload a network. The databus-based connectivity framework decouples applications, as they interact directly with the databus and never directly with each other (DDS-DEF). Software applications need not be aware of other endpoints to participate in a data exchange. Endpoint discovery phase here is automated, as DDS doesn't require explicit configurations to register join or leave.

This data-centric model and automated discovery capability can handle high data volumes in real time with low latency and jitter. The layered databus architecture extends the connectivity across various industrial network levels (ISA-95).

DDS supports unicast and multicast data distribution in broker-less publish-subscribe and request-response patterns. Applications using DDS can use DDSI-RTPS (Real-Time Publish Subscribe Protocol) (OMG-DDS) on the top of either UDP (default) or TCP. DDS has QoS policies integrated to control data distribution parameters such as timeliness, data prioritization, reliability, and resource usage. Gateway standards exist to other connectivity standards such as web services, OPC UA, and oneM2M (under development at the time of writing). Gateways developed for fieldbus technologies (DNP3, C37.118, Modbus, and so on) facilitate system integration and interoperability (IIC-IICF). DDS is already adopted in precision use cases such as in aerospace, autonomous vehicles, medical systems, smart cities, smart grids, and industrial automation.

DDS security

Being agnostic to the underlying network infrastructure, endpoints participating in the databus can be across LAN and WAN. DDS implementations has built-in support for firewalls and other restrictions encountered when going across the WAN. It makes use of transport layer data security controls such as TLS/SSL and DTLS. The introduction of DDS-Security version 1.0, however, makes DDS a pioneering protocol to provide security at the connectivity framework layer for both unicast and multicast distribution patterns, while being independent of the underlying transport layer.

The DDS security standard specifies the following security plugin interfaces (SPI) (IIoT-DATA):

- **Authentication:** Performs mutual authentication of every endpoint participating in a distributed system, so that shared secrets can be established. The default plugins use X.509 certificates issues by a shared certificate authority.
- **Access Control:** Determines whether an endpoint is allowed to perform a protected operation. Protected operations include joining a data domain, creating a topic, reading a topic, and writing a topic. The default plugins use a permission file signed by a shared certificate authority.

- **Cryptographic Control:** Performs the encryption and decryption operations, creates and exchange keys, computes digests, computes and verifies message authentication codes, and signs and verifies signatures. Security functions add to processing cycles. DDS security allows for selectively encrypting and signing data based on its sensitivity. This is a key requirement for implementing security without compromising performance. DDS security gives the choice of selectively encrypting data flows. When confidentiality is not a requirement, for example, when distributing high-frequency sensor data, selected data flows can be signed which helps to minimize the processing cycles. The default plugins provide protected key distribution, and offer AES128 (default), AES256 for encryption, and HMAC-SHA1 and HMAC-SHA256 for message authentication and integrity.
- **Logging:** All security events in a distributed system can be logged for auditing and monitoring at data-level granularity. Logging can be used to detect data corruption, digital signature mismatch, and so on to prevent intrusion.
- **Tagging:** Tagging allows applications to inject metadata that indicates the level of security ("confidential," "restricted," and so on) associated with messages, such that in large distributed networks, participants can access only those data flows that they are authorized to.

DDS Security is implemented in the framework (middleware) layer, can run over any transport layer protocol (TCP, UDP/multicast, and so on), and does not need transport layer security such as TLS/SSL/DTLS.

DDS Security supports both multicast and unicast traffic, and segmentation with multiple independent and isolated communication paths between the same network endpoints. Isolation is accomplished by using DDS domains, which are isolated data spaces on the same network. Within a domain, further segmentation can be achieved by using the PARTITION QoS policy, which allows communication between DDS endpoints tagged with the same partition label (IIC-IICF).

oneM2M

oneM2M defines standards for a common service layer developed rather recently. The main objective of oneM2M is to promote common services across the diverse universe of M2M devices. It defines a common M2M Service Layer that includes the connectivity framework layer functions and can be readily embedded in IoT devices. This service layer exposes a predefined set of functions relevant to applications from across a variety of industry segments such as telematics, intelligent transportation, healthcare, utilities, industrial automation, smart homes, and so on. The oneM2M service layer binds directly with many commonly used IIoT transports, for example, CoAP, HTTP, MQTT, and WebSockets in both wired and cellular infrastructure.

Figure 5.11 shows a simplified oneM2M architecture that supports horizontal integration of applications from various verticals and previously siloed domains for reliable and secure common services (ONE-M2M):

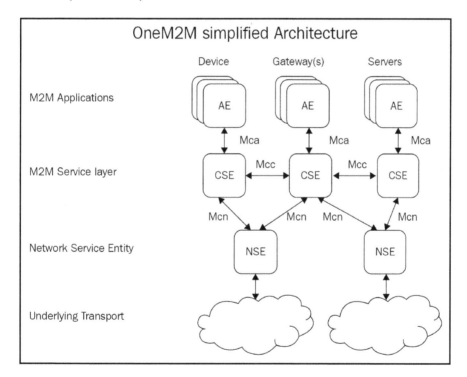

Figure 5.11: Simplified oneM2M architecture

Figure 5.11 illustrates **application entities** (**AEs**), which can be hosted on virtualized or physical instances of nodes (enterprise server, IIoT gateways, and so on). A **common service entity** (**CSE**) receives requests from AEs running on different nodes, and routes the requests to the target AE.

Interworking gateways for oneM2M with OSGi, Alljoyn, **Open Interoperability Consortium** (**OIC**), LWM2M (Open Mobile Alliance), DDS, and OPC UA are being developed at the time of writing.

oneM2M security

oneM2M architecture defines a security model to protect the privacy and confidentiality of data traversing multiple cloud apps and administrative boundaries. The security model supports authentication and identification of applications and CSEs. The security model runs on top of the transport layer and encrypts data streams and communication, either on a segment basis or from end to end, using the underlying transport layer security mechanisms (TLS, DTLS, and so on).

Open Platform Communications Unified Architecture (OPC UA)

OPC Unified Architecture (**OPC UA**) is an open, platform-independent connectivity framework standard maintained by the OPC Foundation and IEC 62541. OPC UA is an evolution of classic OPC (Object Linking and Embedding for Process Control) to support secure and reliable data exchange requirements of industrial automation, and now the industrial internet (OPCF). OPC UA industrial communication architecture provides scalable semantic interoperability between sensors, field devices, controllers, and applications, both on premise and in factory-to-cloud connectivity. For the transport layer, the OPC UA stack can use TCP/IP, HTTP/TCP/IP, and TLS for security.

Classic OPC was designed to provide an abstraction layer for higher-level applications such as HMI, SCADA, historian, and manufacturing execution systems (MES). This helped them discover and control devices running PLC-specific protocols (such as Modbus, Profibus, and so on) using a standardized interface to convert generic OPC read/write requests into device-specific requests and vice versa. OPC UA architecture uses generic device models. Consider the example of the object model for a motor starter. This model includes methods to set system parameters, to read data, and to operate the starter. Thus, applications can control a starter directly without being dependent on the manufacturer's particular implementation.

OPC UA is being deployed in manufacturing, building automation, oil and gas, renewable energy and utilities, and more.

OPC UA security

Security is tightly integrated into the OPC UA framework and includes authentication of users and UA applications, role-based access control, validation of function and user profiles, data integrity and confidentiality, and logging and monitoring of security events.

The UA security model has three levels, namely user security, application security, and transport security:

- UA user-level security grants role-based access to a specific user while setting up a new session.
- UA application-level security is part of this session and includes the exchange of digitally signed X.509 certificates for secure channel establishment and to authenticate an application. The certificates can be self-signed or signed by a CA in the PKI infrastructure.
- Transport-level security can be used to sign and encrypt each message during a communication session. Signing ensures the message's integrity and authenticity, while encryption provides confidentiality.

As shown in *Figure 5.12*, **Global Discovery Server** (**GDS**), a UA server provides discovery services for clients and servers in the IIoT deployment. It also provides automatic X.509 security certificate management services for clients and servers, and role management services to grant role-based access permissions in the UA information model. Users and applications provide their credentials to authenticate and to get a granted role and the corresponding access rights for a UA session. The identity information and access rights are handled via a claims-based authorization mechanism, for example, Kerberos or OAuth2:

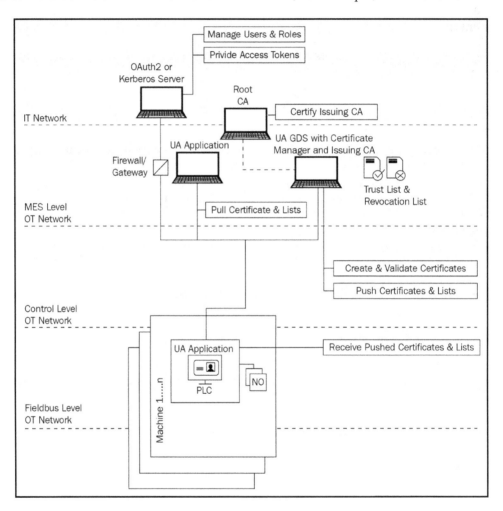

Figure 5.12: OPC UA authentication and access control architecture

This is the scope of the UA security model (OPC-UA):

- Trusted information (CIA triad):
    - Confidentiality, by encrypting messages on the transport layer
    - Integrity and authenticity, by signing messages on the transport layer
    - Availability, by restricting the message size and returning no security-related codes
- Access control (AAA framework):
    - Authentication by username and password or X.509 certificate on the application layer
    - Authorization to read/write values of a node or to browse the information model based on the access rights of the information model, access rights of the user, or of the user's role
    - Accountability by generating audit events for security-related operations

Vendor-distributed OPC UA software stacks include these security mechanisms. Application developers and device manufacturers are responsible for configuring the UA server according to their specific use cases (OPC-WP).

Web services and HTTP

Web services using **Hypertext Transfer Protocol** (**HTTP**), corresponds to the application-specific connectivity framework (IIC-IICF). Latency and jitter characteristics in HTTP cater to human user interactions. Web services may use the RESTful communication architecture. The HTTP open standard specification is maintained by the IETF, and the W3C5 maintains the web (HTML5) specifications. Web services and HTTP are particularly relevant in factory-to-cloud communications.

Web services and HTTP security

Web Services Security (**WS-Security** or **WSS**) is an extension to **Simple Object Access Protocol** (**SOAP**) to apply security to web services. It is a member of the web service specifications and was published by OASIS (WSS-SEC).

The protocol specifies how integrity and confidentiality can be enforced on messages and allows the communication of various security token formats, such as **Security Assertion Markup Language** (**SAML**), Kerberos, and X.509. Its main focus is the use of XML Signature and XML Encryption to provide end-to-end security.

HTTPS, or HTTP Secure, is the secured variant of HTTP supported by IoT cloud providers. In HTTPS, **Transport Layer Security** (**TLS**), or formerly its predecessor, **Secure Sockets Layer** (**SSL**), is used to encrypt the payload, and therefore HTTPS also gets referred to as HTTP over TLS, or HTTP over SSL.

 As a further investigation of the connectivity framework protocols, readers are encouraged to review the assessment templates in the (IIC-IICF) document.

Connectivity transport standards

The high scalability and low CPU power requirements of IIoT field devices have encouraged the adoption of messaging protocols such as MQTT and CoAP for resource-constrained devices. These transports run on top of TCP or UDP and use TLS/DTLS for security. In this section, a brief description of the transports and their security assessment is presented.

Transmission Control Protocol (TCP)

TCP is an open standard maintained by IETF (IETF-TCP) and integral to the internet or TCP/IP protocol stack. TCP provides connection-oriented transport and has been widely used in HTTP-based applications such as e-commerce. In TCP, messages are delivered in order, and it supports retransmission of messages lost in transit, and as such requires considerable time and resources. As a result, message latencies may vary greatly when using TCP.

TCP security

The TLS protocol is usually used to protect transport layer traffic. TLS is an open standard version of SSL version 3 (RFC-TLS). In some cases, TLS may require modifications in the application layer. However, considering its widespread use to protect HTTP-based applications, it is a low-risk option. For additional information on TCP security, readers are encouraged to refer to NIST SP 800-52, *Guidelines on the Selection and Use of Transport Layer Security*: https://csrc.nist.gov/publications/nistpubs/.

User Datagram Protocol (UDP)

UDP provides connectionless transport (RFC-UDP) for network traffic with a best-effort delivery SLA. Compared to TCP, UDP is a lightweight protocol as it does not support retransmission or sequencing messages in order. For resource-constrained IIoT deployments demanding low latency transport, UDP is preferred over TCP. UDP messages are limited to 64 KB; higher-layer protocols have to handle fragmentation and reassembly of longer messages over UDP.

UDP security

Datagram Transport Layer Security (**DTLS**) (RFC 6347) is based on the TLS protocol and offers similar security controls. In ICS networks involving resource-constrained devices, multicast and security are key requirements. The internet draft DTLS-based Multicast Security for Low-Power and **Lossy Networks** (**LLNs**) (draft-KTM) defines a framework to secure multicast communication in LLNs based on the DTLS security protocol (which is already used in CoAP devices, as discussed later in this section).

MQTT and MQTT-SN

MQTT is a lightweight open messaging standard maintained by OASIS (MQTTv3.1.1-OASIS). MQTT is used in M2M and IIoT scenarios where telemetry and diagnostics data is collected from a large number of sensors and other field devices. Consider an example where several applications related to weather, telematics, and transportation are interested in collecting temperature data from sensors. In such scenarios, MQTT provides a publish-subscribe messaging model where clients can subscribe to their topic of interest. MQTT is also used in M2C communications.

MQTT runs on TCP/IP, where an always-on TCP connection is maintained between the clients and a broker server. Clients subscribe to topics of interest. The MQTT broker uses this connection to push new messages to clients who have subscribed to that topic. As shown in *Figure 5.13*, MQTT uses a spoke-hub connectivity model suitable mainly for many-to-one communications:

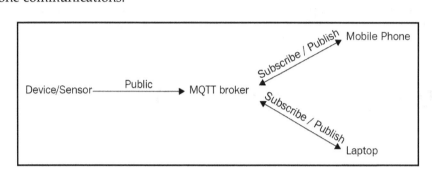

Figure 5.13: MQTT publish-subscribe messaging architecture

For resource-constrained scenarios, such as a WSN, maintaining TCP/IP connections could be too complex for low-footprint **sensor-actuator** (**SA**) nodes. The MQTT-SN standard (MQTT-SN) is an adapted version of MQTT optimized for battery-operated devices with limited processing and storage resources, and low-bandwidth wireless environments where interruptions and failure rates are high.

MQTT security

MQTT is a lightweight protocol with minimal built-in security controls. However, since MQTT uses TCP/IP connections, standard TLS/SSL security is used at the transport layer and IP-based intrusion detection/prevention techniques are recommended for the network layer.

The MQTT CONNECT message contains username and password fields, which the broker can utilize to authenticate and allow only legitimate clients to connect. These fields being in plaintext, transport layer encryption is required to guarantee secured transmission of credentials. Additional CPU usage for using TLS can be a concern for resource-constrained client devices. Session Redemption (RFC-TLS) can considerably improve TLS performance in such scenarios.

Constrained Application Protocol (CoAP)

CoAP, a messaging protocol maintained by the IETF, is designed for resource-constrained nodes and networks such as WSNs (RFC 7252). CoAP is used for M2M communication in energy, smart homes, and building automation, among others.

CoAP is designed to run over UDP and has been modified to run over TCP and WebSockets when UDP is not available. CoAP messages are similar to HTTP, and include GET, POST, PUT, and DELETE. CoAP uses a request-response model where CoAP clients communicate with a CoAP server using specific **uniform resource indicators** (**URIs**). CoAP is designed to interoperate with HTTP and the RESTful web services through simple proxies. A smart light switch, for example, can send a PUT command to change the characteristics of lights (state, color) in a system. *Figure 5.14* shows a sensor network using CoAP:

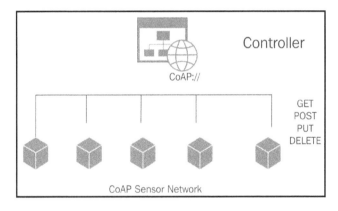

Figure 5.14: Wireless sensor network using CoAP; Source: Packt practical IoT security

CoAP security

In the CoAP security model, to authenticate clients and encrypt client-server messages, underlying transport layer security mechanisms (DTLS/UDP, TLS/TCP) are used. For more details on CoAP end-to-end security, the reader is encouraged to refer to Section 11 of RFC 72522.

Advanced Message Queuing Protocol (AMQP)

AMQP is an open messaging protocol standard maintained by OASIS (AMQP-SPEC). AMQP provides message orientation, queuing, routing, reliability, and security for server-to-server communications. AMQP mandates the behavior of the messaging provider and client for syntactic interoperability (AMQP). AMQP supports both publish-subscribe and point-to-point modes of communications.

AMQP runs on top of a reliable transport such as TCP. AMQP security uses TLS over TCP, and can use SASL as an alternative. AMQP uses client authentication and message encryption. For AMQP security, the reader is encouraged to refer to the AMQP security specification from OASIS (`http://docs.oasis-open.org/amqp/core/v1.0/amqp-core-security-v1.0.html`).

Connectivity network standards

The IIoT connectivity stack model (IIC-IICF) has Internet Protocol as the only protocol standard in the network layer for industrial internet and Industrie 4.0 applications. For multicast communications, **Internet Group Management Protocol** (**IGMP**) is used at the network layer. To secure the network, IPSec is a suite of open security standards defined and maintained by the IETF (RFC 4301).

To provide IP connectivity to low-footprint, resource-constrained devices, the IETF has defined the 6LoWPAN standard (RFC 6282). The standard includes encapsulation and header compression mechanisms that allow IPv6 packets to be sent and received over low-rate wireless personal area networks (LR-WPANs).

Data link and physical access standards

Multiple wired and wireless media-based connectivity standards have been defined, addressing the requirements of resource-constrained, low-rate field and control connectivity. Security support for **wide area networks** (**WAN**), **wireless personal area network** (**WPAN**), and **local area network** (**LAN**) communication standards is presented in this section.

IEEE 802.15.4 WPAN

IEEE 802.15.4 is an open standard for low-rate wireless personal area networks (LR-WPANs), maintained by the IEEE 802.15 working group (WPAN-TG4), which specifies the physical and media access control for LR-WPANs. This standard forms the basis for other upper-layer protocols such as Zigbee, ISA100.11a, 6LoWPAN, WirelessHART, MiWi, SNAP, and Thread specifications (WPAN-WIKI). The physical layer specification defines the RF transceiver management, channel selection, energy, and signal management functions, and supports scalable spoke-hub and point-to-point network topologies. It defines two node types:

- **Full function device** (**FFD**), which acts as a coordinator for WPAN, and
- **Reduced function device** (**RFD**), which can be any low-cost, low-power device.

The 802.15.4 standard defines timeout-based retransmission for reliability. The upper layers can harness MAC sublayer facilities to implement shared secrets between devices for symmetric cryptography, and access control lists to allow only a known set of devices to participate in the communication.

IEEE 802.11 wireless LAN

IEEE 802.11, commonly known as Wi-Fi, is suitable for setting up LAN segments for device-to-device communications within short-range networks, such as factory floors, smart parking lots, smart city lighting, and so on. It is not suitable for low-bitrate RF environments (for example, LP WSN) with battery-operated remote field devices. Wi-Fi is a matured technology used in industrial and enterprise infrastructure. Wi-Fi provides high-bitrate reliable transmission, identity and access control (IEEE 802.1X and MAC-based), and data encryption. In 2018, the Wi-Fi Alliance is adding new enhancements to WPA2 and WPA3 specifications, enumerated here (WPA-WFA):

- Mandatory use of protected management frames to maintain resilience of mission-critical networks
- More resilient password-based authentication, even in cases when passwords do not conform to complexity recommendations
- Dynamic and tailored data encryption to enhance data privacy in open networks
- 192-bit cryptographic strength for sensitive applications

Cellular communications

In IIoT deployments, cellular communication allows wireless wide area connectivity, for example, from an aggregation point to the cloud. The advent of 5G, with unprecedented capacity and throughput, can be an inflection point converging wireline and wireless-based solutions. Unlike its 3GPP-certified predecessors (2G, 3G, and LTE), 5G technology is positioned to support sophisticated IIoT use cases for the smart city, automotive, and health sectors, where human safety is at stake. 5G mobile operators must align with security and location-specific safety regulations across these verticals.

Dynamic network slicing to provide guaranteed access to customized features and resources is a core capability of 5G. Security tailored to each of these slices also needs be factored into the 5G standard. In recent years, there is a growing trend of attacks on the mobile networks, which have originated in the **radio access network** (**RAN**) side. With 100 Mbps capacity, preventing DDoS attacks could be a significant challenge to combat and overcome (MOB-SEC).

Wireless wide area network standards

While cellular and satellite communications are often considered for WAN connectivity, two commonly used industrial IoT WAN technologies are discussed in this section.

IEEE 802.16 (WiMAX)

The IEEE 802.16 standard, commercially known as Worldwide **Interoperability for Microwave Access** (**WiMAX**), was originally defined to provide long-haul wireless transmission, demonstrating up to 30 miles at 70 Mbps throughput (WIMAX). IEEE 802.16s, a new version of the original standard, has been developed primarily to address the security and reliability needs of internet-connected critical infrastructure. **Advanced Metering Infrastructure** (**AMI**) is one of the leading examples of IEE 802.16s used in the oil and gas industry, water and gas utilities, nuclear facilities, rail transportation, military, and so on. In AMI deployments, remote concentrators send smart meter traffic over the WAN infrastructure to central offices, electric substation data acquisition facilities, or to distributed SCADA systems .

Instead of the unlicensed broadband spectrum, IEEE 802.16s is designed to operate below 1 GHz, where utilities and industrial users typically have their own licensed spectrum allocated (MRF: `http://www.mwrf.com/systems/oh-no-not-another-iiot-wireless-technology`). This facilitates added security through spectrum isolation. The protocol also supports AES-CCM payload field encryption, although not much defense is built into the physical layer.

LoRaWAN

LoRaWAN is a **low-power wide area network** (**LPWAN**) specification maintained by the LoRa alliance (LoRa-DEF). LoRaWAN typically uses a star-of-stars topology, where battery-operated end devices use single-hop wireless communication with gateways. The gateways are connected to a network server via traditional IP connections. The WAN may span a single or multiple organizational and regional boundaries. LoRaWAN defines session keys for encryption at three levels:

- Unique network key (EUI64) ensures security at network level
- Unique application key (EUI64) ensures end-to-end security at application level
- Device-specific key (EUI128)

Summary

The industrial internet involves ubiquitous connectivity. Connectivity undoubtedly exposes industrial environments to threats, which may result in serious safety and reliability consequences.

Denying connectivity in the digital era is not an option for enterprises. Industries should instead focus on how to secure their internet-connected infrastructure.

This chapter addresses this question by helping the reader develop deeper insights into building secured IIoT connectivity infrastructure. By analyzing the distinguishing aspects of industrial connectivity frameworks and specifications, this chapter explains how existing industrial deployments can evolve and adopt the secured IIoT connectivity architecture. Multiple security controls and technologies to implement the defense-in-depth strategy for IIoT connectivity were discussed.

A comprehensive understanding of the standards, protocols, and their associated security postures is presented in this chapter to provide the reader with practical insights on securing each layer of the IIoT connectivity stack for their specific use case. Cloud-based services and applications are central to any industrial internet deployment. How to securely integrate cloud-based solutions into an IIoT system will be our focus in the next chapter.

Securing IIoT Edge, Cloud, and Apps

6

"An IoT attack is not a matter of IF, but a matter of WHEN the attack happens and how prepared are we to weather off that attack"
– Arjmand Samuel, Security Lead, Microsoft Azure IoT

The cloud is a key enabler in the evolution of M2M technologies to the Industrial Internet. During the early years of cloud adoption, enterprises were slow to migrate organizational data to multi-tenant cloud platforms, mainly due to data privacy concerns. However, over the last decade, the cost-effective elasticity of cloud platforms have far outwitted privacy fears; and today cloud services are one of the fastest growing IT sectors (GART-CL).

In the case of the Industrial Internet however, the fears extend well beyond data privacy.

On the one hand, the cloud is a key component in typical IIoT architectures. It provides an aggregated view of the entire IIoT deployment, provisions and manages the operational health of millions of connected devices at scale, analyzes and converts machine big data into business insights, and so forth. More importantly, it enables elastic growth of business operations without organizations having to worry about the infrastructure.

However, a centralized cloud-based architecture is subject to single point of failure vulnerabilities.

A multi-tenant public cloud considerably increases the attack surface for an enterprise, as evident from publicly reported cloud security breaches. The attackers can exploit vulnerabilities in hosted applications, access management, service misconfigurations or even a failure to enable existing security features. In some cases, an IIoT deployment may involve multiple **cloud service providers** (**CSPs**), which further add up to the attack vectors. A DDoS attack in the cloud infrastructure supporting a smart city deployment that involves multiple vertical services (energy, medical, transportation, and so on) may have fatal safety consequences.

A silver lining to this is, as a centrally managed infrastructure, the cloud can be secured more predictably (as compared to in-house infrastructures) by implementing the right set of security controls. This chapter discusses the various elements of a defense-in-depth strategy for protecting cloud-based IIoT deployments, where the security responsibilities are shared between CSPs and their customers.

Unlike most other IT disciplines, cloud security involves compliance with several regional and international regulations on sensitive data protection. Non-compliance can be costly to enterprises. While industrial enterprises are accustomed to regulations, before adopting an IIoT cloud platform, it is vital to also evaluate how the platform protects data, prevents threats, and responds in the case of an incident. Well documented chain of custody, forensics, and remediation are key to defining the relationship between the data owner and cloud provider. This chapter includes resources to assess the security compliance stature of IIoT cloud platforms.

This chapter is divided into the following sections:

- Defining edge, fog, and cloud computing
- IIoT cloud security architecture
- Cloud security – shared responsibility model
- Defense-in-depth cloud security strategy
- Infrastructure security
- Identity and access management application security
- Data protection
- Data encryption
- Securing the data life cycle
- Cloud security operations life cycle
- Secure device management
- Cloud security standards and compliance
- Case study of a few IIoT cloud platforms
- Cloud security assessment

Defining edge, fog, and cloud computing

In the early 2000s, when Cisco's (then) CEO John Chambers coined the term **Network as a Platform** (INETNW), the era of cloud computing had just begun to take shape. Cloud computing is one of the disruptive technologies that set the stage for game-changing, "network-enabled" platforms, which are today considered massive growth engines for businesses.

Traditionally, computing resources had been hardware-based assets with fixed compute capacity, and collocated in enterprise premises. This model provided data proximity, data ownership, and data security benefits. However, when a business needs to scale up its compute capacity, then that would translate to significant capex increase and management costs.

A typical cloud computing framework turns this model around. Cloud computing equips third-party cloud providers to offer on-demand compute power, data storage, and application hosting services. Compute resources and applications no longer need to physically collocate on-premise and can be hosted on dedicated hardware or virtualized platforms in remote data centers. Cloud vendors provide managed services for computing and storage resources enabling elasticity with scalable "pay for what you use" models. In our current context, the cloud computing model has two main implications:

1. Cloud computing involves accessing data over public networks, and storing and using data in a shared infrastructure. This necessitates additional controls to protect data in motion, use, and at rest.
2. In spite of geolocation features, data access and compute in cloud platforms contributes to high latency, which could be unacceptable to time-sensitive applications such as industrial control systems.

IoT sensors and other field devices generate a massive volume of data. **Fog computing**, a term coined by Cisco (CSC-FOG), brings compute and intelligence to analyze this data closer to industrial premises. Fog computing is supported in a wide variety of device form factors, for example, routers, edge gateways, controllers, switches, and so on. These fog devices have compute, storage, and of course network connectivity.

Edge computing is a more generic term representing similar capabilities as fog computing, namely, where computing happens at or near the source of data. Today, public cloud vendors offer edge services, wherein the intelligence is synchronized between the cloud and the industrial edge.

Some important capabilities of edge and fog computing are:

- **Minimize latency**: Analyzing data closer to its source can reduce latency from minutes to milliseconds. In a power grid distribution network, for example, protection and control loops are highly time-sensitive. If devices closest to the grid sensors detect a problem, control commands to shut it down can be sent to actuators in quasi-real-time.
- **Optimize bandwidth utilization**: Industrial applications generate a massive volume of time series data, not all of which requires massive computing and processing power. Local processing and analytics significantly reduce the burden of uploading this data to the cloud.
- **Address data security and reliability**: Local processing reduces the attack surface of data in motion and use. Besides, not all asset owners are open to hosting and analyzing data in third-party facilities. Edge computing offers reliable performance where internet connectivity is sporadic or absent.
- **Normalize data processing**: IoT data sources can be disparate, may involve non-IP protocols, and are context sensitive. Edge processing allows protocol translations and context-based processing to selectively upload relevant data for cloud computing, analytics, and storage.

IIoT cloud security architecture

Cloud-based platforms centralize compute, storage, and management functions; this improves the overall economics of scalable deployments. For industrial IoT uses cases, however, cloud security must be architected while considering the unique time-sensitive characteristics of industrial applications, and must be in alignment with safety, reliability, and data privacy regulations. *Figure 6.1* illustrates the various elements of an IIoT cloud security architecture, which spans from the industrial premises to centralized data centers where the cloud services are hosted:

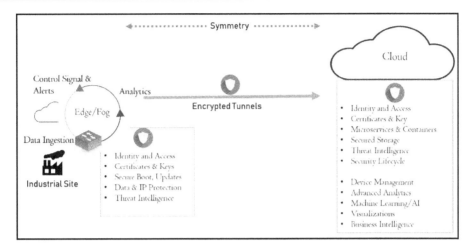

Figure 6.1: Elements of an IIoT cloud security infrastructure

This security architecture has four main functional components.

Secured industrial site

Cloud security depends on the trust controls implemented in the industrial site. A compromise in the trustworthiness of industrial assets, connectivity infrastructure, or machine data impacts the entire edge to cloud value chain. Security controls to protect the field, control, and aggregation layers of an industrial site have been discussed extensively in `Chapters 4`, *Endpoint Security and Trustworthiness*, and `Chapter 5`, *Securing Connectivity and Communications*.

Secured edge intelligence

The industrial edge plays a significant role in securely connecting and complementing cloud intelligence with on-premise operations. The edge layer may consist of one or more devices, such as a gateway to ingest high volume of time series machine data (for example, from temperature and pressure sensors), perform analytics on-site to remove unnecessary exposure of data, and offer low-latency controls for time-sensitive applications. An edge-and-cloud synchronized deployment model removes many limitations of a cloud-only IIoT strategy. It allows operators to push down security policies, analytics intelligence, and device models built in the cloud to the edge. Processing at the edge eliminates latency associated with a round-trip to the cloud.

The edge layer may also provide secured device management functions such as device onboarding, and identity and access control. Trustworthiness of on-premise edge devices must be ensured with physical security, tamper-resistant hardware, secure boot, and signed firmware upgrades. An edge device needs to implement security best practices such as blocking unused ports, whitelist-based access policies, firewalls, threat intelligence, managing keys and certificates, and securely synchronizing device information with the data center.

The case study section of this chapter showcases how an edge cloud combined strategy is implemented by many leading CSPs, and the associated security blueprint of edge cloud architectures.

Secure edge cloud transport

Data in motion from the industrial edge and the data center needs to be protected from man-in-the-middle attacks. Encryption of confidential data and secured connectivity mechanisms (discussed in Chapter 5, *Securing Connectivity and Communications*) are highly recommended. We have already cited technologies such as AT&T's NetBond; which extends Virtual Private Networks from the edge into the cloud infrastructure of most CSPs. Adequate crypto controls for **over-the-air** (**OTA**) firmware and software updates (discussed in Chapter 4, *Endpoint Security and Trustworthiness*) can protect the edge gateway and endpoints behind it.

Secure cloud services

Protection of the infrastructure, platforms, and application across the deployment life cycle of a cloud platform is discussed in the subsequent sections of this chapter.

For data privacy and IP protection, industrial enterprises may use the private cloud model; using either on-premise data centers or single-tenant cloud infrastructures. In the case of a private cloud or private-public hybrid model, the edge and cloud layers may overlap in some cases. However, the security controls discussed in this chapter are applicable across these models.

Cloud security – shared responsibility model

To protect cloud-based solutions, the tenant (customer) and the CSPs usually share the security responsibilities. The three common models of cloud service offerings are listed as follows:

- **Infrastructure-as-a-Service (IaaS)**
- **Platform-as-a-Service (PaaS)**
- **Software-as-a-Service (SaaS)**

The split in responsibilities varies according to the cloud service level agreement between the customer and cloud provider, as specified in the ISO/IEC 17789 standard. Since the customer is in control of the edge functionalities, a separation of duties is key to ensure the implementation of the right security controls. To avoid any ambiguity, the ISO/IEC 27017 standard recommends a cloud service agreement between the customer and the provider to clearly enumerate these shared roles and responsibilities.

In the case of the IaaS cloud service model, the customer is typically responsible for the security of data, application software stack, systems, networks, and also security elements such as firewalls and identity and access management. The cloud provider is responsible mainly for protecting the infrastructure.

In a PaaS service model, the cloud provider is responsible for securing the platform including OS, middleware, and runtime environment, and DevOps. The customer is responsible for secured configurations, user roles, and access management, and for managing the application life cycle.

Security functions for a SaaS cloud service model are configured and controlled entirely by the software provider.

Figure 6.2 illustrates the shared responsibility model for **Amazon Web Services** (**AWS**):

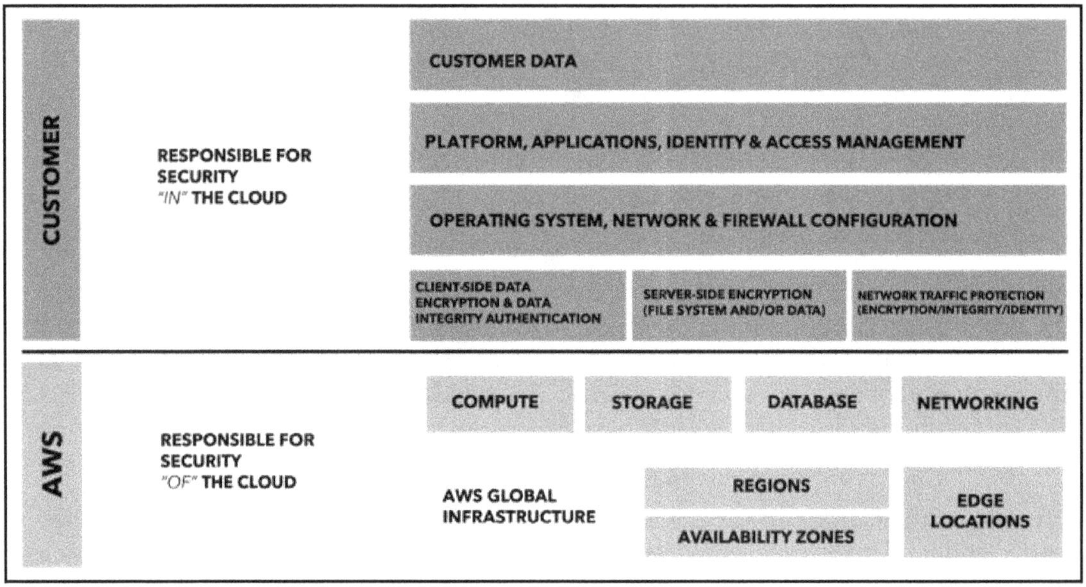

Figure 6.2: AWS shared responsibility model; Source: aws.amazon.com

Defense-in-depth cloud security strategy

As more and more enterprises are moving their data, compute, and storage to the cloud, CSPs now have a greater onus to protect customer assets using best of breed cybersecurity controls. However, conventional cybersecurity countermeasures, such as patching and upgrades, are *reactive*, wherein resolution comes after the compromise has happened.

Repeated reports of DDoS and data breach incidents highlight a need for more robust and security compliant cloud architectures, more so with the introduction of Industrial Internet applications. Today, industry leading CSPs such as Microsoft Azure, AWS, and IBM Cloud. have service offerings specific to the IoT marketplace. The new IoT-specific cloud capabilities, such as device life cycle management, big data analytics, and visualizations must be augmented with measures to protect not only the cloud infrastructure but also the critical infrastructures that are now integrated with these cloud platforms.

Cloud security architecture supporting critical infrastructures, biomedical facilities, and industrial operations must meet a high level of regulatory and cybersecurity compliance. That's when the defense-in-depth strategy becomes critical. Security measures to detect, prevent, and/or control exploits must be implemented across multiple layers, such as infrastructure, application development, data protection, device management, DevOps, and so on.

In the subsequent sections, the various key concepts of cloud security are discussed in the context of Industrial Internet use cases. Readers can use these concepts to assess and evaluate the security readiness of various cloud platforms for a given IIoT use case.

Infrastructure security

The first line of defense is to implement security controls to protect the security of data-center assets, such as server farms, routers, switches, wiring closets, network firewalls, and so on, from both natural and human threats. Anti-tailgating measures, video surveillance, physical access-controlled barriers, password protected consoles, port locking, and so on are a few examples of physical security measures. Connected assets should also implement hardware-based root of trust, tamper resistance, secure boot and updates, and other endpoint security controls described in `Chapter 4`, *Endpoint Security and Trustworthiness*. ISO 27002 section 11, PCI DSS 3.2 requirement 9, and other standards (CSCC) provide guidance on these controls.

In the case of multi-tenant architectures, compute, network, and storage resources are shared but require adequate isolation between tenant workloads. Depending on the SLA, isolation can be implemented at the bare metal and physical hardware level, in VMs, or by using containers. Containers using the same OS kernel can pose considerable integrity risks. For sensitive workloads, containers can be run on the top of separate VMs or bare metal hardware to provide adequate security and isolation from other workloads.

A multi-tenant implementation can protect data at rest using encryption. Network segmentation, appropriate firewall rules, VPNs, TLS encrypted transport, connectivity framework mechanisms, and **Web Application Firewalls** (**WAFs**) are some other advisable controls to protect the infrastructure layer.

For protecting cloud data center connectivity, including routers, switches, VLANs, and other network elements, the defense-in-depth measures discussed in `Chapter 5`, *Securing Connectivity and Communications*, are equally applicable.

Identity and access management

Trust underpins the reliability and resilience of M2C communications.

Cloud-based IIoT deployments have a large attack surface prone to threats such as masquerade device identity, escalate privilege to compromise a device or application, snoop data in transit, send malicious data and control commands, and so on.

Devices and services must mutually authenticate to establish a trust relationship. Similarly, developers, applications, and users must also authenticate their identity before they can take action based on device data or send control commands. Roles and responsibilities of identity and access management are typically shared between the cloud vendor and the tenant or customer. For an IIoT deployment, identity, authentication, and authorization best practices include:

- Identity management using digital certificates and PKI infrastructure, federated identity schemes, and role and group-based identity and access. While many cloud vendors can generate device certificates, it is advisable for devices to have their own digital certificates, preferably hardware-based.
- Mutual authentication between client and server ensures that the devices and applications are communicating with the intended server, and the server is also receiving data from an authenticated data source. Multifactor authentication is recommended when feasible.
- Cloud implementations should authenticate devices and grant access to only those topics to which they are authorized to subscribe.
- Privilege levels are defined and assigned based on user roles and responsibilities, in accordance with the principles of least privilege and segregation of duties based on user roles.
- Access policies are enforced based on user roles, device groups, and so on. Access policies implemented in the cloud need to be mirrored at the corresponding edge device.
- Future-proof authentication and access control by supporting strong crypto libraries, encryption algorithms, strict isolation between user accounts and namespaces in multi-tenant environments, and identity life cycle management (include certificate revocation).

 Cloud security alliance has published a detailed guidance titled *Cloud Customer Architecture for Securing Workloads on Cloud Services*. Interested readers are encouraged to use it as a further reference on cloud defense-in-depth strategies.

Application security

In any cloud offering, the application software stack is a key component. IIoT applications typically act upon the intelligence hidden in the data. In general, application software interfaces with the stream and batch analytics engines, machine learning models, and so on to generate control commands, business insights, and also data visualizations.

Enterprise information systems such as remote asset tracking, asset performance management, anomaly detection, and business intelligence systems are part of this application layer. By using a remote monitoring app, for example, an operator can keep track of a turbine's temperature and pressure states, receive alerts if these states exceed a certain threshold, and send control commands to operate the turbine within safety boundaries.

Today, many IIoT solution providers are offering platform-agnostic SaaS products running on the top of cloud platforms such as AWS and Microsoft Azure. These SaaS products essentially offer an abstraction layer to build IIoT solutions customized to various use cases. This expedites time-to-market since industrial users can adopt IIoT without having to build and manage the entire software infrastructure.

Now the question is, how is security built into the cloud-based software application stack?

The software stack supporting IIoT apps involves a high degree of complexity, and hence is prone to bugs and errors. To offer a "single-pane-of-glass" user experience, it supports both mobile and desktop operating systems, and as such caters to web, desktop, and mobile interfaces. The sheer complexity of these apps increases the overall attack surface, exposing the deployment to threats such as unauthorized access, buffer overflow, SQL injections, parameter tampering, and data exfiltration.

To secure the IIoT application layer, both the customer and CSP have a role to play. These roles and responsibilities vary according to the cloud service model used.

A PaaS user who develops software applications on top of the cloud platform needs to (CSCC):

- Understand the security functionalities built into the cloud platform. The support of security microservices for containerization (including hypervisors), crypto libraries, DevOps (automated software life cycle management) tools, and run-time environments must be carefully evaluated. Many cloud platform providers publish product briefs containing the security features. It is recommended to use the Cloud Platform Security Assessment (provided later in this chapter) as part of the platform selection criteria.

- Adhere to secure **software development life cycle** (**SDLC**) guidelines, for example, threat modeling, attack surface evaluation, and accounting for data and service isolation.

- Secure coding using **OWASP Secure Coding Practices** (**OWASP-SEC**) and SEI CERT Top 10 Secure Coding Practices (SEI-SEC).

- Secure application interfaces using API runtime workflow analysis. Additional guidance on securing APIs is provided in the CSCC Cloud Customer Architecture for API Management (CSA-API).

- Implement cryptography to encrypt sensitive IO and also implement identity and access control.

- Implement WAF to detect and protect against malicious traffic.

- Perform attack surface reviews, static analysis, and exhaustive testing, including fuzz and penetration testing, web application scanning, and system testing on supported platforms (fixed and mobile).

- Ensure that the platform supports strict isolation between development and production environments.

For SaaS products, the solution provider is mostly responsible for security spanning the software life cycle. Ideally, all released application software should be security certified and attested with credentials by a central authority. Such SaaS certifications would provide sufficient transparency into the security controls built into the software. In the real world, however, that is not the case.

In the absence of such transparency, the next best option is to partner with the SaaS provider and conduct product acceptance tests specific to your use case before deploying it in the production environment. The acceptance tests should include a series of security-specific test cases, including penetration testing scenarios.

A SaaS customer must have visibility into the security capabilities and security testing that the SaaS platform has performed as part of the release, while the acceptance test criteria would depend on her specific use cases.

Microservice architecture

Many cloud platforms today use the microservice architecture. As independently deployable, small, modular services (MS-DEF), microservices accelerate the overall enterprise software development process. By abstracting a unique set of functions into reusable entities, microservice architecture also improves the overall security posture of the application software.

Certain industrial cloud platforms include security-specific microservices. Security microservices provide a set of standardized software tools to integrate security into the application software development process. As an example, `https://www.predix.io/` has a catalog of security microservices, which include tenant management, **user account and authentication** (**UAA**), **access control services** (**ACS**), web application security, credential store and vault, cybersecurity analytics and monitoring, audit, blockchain data integrity, and blockchain-as-a-service, among others.

Container security

Along with microservices, container-based deployment environments (for example, Kubernetes) are also increasingly preferred to secure and streamline DevOps. (*DevOps unifies software development and operational activities in both incubation and production environments*). Container-isolated applications access the same OS kernel and therefore container threats and associated security controls in a container-based deployment must be carefully evaluated.

In a container-based deployment, the three main isolation techniques are namespaces, control groups, and network-based isolation. A namespace defines the virtual boundary between processes executed within a container. Control groups define resource allocation per container. Exposure to network traffic associated with a given container should also be reduced by using proper network configurations (for example, VLANs, firewalls, adapters to control physical resource access, and so on).

Credential store and vault

Cloud security standards require applications and services to regularly rotate API keys and secrets (such as passwords, certificates, and so on), encrypt data at rest, and maintain credential access audits. Many PaaS providers offer a secured and centralized store and vault service to encrypt, store, and manage access to tokens, passwords, API keys, and so on. Logs of vault usage are usually included in such a service for future auditing. To minimize configuration errors, it is recommended that application developers use a centralized data encryption and access control service for credentials. Lease renewal and revocation of access can also be leveraged using this vault service.

Data protection

In a data-driven economy, data itself is an asset. IIoT is about unlocking the intelligence inherent in data, using cloud-enabled analytics. Every organization has an onus to protect its own data, and also customer data. In the case of the healthcare industry, medical facilities must protect sensitive data related to patient biometrics, health records, credit cards, and so on. In the transportation and insurance industries, customers' **Personally Identifiable Information (PII)** needs to be safeguarded. Unauthorized visibility into machine data can lead to sensitive technical information leakage, which can be misused against the organization that owns the data.

That's why in IIoT deployments, where sensitive data may be transported, processed, and stored across multiple organizational boundaries, data protection and governance must be clearly defined and prioritized. Cloud service providers must guarantee the protection of data in use and data at rest (storage) for tenants. However, that's not enough.

Security policies and procedures must be added on top to protect the data flow from end to end. At any given time, the data flow needs to be verifiable to ensure that the device is sending/receiving data to/from intended endpoints on the network and that it hasn't been compromised (for example, as in the case of a bot sending high volume DDoS attacks). The cloud platform needs to secure their ingress and egress points to detect data anomalies and protect machine-to-cloud communication.

 To cater to the distinguishing demands of the Industrial Internet, involving millions of devices and zettabytes of big data, many cloud providers are offering IoT-specific cloud services and security features. These are discussed in the case study section later in this chapter.

Data governance

Data governance defines protection for data, service, and platform integrity and nonrepudiation for both the cloud platform provider and its tenants.

Inadequate protection of data from unauthorized access may lead to serious operational consequences, while too much protection can be costly and negatively impact system performance. Data governance policies for a cloud platform can take a risk-based approach based on data classification, a granular understanding of regulated data such as PII and customs and trade-related data, and also provide adequate protection in accordance. Multiple levels of data access permissions can be defined based on the legal and regulatory sensitivity of various data types.

A reliable data governance framework can be assessed using the following guidelines:

- Standardized rules, code, and processes to consistently protect data across the platforms
- Well-defined roles and responsibilities pertaining to data ownership and stewardship, compliance to local and international regulations, and processes to enforce these
- Automated tagging and metadata-based policy enforcement

Data encryption

Data encryption protects data confidentiality; however, applying encryption to all data is not always required, nor is it efficient or cost effective when not needed. The cloud platform provider and tenant can mutually decide on a use case-specific data encryption policy, considering the scope of encryption, where to apply encryption, and also the organizational and regulatory requirements.

The scope of encryption defines which data types need encryption, encryption key usage, and so on. If these parameters are user configurable, then the platform provider needs to implement a default encryption mechanism to enable less educated customers protect themselves. When data needs to be persistently stored outside the data center and on-premises, such as in a mobile device, then encryption methodologies must be decided as part of the deployment requirements (device policies and so on).

Encryption of data in transit typically uses connectivity framework mechanisms (for example, DDS Security), TLS, IPSec tunnels, or encrypted VPNs. These encryption techniques have relatively low performance overheads, and hence are always recommended for sensitive data regardless of whether the data traverses public or private networks.

Encryption of data at rest can be done selectively and at OS/storage level, middleware level, or application level. Filesystem encryption such as Linux Unified Key Setup is an example of storage-level encryption. It protects against physical tempering and data theft but not run-time vulnerabilities. Transparent Data Encryption in Microsoft SQL Server and DB2 Native Encryption in IBM DB2 are some examples of middleware encryption (CSCC). However, in IIoT deployments using noSQL (MongoDB, Cassandra, and so on) and Hadoop-based schemas, application-level, and filesystem encryption are sometimes provided by third-party tools, for example, Gemalto.

Debug tools and console interfaces provide attack surfaces for application-level encryption. The attacker can use the debug interfaces to disable encryption or gain access to secret keys. Crypto errors from developers can also expose vulnerabilities.

 US **National Institute of Standards and Technology** (**NIST**) Special Publication 800-175B provides useful guidance on strong cryptographic methods.

Key and digital certificate management

Malicious use of keys and digital certificates undermines data confidentiality by allowing attackers to break the encryption. Keys must be securely created and deleted, stored, regularly rotated, and access controlled. It is important to understand the storage protections used for keys. Openstack's Barbican and Hashicorp's Vault are examples of open source key management solutions. Amazon Web Service Key Management Service and Microsoft Azure Key Vault are some proprietary examples.

HSMs provide most secured key storage. Crypto processor chips in HSMs provide tamper resistance by deleting keys after tamper detection.

Securing the data life cycle

Data generated by connected assets has a life cycle. Device-cloud communication involves data acquisition, processing, retention, and deletion. In order to protect the privacy of data across its life cycle, policies need to enumerate the responsibilities of all parties covering the entire period of contract engagement.

Encryption of sensitive data protects data during acquisition, protection, and retention phases.

Data activity monitoring services provide logging and auditing traces associated with the data access, changes, and events, often at a data-element level of granularity. Thresholds and rules define the normal activity to flag alerts in the case of data anomalies. In multi-tenant environments, the visibility of these events should be limited only to associated tenants and users. While the cloud platform provider may provide proprietary data monitoring solutions, some well-known third-party solutions include IBM Guardium Data Activity Monitoring and Imperva SecureSphere (CSCC).

PaaS and SaaS solution providers should also have well-documented data deletion policies, in adherence to local and international regulations. Adversaries could make an extreme attempt to gain access to the data. To protect against such threats, it is advisable that platform providers do not repurpose decommissioned hardware. Data deletion policies associated with account deactivation or at the end of the contractual agreement also need to build in adequate security controls.

Many data privacy regulations, including the GDPR (for EU users), give end users rights to migrate and delete personal data. This may apply to organizations as well. Data migration and deletion responsibilities should be well documented in the service agreement contract.

Cloud security operations life cycle

Cloud security is not a one-time solution. It has to align and persist throughout the active lifespan of an IIoT deployment, involving development, **Continuous Integration/Continuous Deployment (CI/CD)** and other secure DevOps functions, design re-engineering, and so on.

Business continuity plan and disaster recovery

Prevention and response to malicious activities is vital. However, incidents leading to outages do occur, sometimes even due to natural factors such as flood and fire. In an era of accelerated deployment cycles, lack of data center availability following an incident is also a serious reliability issue. **Business Continuity Plan (BCP)** and **Disaster Recovery (DR)** is an essential component of any deployment.

To address business continuity, certain CSPs have out-of-the-box high availability solutions. To mitigate single points of failure, as common high availability strategies, CSPs provision load balancing between their geographically separated data centers, in addition to data replication, and database redundancy. Some CSPs deploy multiple **Points of Presence (PoP)** in two availability zones, which are geographically diverse. The PoPs are maintained in **active-active** mode, where all data is continuously replicated among the PoPs. In the case of an incident in one PoP, operations instantly migrate to the peer PoP, and the active-active mode eliminates any **spin up** delays. In the case of a major security breach in a zone, the redundant zones ensure availability. Tenant organizations must ensure that multi-tenant security features are not compromised under any of these circumstances.

Some cloud providers offer only the underlying redundant infrastructure, such as geographically diverse redundant data centers with load balancing and data replication capabilities. In such service models, the tenant or customer is responsible for configuring and deploying the high availability solution.

Secure patch management

While in OT environments patching bug fixes is a practical challenge, it need not be so for cloud platforms. Some cloud providers implement procedures to continually keep track of newly released patches from OEMs and software vendors using public records and partner channels. A patch can be applied to the hardware, firmware, operating system, software, as well as to the component libraries. Once a patch is detected, it needs to be safely and efficiently deployed in the production environment. GE's Predix platform, for example, in some instances maintains two identical production environments, let's say blue and green. At a given time, only one of these, say blue, is live to serve production traffic. Green on the other hand is routinely prepared with a fully patched version of the software or service. When ready, green is promoted seamlessly to production, replacing blue, which is ultimately wound down and removed. In virtual environments involving VMs, similar approaches are used to minimize production downtime and expedite the remediation process.

Security monitoring

Traffic visibility provides insights into abnormal trends to successfully prevent or contain an attack. Cloud platforms need to continuously monitor traffic ingress and egress points, isolation points between virtual networks, network segment boundaries, and DMZs.

In a databus-based cloud IoT implementation, the databus can be monitored to detect malicious activity. For example, the DDS Security specification provides a log of all security relevant events. In a message broker-based cloud IoT implementation, the broker can be monitored to detect malicious behavior. For example, version 3.1.1 of MQTT spec provides some example behaviors worth reporting:

- Repeated connection attempts
- Repeated authentication attempts
- Abnormal termination of connections
- Topic scanning
- Sending undeliverable messages
- Clients that connect but do not send data

For end-to-end traffic visibility, data analytics and machine learning models can monitor traffic stats and security logs to detect threats and expedite responses.

Vulnerability management

Vulnerabilities, though unwanted, are a reality of the software-defined world. Design flaws, programming, and runtime errors in software and firmware expose gaps, which adversaries can exploit. A cloud platform has to manage vulnerabilities in hardware, firmware as well as in open source software, commercial software, software-as-a-service, and in custom code. Inadequate strength of cryptography, virtual machine escape, session riding and hijacking, vendor lock-in, and internet dependency are some of the common vulnerabilities in the cloud.

For any IIoT system, it is important to understand the vulnerability management policies and processes of the cloud provider. A standard process needs to be applied across the infrastructure, platform, applications, and services layers to discover vulnerabilities and distribute patches.

A comprehensive vulnerability management process must:

1. Establish a set of vulnerability management policies, to account for industry and regulatory compliance obligations, and define assessment techniques used to identify vulnerabilities.
2. Scan at multiple levels for network, host, source code, and traffic vulnerabilities. Scanning based on the cloud delivery model includes the following:
   - **SaaS model**: Scan operating systems, hardware, network infrastructure, access management applications, instance resources, upgrades, patches, and code.
   - **PaaS model**: Scan operating systems, hardware, network infrastructure, and instance resources.
   - **IaaS model**: Scan the entire infrastructure, including operating systems, hardware, network, and virtual machines.
3. Audit network security technologies to verify proper configuration.
4. Mitigate vulnerabilities in accordance with their risk priority by securely applying patches and upgrades.
5. Perform penetration testing to identify vulnerabilities and compliance violations.
6. Perform vulnerability scanning periodically to ensure a known vulnerability doesn't re-emerge. Scanners need to be updated to accommodate new regulatory and compliance concerns on an ongoing basis.

Vulnerability management provides additional assurance to mitigate elevated application and infrastructure risks.

Threat intelligence

In an industrial IoT system, the cloud is a crucial link in the security chain of controls. That's why in addition to implementing defense-in-depth security controls for the infrastructure, platform, application, processing, and operations such as monitoring, vulnerability scans, patch management, and business continuity; it is also vital to be vigilant about emerging threats. That's where **Threat Intelligence** (**TI**) comes in. Gartner defines TI as:

> *"...evidence-based knowledge, including context, mechanisms, indicators, implications and actionable advice, about an existing or emerging menace or hazard to assets that can be used to inform decisions regarding the subject's response to that menace or hazard."*

> *"Definition: Threat Intelligence,"*
> *-Gartner,*
> `www.gartner.com/doc/2487216/definition-threat-intelligence`

In a rapidly evolving threat landscape, in order to preemptively manage imminent threats in runtime environments, cloud providers are responsible for implementing TI practices. TI involves ingesting threat information from vendor sources, field data, industry contacts, and trusted sources. (*Author's note: In this context, it is interesting to note that in TI practices, privacy and security priorities may appear to conflict*).

Analysis and proper interpretation of this threat data is the key to enhance incident response and threat prevention processes. Using TI, CSPs can offer significant protection to both platform and tenant assets. However, just as the threats evolve, TI processes and policies also need to be revised continually with the regular deployment of advanced intelligence capabilities.

Incident response

Before finalizing the contract, the industrial customer needs to evaluate the cloud platform provider's incident response process. A robust incident response process implements proactive measures to preempt imminent attacks and rapidly resolve them before they might occur. Threat intelligence, penetration testing, vulnerability management, and regular training to keep the responders informed of the evolving threat landscape must be used judiciously.

In the case of unavoidable incidents, controls must be in place for fast resolution, proper communication and coordination with stakeholders in the customer organization, and rapid triage involving multiple channels such as technical, legal, PR, and forensics. Incident data stored for historical purposes should be protected with strict **role-based access control (RBAC)** measures and encrypted in compliance with regulations. Any data that can be shared publicly can be published in authorized portals for public access. Provisions for official communication between customers and cloud providers on incidents need to be formalized during the contract process.

Secure device management

Most IIoT deployments involve connected devices at the scale of thousands if not millions. Management of these devices at scale is one of the core offerings of most IoT cloud providers. The end-to-end life cycle management of devices includes secured provisioning, identity and access control, configuration management, remote monitoring of device health, and retirement of unused devices. An automated device provisioning service registers new devices with geographically diverse PoPs, manages device configurations, secures devices by pushing OTA patches and updates, and also re-provisions devices when they reconnect or relocate.

For secured and efficient access to device state information and health data, and to facilitate analysis and business application development, a virtual replica of each device is maintained in the cloud. This replica is referred to by various names by various cloud platforms, for example, "digital or device twins", "device shadows", and so on. The digital replica in the cloud and the edge are state synchronized with the physical device in quasi-real-time. This mechanism gives greater visibility into device state, security posture, its software/firmware versions, and also device health.

Figure 6.3 illustrates secured device management and device health monitoring using digital twins:

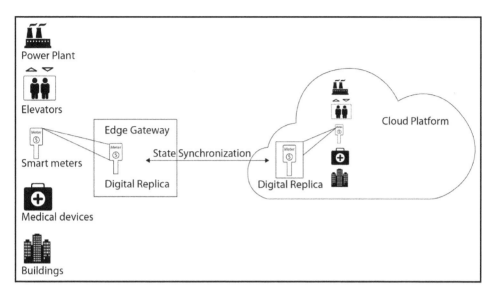

Figure 6.3: Digital replica of physical device state synchronized at edge and in the cloud

Cloud security standards and compliance

Multiple security standards have been developed to protect customer assets when using cloud services. These standards can be broadly classified as advisory, security frameworks, and technical specifications. Customers need to evaluate to what extent the cloud service providers are in compliance with these standards. A list of the security standards is provided here:

- ISO/IEC 27001, a high-level management systems standard series and its associated cloud service specific standards ISO/IEC 27017 (for security) and ISO/IEC 27018 (for protection of personal data)
- Standards addressing specific aspects of cloud computing: ISO/IEC 27033 for network security, ISO/IEC 27034 for application security, ISO/IEC 19086 for cloud service SLAs
- Technology-specific security standards such as OASIS KMIP (key management), FIPS 140-2 (approved cryptographic modules), and OASIS SAML 2.0 (security assertions, used in IAM implementations)

- ISO/IEC 20889 standardizes de-identification techniques
- US NIST Special Publication 800-175B provides guidance on strong cryptographic methods.

Some useful documents on cloud security standards are as follows:

- CSCC white paper *Cloud Security Standards: What to Expect and What to Negotiate V2.0* (http://www.cloud-council.org/deliverables/CSCC-Cloud-Security-Standards-What-to-Expect-and-What-to-Negotiate.pdf)
- Cloud Control Matrix (https://downloads.cloudsecurityalliance.org/initiatives/ccm/CCM_v3_Info_Sheet.pdf)
- Cloud Customer Architecture for Securing Workloads on Cloud Services from Cloud Security Council
- SAFEcode/CSA: Practices for Secure Development of Cloud Applications
- 'Cloud Computing: Benefits, risks and recommendations for information security': published by European Union Agency for Network and Information Security (ENISA

Case study of IIoT cloud platforms

Secured management of an IIoT system involves many moving parts. This leads to complexity requiring domain expertise in multiple disciplines, high cost of development and integration, and a very long time to market. To mitigate this difficult terrain, many cloud platform providers have expanded their portfolio beyond centralized data analytics to include end-to-end services specific to Industrial IoT workloads. In collaboration with their ecosystem partners, the CSPs are able to offer a service set that includes zero-touch provisioning at the scale of millions of IoT devices, device management, physical WAN connectivity using cellular and fixed lines, VPN-based edge to cloud connectivity, single billing, and so on. In this section, readers can review three IoT-specific cloud platforms AWS IoT, Azure IoT, and Predix from GE Digital to gain real-world insights into cloud-based security architectures and services.

Disclaimer: These case studies have been compiled based on publicly available information assets at the time of writing and do not necessarily represent the views of the vendors concerned. The case studies are included with the sole purpose of providing practical relevance to the topics discussed in this chapter. The author is not affiliated with any of the cloud platform vendors cited. The referenced sources are used with the permission of their respective owners where applicable.

Case study 1 – Predix IIoT platform

GE's Predix is a PaaS cloud solution designed primarily for Industrial IoT applications. As an industrial-grade cloud platform with PoPs around the globe, Predix has built in compliance with country and industry-specific security standards, such as CSA/CCM 3.01, ISO 27001/27002, ENISA, HIPAA, and so on (PDX-BRF). The Predix platform uses Cloud Foundry-based architecture, provides security-specific microservices for industrial applications, and employs a software-defined infrastructure abstraction to provide on-demand capacity for tenants.

Predix services extend from the edge to the cloud. Predix Machine provides edge intelligence functions for on-premise devices. Predix machine runs on hardware of various form factors, such as sensors, controllers, gateways, and so on, and provides analytics-based actions and insights with low latency. For example, if the temperature of a gas turbine exceeds the safety threshold, a corrective control command can be issued in real time, without having to rely on internet connectivity or incurring the latency associated with a round trip to the cloud. The edge security stack is built on top of GE's security solutions and understands fieldbus protocols such as MODBUS, DNP3, and so on and also open connectivity standards like OPC UA and DDS (PDX-ARC). As such, it is capable of providing perimeter protection with deep packet inspection, and continuous traffic monitoring to detect anomalous behavior:

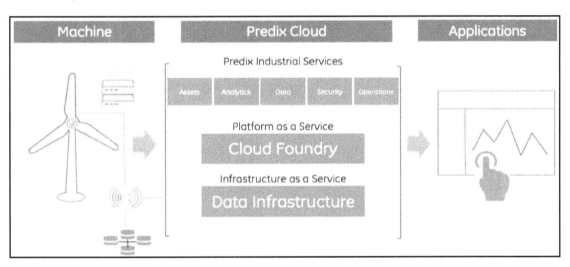

Figure 6.4: Predix industrial IoT PaaS edge cloud architecture; Source: Predix.io

Predix Machine supports device provisioning for edge devices at scale, certificate or OAuth2 authentication, and fine-grained access control for applications, data, and analytics (PDX-IO).

Predix Cloud provides the development and runtime environment for identity and access control, analytics, machine learning, device management, security monitoring, and asset performance functions. Predix uses digital twin, a digital replica of the physical machine. Digital twin is a container of aggregated data from asset model, asset data, contextual data (such as environmental measurements), and reference data used to deliver insights and outcomes that are essential to build apps around performance, optimization, and business transformation.

Case study 2 – Microsoft Azure IoT

Microsoft Azure IoT supports both PaaS and SaaS service models. For industrial applications, Azure IoT Suite provides a cloud-based platform to provision and manage IIoT deployments at scale. Azure IoT Central is the fully managed SaaS solution for relatively-less-complex deployments. Both PaaS and SaaS solutions use the same set of Azure IoT services, namely Azure IoT hub, stream analytics, time series insights, machine learning, logic apps, and so on.

The Azure IoT cloud service is called the IoT hub. It provides broker-based data ingestion and cloud gateway services, which support the secured IoT messaging protocols HTTPS, MQTT, and AMQPs (AMQP over WebSocket Secure or "wss"). The IoT hub manages end-to-end device management workflows at scale to automatically provision devices to the cloud, manage configurations, monitor device health, and retire unused devices.

Azure IoT has a certification program for devices and equipment. Azure IoT certified devices work out of the box with Azure-certified services. The automated device provisioning service supports new device registration with geographically diverse IoT hubs, manages configurations using centrally stored device state in the cloud (device twin), and re- provisions devices as they reconnect or relocate. IoT hub supports hardware root of trust-based identity, per device X.509 certificates, and shared access policies for authentication and access control.

Azure IoT Edge is a fully managed edge analytics solution. Azure IoT Edge maintains state synchronization with the IoT hub in terms of access policies, device twins, and device management functions. Azure IoT Edge is based on Docker-compatible containers, and agnostic to underlying hardware and OS (both Windows and Linux compatible). It runs on on-premise secured device operating environments supporting tamper resistant hardware-based RoT, secure boot and updates, vulnerability scanners, encrypted communication using TLS or by using IPSec tunnels and VPNs, IP and policy-based whitelisting, and so on.

Azure IoT Edge provides reliable low-latency stream analytics, machine learning, and actuation command feedback, which is critical for real-time industrial control loops:

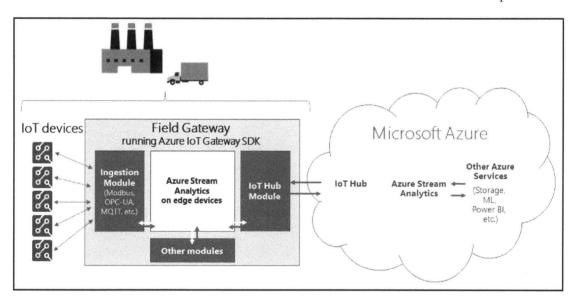

Figure 6.5: Microsoft Azure IoT edge to cloud architecture; Source: Azure.microsoft.com

Azure IoT hub and IoT Edge maintain a digital replica or "device twin" for each connected device. Encrypted bidirectional communication between edge and cloud maintains state synchronization in real time. Device twins are used to obtain real-time insights into device health, configuration management, pushing down secure updates, and so on.

Case study 3 – Amazon AWS IoT

Amazon AWS IoT is a PaaS cloud service designed for both consumer and industrial IoT applications (AWS-IOT). The platform uses serverless microservice architecture and a message broker for device communication and monitoring at scale. The message broker supports MQTT over TLS and MQTT over WebSockets in publish-subscribe mode and HTTPS in secured publish mode. Devices and applications mutually authenticate with the AWS IoT Core cloud service. X.509 certificates and private/public key pairs are used for IoT device identity. For application layer access, HTTP, or WebSockets IAM users, groups and roles are used. Amazon Cognito identities are used to control API access:

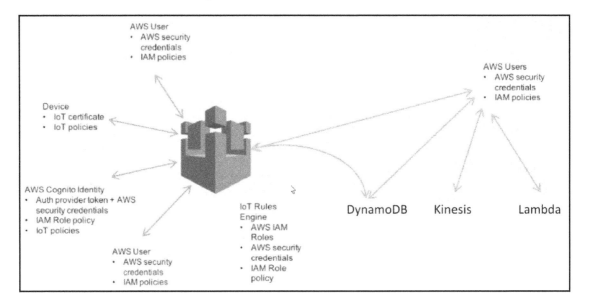

Figure 6.6: AWS IoT identity and access management workflow; Source:
https://www.slideshare.net/AmazonWebServices/best-practices-with-iot-security-februart-online-tech-talks/4

Customers have the option to use digital certificates and keys created by AWS IoT, or use keys and certificates installed in device hardware. For device-to-cloud communication, TLS 1.2 is used for message encryption, where client-side certificates should be at least 2048 for RSA and P-256 and P-384 curves for ECC (AWS-IAM). The platform provides a recommended list of cipher suites and 2048-bit primes for Diffie-Hellman. Access policies are enforced to authorize access to resources and actions (for example, to participate as publisher, subscriber, or both roles).

The AWS IoT platform has both IIoT edge and cloud components. For microcontroller-based edge devices, AWS IoT open source RTOS provides libraries for local and internet connectivity, crypto functions, and over-the-air signed software updates. The AWS IoT edge (Greengrass) gateway provides on-premise analytics and machine learning-based actions for low-latency applications. This edge software provides reliable edge services without relying on internet connectivity. The platform maintains synchronization between edge and cloud applications, access policies, device state information, and so on:

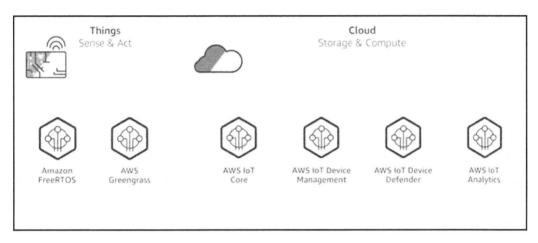

Figure 6.7: AWS IoT edge things and cloud services; Source: https://aws.amazon.com/iot-core/

Advanced analytics, machine learning, application development and deployment, and visualization services are provided in the cloud. Cloud-based AWS IoT Core provides device provisioning, device identity and access management, configuration management, remote monitoring, OTA updates, and so on. The AWS IoT "device defender" service is specifically designed to detect data flow anomalies at the granularity of individual devices.

Cloud security assessment

In this chapter, we discussed multiple security controls for a cloud service to meet the industrial grade of trustworthiness. *Table 6.2* provides an assessment matrix that can be used in conjunction with cloud security standards compliance to evaluate the security readiness of an IIoT cloud service:

[Cloud Platform]: Security Capability Matrix	
Edge Security	[Practices implemented at the cloud-edge device such as secure boot, secure O-T-A firmware/software updates, edge access policies etc.]
Identity and Access Management	[Controls/protocols implemented for managing identity, authentication (e.g. Oauth tokens, SAML federated access etc.) and at what granularity access/authorization policies are enforced (applies to both edge and cloud)].
Infrastructure Security	[Multi-tenant/Datacenter security controls at hardware, virtualized environments e.g. container-based isolation, network, storage, monitoring etc.]
Application Security	[Application layer controls such as -- Microservice/Container architecture, app user access controls, secure development lifecycle, WAF etc.]
Data Protection	[Extent of encryption support for data-in motion/use, at rest, policies for data governance, retention, deletion etc.]
Secure Device Interaction	[How device lifecycle management is secured]
Threat Intelligence	[Documented TI capability (1 or 2 sentences max)]
Incident Response	[Incident response support (1 or 2 sentences max)]
Business Continuity	[Business continuity support (1 or 2 sentences max), use of PoPs/availability zones etc.]
Vulnerability Management	[Support for Vulnerability scanning/secure patch management particulars]
Security Monitoring	[Document supported security monitoring capabilities]
Standards Compliance	[Published list Cloud security standards the solution conforms to]

Table 6.1: Cloud security assessment matrix

As an illustration of the use of the table, *Table 6.3* shows the mapping of the published security capabilities (at the time of writing) of the Predix IIoT platform in the security assessment matrix (PDX-BRF):

GE Digital Predix: Security Capability Matrix	
Edge Security	Secure operating environment using hardware RoT, secure boot, secureOTA firmware/software updates, edge access policies synchronized with those in the cloud, perimeter protection using GE's industrial firewalls for network segmentation and deep packet inspection.
Identity and Access Management	Identity management through SCIM APIs, PKI, digital certificates; Oauth 2.0 token for access to relevant applications, SAML federation capabilities, key management; tenant-aware fine grained access control for application, data and analytics.
Infrastructure Security	Cloud-Foundry based multi-tenant design, tenants logically isolated at run-time and storage, native logging support to monitor traffic across VLANS and VPCs for anomalies and audit.
Application Security	Microservice design, security specific microservices in Predix.io catalog, application and user level access policies for resource access, Predix secure development lifecycle (PSDL), application security review enforcement.
Data Protection	Encryption of sensitive data, TLS and digital certificates for user level encryption for data in motion. Dataflow monitoring for anomalies, policies enforced for data governance, retention and deletion.
Secure Device Interaction	Digital Twins, device provisioning and management over secure tunnels, device monitoring for anomalies.
Threat Intelligence	TI program to ingest and interpret multiple streams of threat information to preempt attacks
Incident Response	End-to-end coordination of incident response which includes incident notification, investigation, forensics, and close-out
Business Continuity	Geographically diverse PoPs and availability zones deployed for Predix Cloud using active-active model for seamless cutover.
Vulnerability Management	Vulnerability scans of open source, as well as in-house and commercial off-the-shelf (COTS) technologies
Security Monitoring	Continuous traffic monitoring to detect traffic anomalies at the edge and the cloud.
Standards Compliance	https://www.predix.com/sites/default/files/predix-the-industrial-internet-platform-from-ge-digital-brief.pdf

Table 6.2: A sample cloud security assessment Matrix

Summary

As the Industrial Internet evolves, so do the security requirements. Secure cloud platforms enable industrial enterprises to unlock the potential of the data that already resides in the organization. While IIoT edge-cloud services enable industrial enterprises to manage scaled deployments, they also significantly increase the attack surface, exposing the deployment to new attack vectors. This chapter presented readers with insights into the security controls in edge-cloud architectures. The defense-in-depth strategy for secure cloud platforms, security measures specific to the infrastructure, application, data protection and encryption, and the DevOps life cycle were discussed using real-world case studies. The chapter includes a list of important cloud security industry standards that cloud services need to comply with, in addition to regional and international data protection and privacy regulations. A cloud security assessment matrix developed in this chapter can be a useful resource for readers in a cloud-based solution design or selection process.

The next chapter focuses on securing processes and the governance model to orchestrate the multi-layered IIoT defenses in a practical and meaningful security framework.

7
Secure Processes and Governance

"Security gets orders of magnitude more attention today than only a short time ago."
– Stan Schneider, CEO, RTI

IIoT attributes intelligence and autonomy to machines. In a world where smart machines make autonomous decisions, trustworthiness is critical and must be ingrained in their DNA. This distributed autonomy calls for a decentralized approach to IIoT security, where safety and integrity controls are built into every node, endpoint, and in every technology that renders intelligence and connectivity.

In this book, IIoT security is decomposed into endpoint, access, connectivity, and edge-cloud layers. Earlier chapters have already analyzed the security controls at each layer, where readers can find actionable tools to evaluate and implement security in the respective layers. However, the question that still remains unanswered is: how do we orchestrate multi-layered controls to achieve a sustainable security framework?

And that's where secured processes and governance come in.

Typical IIoT use cases involve several complex processes, from design to operations. A smart energy use case, for example, encompasses field-level intelligence, on-premise supervisory and control intelligence, and edge-cloud intelligence. In the case of an IIoT **system of systems** use case such as a smart city, multiple verticals, such as energy, transportation, connectivity infrastructures, and smart homes, must reliably interoperate. The solutions involve an ecosystem of vendors and platforms and thus a high degree of technological and vendor complexity.

To orchestrate the various security controls in a complex technology-vendor matrix, effective security governance must protect the entire life of the solution; starting from component design and development, through system and platform integration, and finally in the operation phases.

In addition to this, IIoT security also involves multiple stakeholders at industry and organizational granularities: those who define the overarching standards and reference architectures. For example stakeholders responsible to build system components and platforms, and also those who adopt and own the deployment (as example, an energy company who implements a smart energy solution or the administrators of a smart city).

The main objective of this chapter is to keep this rich ecosystem in perspective and arrive at a practical and adaptive security governance framework, in order to realize the true potential of a secured IIoT deployment. This chapter analyzes the governance mechanisms that glue and catalyze IIoT security controls into a singular architecture. Security governance is considered across multiple phases of an IIoT solution, taking into account various roles and dynamics involved in each phase. In this chapter, we will cover:

- Challenges of unified security governance
- Securing processes across the IIoT life cycle
- Understanding security roles
- Elements of an IIoT security program
- Security maturity model
- Implementing an IIoT security program

Challenges of unified security governance

Chapter 2, *Industrial IoT Dataflow and Security Architecture*, elaborates on how IIoT security involves much more than just the protection of information assets. Securing IIoT translates to establishing end-to-end trustworthiness. In addition to information security, trustworthiness relies on resilience, safety, reliability, and privacy. IIoT security governance policies must be designed to ensure adequate trustworthiness, by converging IT security understanding and domain-specific OT expertise.

For the industrial internet or the Industrie 4.0 ecosystems, how-much-ever we may hope for overarching, industry-wide security governance; in reality, such a unified model is not viable for various reasons. Some of that reasoning is presented here.

Security, in general, comes at a cost. It involves training a workforce and investing extra resources and cycles to implement security. This, in turn, impacts time-to-market. In a fast-paced innovation landscape (as in the case of IIoT), security governance should be able to strike the right balance between investments and trustworthiness. Security must be right-sized by assessing the risks based on how the solution is deployed and how customers engage with and use it.

In earlier chapters, readers were presented with a list of security controls at each layer. Based on risk assessment, instead of enabling every control at each layer, security policies should be able to define and enforce a subset of controls that are necessary to establish trust in a specific solution.

One more challenge of IIoT security governance is industry regulations and standards are lagging behind innovations. Although multiple information security standards and industrial regulations exist today, unified security standards and policies for IIoT are still at an evolutionary stage. Many IT regulations are still country- or region-specific, while the marketplace remains global. Consider the example of **Global Data Protection Regulation (GDPR)**. As a policy, it aims to protect only customers in the EU region; however, in effect, it impacts providers from around the globe who have a market in the EU region.

This further puts the onus of securing IIoT on an organizational level. Organizational security policies must comply with existing standards and any relevant industry/region-specific regulations. Instead of unified security governance, we must be looking at business specific governance, where security policies account for the overall business case, and are applied to relevant processes and stakeholders. Subsequent sections of this chapter further elaborate on this homogenized approach.

A practical security governance model must be able to right-size security for a specific business use case to ensure trust and compliance.

Securing processes across the IIoT life cycle

In a fast-paced software-defined economy, innovation and time-to-market often take precedence over security and reliability. The latter are either added after the fact or left to users to integrate. This, however, would not suffice in the case of regulated, mission-critical industry segments. For industrial products, safety and reliability controls must be ingrained at every phase of development and must satisfy rigorous standards and regulatory compliance.

The same holds true for IIoT. For IIoT systems, trustworthiness is not something we can "bolt on" post-deployment. Every phase of the solution life cycle needs to comply with the minimum safety, resilience, and security requirements. This section analyzes various strategies to achieve this. *Figure 7.1* shows the various phases and processes of a typical IIoT solution. While standards are yet to evolve to evaluate the security of these processes and policies, this section presents some practical best practices:

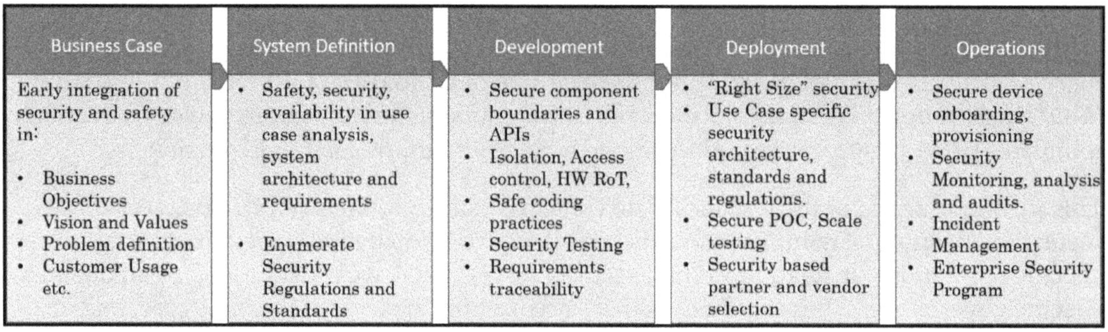

Business Case	System Definition	Development	Deployment	Operations
Early integration of security and safety in: • Business Objectives • Vision and Values • Problem definition • Customer Usage etc.	• Safety, security, availability in use case analysis, system architecture and requirements • Enumerate Security Regulations and Standards	• Secure component boundaries and APIs • Isolation, Access control, HW RoT, • Safe coding practices • Security Testing • Requirements traceability	• "Right Size" security • Use Case specific security architecture, standards and regulations. • Secure POC, Scale testing • Security based partner and vendor selection	• Secure device onboarding, provisioning • Security Monitoring, analysis and audits. • Incident Management • Enterprise Security Program

Figure 7.1: Security practices in IIoT processes

Business cases

Typically, every product or solution begins with a business case. Security and reliability should be considered when defining the problem, business objectives, vision, values, and customer usage in the business case. For example, the level of safety and security assurance expected from an autonomous vehicle software is different from those expected from a software controlling robot arms on a factory floor.

Defining a business case is usually considered a non-technical, management function. However, ensuring security alignment of business objectives, values, and vision can save valuable cycles if otherwise deferred to subsequent phases.

This rationale is applicable to both solution providers and those adopting an IIoT solution in their business model.

System definitions

The system definition phase (in our current context) includes use case analysis, requirements identification, and system software design. Each use case typically demands a unique set of safety, security, and availability capabilities. A system definition must decompose the overarching system requirement into functional, safety, security, and availability requirements. Requirements must also define boundary conditions and exception handling with respect to safety and security. For example, during a cyberattack in a data center, shutting down one of the redundant servers may be acceptable. However, for a mission-critical industrial scenario, the sudden shutdown of any equipment may result in safety violations. In such cases, a safer option would be to gracefully disconnect the equipment from the network to prevent further damage, while the equipment may still continue to run.

System requirements need to explicitly capture the safety requirements of IIoT use cases. The development phase should implement and explicitly test against these requirements.

Requirement traceability is also vital to ensure adequate implementation and test coverage of functional, safety, and security requirements. *Figure 7.2* illustrates the backward-traceability of safety, security, and availability functionalities from the test to requirements phase:

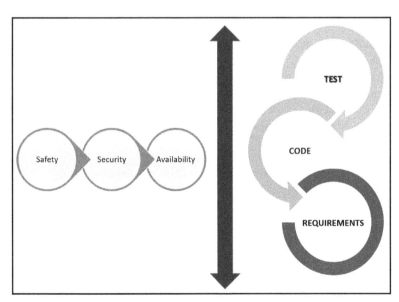

Figure 7.2: Requirement traceability for safety, security, and availability features

The system definition phase should enumerate the industry standards and regulations the system will be built against. Examples of industry standards for embedded systems include IEC 62443 (Industrial Network and System Security), ISO 27001 (Information Security Management), IEC 62351 (Information Security for Power System Control Operations, Smart Grids), IEEE 12207 (Systems and Software Engineering replaced MIL-STD-498), ISO/IEC 9797 -1 (Security Techniques—Message Authentication Codes), and DO -326a IEC 62443 (Airworthiness Security Process Specification).

If the system definition phase includes prototypes and/or simulations to validate the software architecture, security functionalities should be integrated as part of these activities instead of postponing those to later phases.

Adopting a zero-tolerance policy may be useful to ensure the management of security vulnerabilities at the end of each phase, by preventing them from percolating to subsequent phases. A zero-tolerance policy requires each phase to comply 100% comply with the security and safety criteria before that phase is declared as complete.

Development

This is the most crucial phase of the IIoT life cycle. Security adherence during the development phase helps pre-empt issues early in the life cycle. A common misconception is too much security stifles innovation, adds cost, and delays product release. Quite on the contrary: studies have shown that up to 80% of defects and vulnerabilities get introduced during the development phase, and the cost of remediation is significantly higher when these defects are uncovered during post-development phases. Moreover, networked, embedded devices are perfect targets as they provide access to high-value industrial assets. Breaches in such devices often escape detection. Therefore, enforcing safe coding practices during development not only improves system resiliency, but also reduces the cost of compliance and time-to-market.

Some practical challenges in this phase are that software developers and architects often lack adequate skills to effectively design and code against security threats. Training the development workforce on security techniques cuts into productivity. Also, ethical hackers and penetration testers often expose vulnerabilities, but only after the software has been fully implemented.

These challenges must be overcome using safe coding practices, such as:

- The architecture provides the framework to define safety and security controls in software boundaries, the API layer, and data flows. Identify available reference architectures that best suit your solution.
- Developers need to be aware of intended customer usage, threat models, and attack vectors, and trained on the SDLC.
- Define security and reliability rules and policies, based on existing standards from MISRA, NIST, CERT, CWE, NASA, and OWASP. Compliance with these standards can be validated and certified using peer reviews, static and dynamic code analysis, and testing.
- Automation is highly recommended. Use tooling and automation to streamline development workflows and easily detect regressions.
- Evaluate the security posture of open source versus third-party software and libraries. In some cases, a hybrid of open source and third-party software may be preferable.
- Prevent buffer/datatype overflow, null pointer dereferences, memory leaks, uninitialized data usage, platform/OS specifics exposing privilege escalation scenarios, concurrency, and unwanted functionalities.
- Enforce measurable verification controls and audit trails, such as structured coverage, static and dynamic code analysis, unit/system/robustness tests, and code coverage analysis.

Deployment

The deployment phase is when the rubber meets the road. The vital first steps of a secured IIoT deployment are the following:

- A well-defined business problem
- A clear understanding of how the solution integrates and operates with an organization's workflow

As noted before, an IIoT deployment involves multiple subsystems, platforms, technologies, and an ecosystem of vendors. This provides a perfect environment for mistakes and inadvertent exposure to threats. This book extensively discusses methods to properly plan and ensure security at various layers. However, a valid question at this stage is "what" should be secured and by "how much." Securing "everything" is ideal, but not practical. It leads to unwanted cost barriers and often frustration. During deployment, it is vital to assess the scope of security specific to use cases, using risk analysis.

Based on the problem definition and use case specifications, we need to come up with the deployment architecture. An architecture provides visibility into the various layers, components, and technologies used in the solution; it provides a perspective on customer usage and expectations; and most importantly, it gives us a flexible framework to plan for future expansion and adjustments. Adequate security controls and vendor selection can be based on these insights. It is advisable to have the deployment based on the IIoT reference architectures (defined by IIC and also discussed in `Chapter 2`, *Industrial IoT Dataflow and Security Architecture*)

In the absence of product- or deployment-specific security certifications, solution acceptance testing (also known as pre-production testing) of the deployment is critical. A security acceptance criteria can set the expectations that a deployment must conform to, in terms of functionality, safety, security, availability, and compliance.

Acceptance tests are typically performed in test-benches where endpoints and other operational parameters can be simulated and easily scaled to detect any defects.

Vulnerabilities often leak through product releases. Often, new attack vectors get introduced in a scaled production environment. Secure boot, hardware root-of-trust, trust chains, PKI/cert provisioning, IAM, device onboarding, and secure software/firmware updates need to be validated during this phase. Proper automation is very helpful for verifying bug fixes and detecting regressions.

In addition to acceptance tests, penetration testing is also recommended in the pre-production environment.

Many IIoT deployments involve disruptive innovations and require **proof of concept (POC)**. During POC, functional verifications are the primary goal. However, it is prudent to validate the security capabilities of the solution as well during POC, instead of deferring security for post-POC stages.

Evaluating security products

Industry standards such as the common criteria and **Federal Information Processing Standard (FIPS)** are typically used to technically evaluate and certify security products in third-party labs. Evaluations with restricted configurations and enabling only a basic feature set is practically meaningless. Simulating the pre-production and deployment environments is highly desirable for security evaluations; care should be taken to evaluate how these products adapt to changes in the production environment and also when an attack is in progress (IIC-IISF).

Operations

Industrial operations are founded upon resilience, robustness, and longevity. Industrial control systems, devices, and equipment are expected to operate for decades, and ideally with zero downtime. After successful POC and pre-production testing, in the operations phase, devices are physically installed and configured at scale.

Securing the supply chain is important during operations. In an ecosystem where technologies, software, and hardware are supplied and maintained by multiple vendors, tracing accountability often gets tricky. Audits and security policies for the supply chain need to be in place to ensure such traceability. Blockchain (discussed in Chapter 8, *IIoT Security Using Emerging Technologies*) is an emerging technology that could automate supply chain attestation and accountability.

Onboarding, provisioning, and configuration management of devices at scale are key operational functions that may expose undetected vulnerabilities. As discussed in Chapter 6, *Securing IIoT Edge, Cloud, and Apps*, today multiple CSPs offer automated device provisioning and configuration management functions. In cases where third-party cloud providers are used for device provisioning at scale, it is important to evaluate security in their audit and provisioning workflows.

To detect anomalies and remediate incidents, continuous security monitoring and incident management are key functions. While using third-party monitoring and management solutions, the reliability of such a solution should be tested in the production environment before an incident actually occurs. Some monitoring and management solutions use machine learning-based (discussed in Chapter 8, *IIoT Security Using Emerging Technologies*) analytics, which execute 24/7 and should be tested against false positives and usability prior to an incident.

Last but not least, IIoT introduces new digital technologies, platforms, and workflows that are less prevalent in traditional OT environments. The OT workforce responsible for operations should be properly trained and certified to the ensure long-lasting secured life cycle of an IIoT deployment.

Understanding security roles

A sustainable IIoT security implementation depends on the well-orchestrated efforts of various ecosystem partners and stakeholders. The preceding section of this chapter (*Securing processes across the IIoT life cycle*) discussed actionable steps to integrate security across IIoT life cycle processes. These processes are also linked to multiple roles; each role is associated with its respective security onus. Effective security governance depends on role-based accountability. This section dissects and evaluates security responsibilities based on four broad role categories. *Figure 7.3* illustrates these broad roles as four pillars (*Author's note*: the diagram only presents the roles, not necessarily the relational connections between these roles):

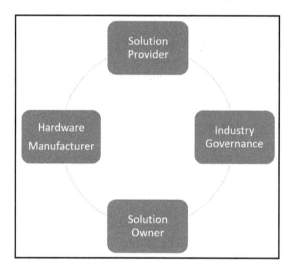

Figure 7.3: IIoT security responsibilities based on broad roles

Solution provider

Solution provider in *Figure 7.3* is a generalized category representing providers of IIoT endpoint technologies, crypto solutions, software applications, cloud-based functionalities, IIoT platforms, system integration, and communication infrastructure.

Solutions providers are responsible for ensuring trustworthiness at every stage of the product life cycle, starting from the business case and system definition phase, through development and delivery. Solution providers need to ensure their products and services use hardened architecture, SDLC, secured and easy patching mechanisms for industrial production environments, seamless upgradability to newer versions, adequate identity and access control at all layers, cross-vendor interoperability and integration, and secured scaled performance in production. By enforcing a zero-tolerance policy (discussed in the section: Securing processes across the IIoT life cycle), solution providers can ensure mission-critical solutions are delivered only with full security compliance.

For subscription-based models, solution providers can offload asset owners from security maintenance workflows, such as secure updates, configuration management, device on-boarding, and upgrades. Backward-compatibility and flexibility to integrate new capabilities without breaking existing security features must be supported without causing unacceptable production downtime. Consider the example of data encryption in communication channels. Today, most solutions use TLS 1.2 for encryption. This, however, should not prevent vendors from seamlessly upgrading to TLS 1.3 or 2.0-based encryption capabilities when the new version is released.

Hardware manufacturers

Hardware manufacturers are providers of individual hardware components, such as CPUs, MCUs, FPGAs, ASICs, and boards. They may also provide hardware drivers and other software or firmware, and OEM equipment for the IoT marketplace.

The IIoT hardware supply chain involves chipset manufacturers, OEMs, and delivery stops. Digital signing using X.509 certificate-based trust chains or blockchain technology should be used to ensure hardware identity and attestation. Device manufacturers are also responsible for ensuring tamper-proofing, hardware-based device identity and root of trust, PKI/certificates, hardware-based secured storage, secure boot, updates, and upgrades (these techniques are explained in `Chapter 4`, *Endpoint Security and Trustworthiness*). For resource constrained devices, manufacturers should be able to provide HSM using crypto accelerators and hardware-based isolation.

Manufacturers should also ensure that only the most critical set of hardware functionality is shipped, thus eliminating the increased attack surface from unused features. The ability to upgrade the software and firmware of released products while in operation is a key capability manufacturers must plan for to future-proof security.

Industry governance

Industry governance is a generalized category for industry bodies responsible for driving IIoT reference architectures, standards, industry- and region-specific regulations, and common frameworks.

Common security frameworks and practical guidelines are vital for ensuring security and interoperability in the all-pervasive IIoT landscape. Currently, both the IIC and Industrie 4.0 (EU-centric) are exclusively focused on IIoT. OneM2M is a consortium specific to the telecommunications industry. IEEE, IETF, ISO/IEC, the OPC foundation, OMG, and OASIS have added IIoT-specific protocols and standards definitions to their existing standards portfolios.

A critical element of industry governance is to prioritize security architectures and integrate security definitions during the initial draft phase itself, rather than bolting on security in subsequent revisions. When added as an afterthought, the security robustness of the standards is often compromised. When security is added as an enhancement, software and hardware stack providers are also denied an adequate bake-in period for security hardening.

In a fast-paced technology landscape where innovation tends to leapfrog standardization, industry governance is a challenge. The technology industry is also replete with overlapping standards. As an overarching technology, IIoT has driven convergence of the cyber and physical worlds, and also that of IT and OT practices. The richness of such a grand convergence emphasizes the need for simplified and converged standards at an industry level to make security implementation easy and practical.

Converged governance is also desirable in regulatory compliance. Government organizations, such as NIST and the **European Commission** (**EC**), can play a vital role in defining regulations that consider the global IIoT marketplace.

Solution owner

A solution owner is responsible for a specific IIoT use case deployment and collectively represents the solution architects, deployment planners, business-level managers, and operators of the solution.

The solution owner is the final and yet most important pivot of the IIoT security "quad-role" shown in *Figure 7.3*. The solution owner is responsible for assessing and managing the risks to right-size security in the deployment architecture. It is also the solution owner's responsibility to integrate secured technologies and solutions, validate security compliance, and finalize security SLAs with any third-party "as-a-service" providers. Any security incidents during the operational life cycle of the IIoT deployment must be resolved by the solution owner. The security imperatives discussed in the deployment and operation processes of the previous section tie in to the solution owner.

There is no reasonable mechanism to future-proof security. That's why the solution owner is responsible for implementing a right-sized security program that is living and adaptive enough to keep up with newer attack vectors. Unlike industrial OT, software-defined information technologies have a much shorter lifespan. So as IT intelligence penetrates into OT environments, solution owners must plan for ways to keep up with latest technology, firmware, and hardware versions to ensure a safe and secured production environment.

Elements of an IIoT security program

The security posture of an IIoT deployment depends on how safely it can weather instabilities during the operation phase. In spite of multiple layers of security checkpoints in the pre-operation phases, vulnerabilities do exist at runtime. In enterprise IT deployments, a security program provides well-orchestrated governance, protecting organizational assets and infrastructure from external and internal threats during the operational phase. Data availability, privacy, and integrity are the primary goals of an enterprise IT security program.

As we have already discussed in this book, the stakes in an IIoT deployment are much higher than enterprise IT. IIoT involves critical infrastructures and human safety. In addition to data availability, privacy, and integrity, an IIoT security program must ensure resilience and reliability in the event of an attack, which can be from external or internal adversaries, or due to inadvertent misconfigurations or natural catastrophes.

Figure 7.4 shows the components essential in defining and sustaining an IIoT security program. This section elaborates on each of these components:

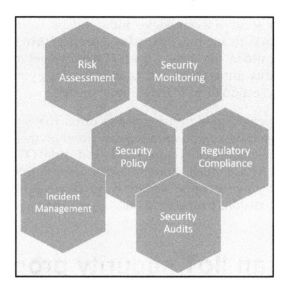

Figure 7.4: Elements of an IIoT security program

Risk assessment

In the absence of infinite resources, a sustainable security program depends on the effective assessment of risks. IIoT deployment involves significant investment, in terms of assets, complex technologies, and infrastructure. It is practically impossible to secure everything at runtime. Risk assessment enables right-sizing security by determining where security investments must be directed.

Every organization deploying IIoT needs to have a precise understanding of associated attack surfaces and attack vectors. Chapter 2, *Industrial IoT Dataflow and Security Architecture*, delves deep into the various components of risk assessment by using attack trees, fault-tree analysis, and the STRIDE and DREAD threat models.

An IIoT deployment architecture has various levels of complexity. To better manage the risk assessment process, a multi-tiered, multi-segmented architecture can be decomposed into device types (for example, sensors, field gateway, cloud/edge gateway, and router), processes, and services and zones (for example, the field gateway zone, the control and supervisory zone, and the cloud gateway zone).

Threat modeling provides structured visibility into threats and associated risks. Based on threat modeling, risks and the associated cost of mitigation can be assessed to prioritize and manage risks.

Regulatory compliance

Standards and regulatory compliance is essential to ensure safety, resiliency, reliability, and data privacy. An IIoT deployment must comply with regulations and standards specific to its industry vertical, in addition to any geography-specific regulations. HIPAA for the medical industry and FAA safety regulations for aviation are some example of industry-specific regulations.

The executive team charged with a security program needs to identify and enforce the implementation of regulatory compliance at an asset, infrastructure, and overall architecture level. When appropriate, a security program should make sure the products and services are certified using industry standards such as Common Criteria and FIPS 140-2.

Security policy

Security policy is an overarching term for guidelines authored and defined to protect a deployment. An organizational security policy takes into account industry standards and regulations, organizational directives, the targeted steady-state production environment, and expected behavior.

The security policy includes both technical and nontechnical security controls. Permitting visitor entry only during specific office hours is an example of a nontechnical security control. An organizational security policy needs to be implemented at physical, workforce/employee, device, and communication layers. Access control to industrial premises using authentication (ID badges, and so on), surveillance cameras for event-monitoring, and keyed access to equipment closets are examples of a physical security policy. Limiting corporate network access to only authorized computers and mobile devices, privilege-based resource access by employees, and vendor access to the corporate network using VPNs are part of the people-level security policies. Examples of device-level security policies are device enrollment and provisioning rules, device-to-device communications, and filtering and access control lists for gateways. In the communication layer, the security policy needs to define mechanisms to protect data at rest, data in motion, and date in use, which encompasses both customers' and an organization's sensitive data.

A security policy defines both preventive and detective controls. Preventive controls aim to prevent an action that violates organizational directives. Detective controls define corrective actions in the event of an incident or policy violation.

A security policy can be segmented into three cascading categories: regulatory, organizational, and machine policy (IIC-IISF). Regulatory policy, such as HIPAA and NIST 800-53, mandate compliance at industry, country, or global levels. Organizational policy specifies technical and nontechnical behavior for the organization, for example, compliance to ISO 9001, DMZs between network segments, and privilege-based USB and network port access. Machine policy defines technical security controls on one or more devices.

Figure 7.5 illustrates the security policy as an overarching concept, which can be decomposed into sub-levels based on hierarchy, levels, and/or type of controls. A practical security program needs to consider these aspects to adequately define and author use case-specific security policies:

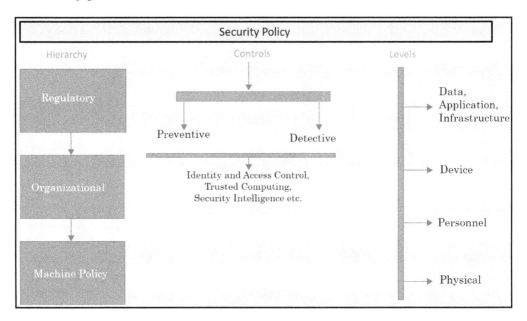

Figure 7.5: Underlying components of security policy authoring

Security monitoring

The monitoring of operational data provides valuable insights about device health, asset performance, and asset tracking. However, to secure an IIoT deployment, in addition to operational data, it is also essential to monitor the security data (IIC-IISF). Monitoring security data helps to detect event sequences, for example, a successful login from an unexpected endpoint, followed by a network whitelisting violation, which together indicate a potential attack in progress.

The primary sources of security data are monitored by endpoints and the network. Some examples of security data are device access and activity logs, event timestamp and device location, network traffic volume, and connection setup and teardown timestamps.

Data captured from endpoints is usually transported to remote monitoring stations over a secured channel, processed either in real time or in batches, and used by security analytics systems. The storage of security data needs protection from unauthorized access. To maintain an audit trail, logging of both local and network events and activities should be configured. To preserve the integrity of the log data, logging can be remotely stored in a network-accessible log server.

Monitored security data can provide predictive insights, suggesting the potential of an attack, or insights into an attack in progress, and also for post-attack forensic analysis. For example, in a device, unexpected configuration changes, suspicious user account creation, and frequent audit function shutdowns collectively predict the potential of a future attack. Denial-of-service and failed authentication events suggest an attack is in progress. An audit trail of source-destination information of network traffic can be used by security investigators to obtain forensic insights into the footprints of a past attack.

Security analysis

Security analysis is inherently tied to security monitoring. For physical assets and personnel, security monitoring and analysis can be manually performed and supervised. However, the monitoring of a highly-scaled number of IoT devices mandates automated security analysis with limited human supervision. Currently, there are multiple security analytics solutions based on machine learning and deep learning. Considering the high volume and ingestion rates of security data, security analytics should be performed on-premise or very close to industrial assets (such as by using fog computing). A security analysis solution is most useful when it provides an actionable response, which in its turn can be tied to the incident management system.

Security analysis can utilize either:

- Behavioral/anomaly-based models or
- Rule/signature-based models

In an anomaly-based model, the analytics software is trained based on monitored security data to learn the "normal" operational state. After the learning completes, if the operational state deviates from the "normal" beyond a predefined threshold, an alert or an alarm is triggered. The anomaly-based approach is suitable for safety and reliability-critical industrial systems where behavioral patterns change less frequently. Network intrusion-detection or filesystem monitoring systems are examples of this approach, which uses machine learning algorithms to flag anomalies. In the case of rule or signature-based analytics, a predefined library of rules and signatures is used. When the monitored security data does not match the signatures, an alert condition is flagged.

Industrial enterprises often face the challenge of reliably detecting and flagging an anomalous condition using security analytics. Creating a simulated model that precisely replicates a real-world system by factoring in various nuances usually does not work that well. Besides, every industrial use case has their vertical and organization-specific operational variations. This often requires bespoke or highly customized solutions. A combination of behavioral- and rule-based models can help alleviate this challenge in scenarios where an operational state cannot be learned using rules alone.

Another challenge with reliable anomaly detection is in defining an optimal threshold. A threshold that is too close to "normal" has a higher likelihood of generating false positives. On the other hand, having the threshold on the higher side may allow valid anomalies to escape. By using large datasets, the proper tuning of models, and occasional adjustments in the model, we can keep up with real-world variations and provide reliable anomaly detection.

Incident response and management

A security program must include an incident management plan, which identifies and enumerates actions in response to a security breach. Incident management draws insights from the analysis of security data and needs to take a well-defined set of actions **prior to** a potential incident, **during** an incident, and **after** the incident has been resolved. These three stages and associated activities are illustrated in *Figure 7.6*:

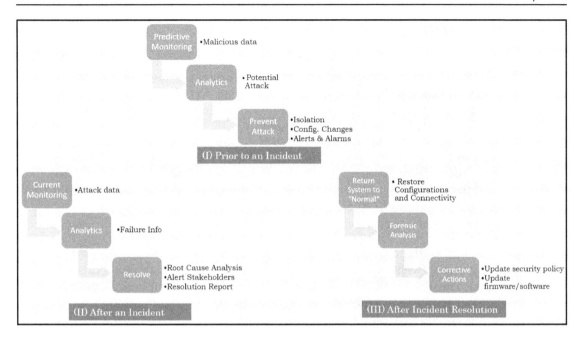

Figure 7.6: Incident management workflows before, during, and after an incident

Based on predictive monitoring and analysis, when a potential attack is detected, its severity and footprint should be minimized by raising alerts and notifications, isolating network segments at risk, and applying policies on devices reachable from the compromised endpoint.

During an attack, the **incident response (IR)** team investigates, collects and stores logs, and notifies impacted stakeholders. The IR team subsequently performs root cause analysis to resolve the incident.

On resolution, the system needs to be returned to a normal state, data recorded before and during the incident are sent for forensic analysis, and corrective measures such as security policy, configuration updates, secure firmware, and software updates are applied.

Incidents involve different degrees of downtime and outages, which could often severely impact the safety and reliability performance of an IIoT deployment. When preventive measures fail, the goal of IIoT incident management is to minimize its impact and identify corrective measures to counter future reoccurrence.

Security audits

Security audits aim to assess compliance with legal, legislative, and regulatory standards and guidelines. In addition to compliance assessment, audits help flag procedural and technical deficiencies should they exist in the security plan. Periodic audits of device configuration, identity certificates, and device states following a firmware are necessary to protect the operational health of the deployment.

In most security audits, the internal audit team members evaluate operational processes, workflows, and information flows to assess compliance and scope for improvements. Certain regulations and industry standards mandate external audits to confirm compliance. In an external audit, a neutral third party evaluates compliance, assesses security operations, and recommends changes to bridge security gaps.

A security audit is also triggered by a security incident and may be included as part of forensic investigations. Event logs, configuration changelogs, and analysis reports are necessary to prove an audit trail. In traditional OT environments, automated event and changelogs are not always implemented. With the introduction of connected IT technologies, it is crucial to deploy logging and log history storage using secured servers.

Security maturity model

The various connected assets in an organization do not require the same level of security measures. For example, security measures for critical infrastructure and those for a handheld mobile device need not be of the same degree. Every organization needs to balance what is ideally desirable with what's practical and actionable in terms of resources. To guide you in the process, the IIC has defined the **IoT Security Maturity Model (IIC-SMM)**, a conceptual framework to organize various considerations to determine the maturity level of a given system.

The security maturity model can be used to identify the comprehensiveness and alignment necessary for different maturity levels appropriate for a specific industry. The framework can also be applied in the context of a specific organization, or a production environment, or at a specific system level to define what the current state of security is and the security target state. The following is an excerpt from IIC's *"IoT Security Maturity Model: Description and Intended Use"* whitepaper.

"Not all IoT systems require the same strength of protection mechanisms and the same procedures to be deemed secure enough. The organization determines the priorities that drive the security enhancement process, making it possible for the mechanisms and procedures to fit the organization's goals without going beyond what is necessary. The implementation of security mechanisms and processes are considered mature if they are expected to be effective in addressing those goals. It is the security mechanisms' appropriateness in addressing the goals, rather than their objective strength, that determines the maturity level. Hence, security maturity is the degree of confidence that the current security state meets all organizational needs and security-related requirements. Security maturity level is a measure of the understanding of the current security level, its necessity, benefits and cost of its support."

-IIC:PUB:IN15:V1.0:PB:2018040

Interested readers are encouraged to refer to the IIC-SMM series of documents to gain more insight into the security maturity model for IIoT deployments.

These documents provide information to answer the following set of questions (IIC-SMM):

- Given the organizational requirements and threat landscape, what is my solution's target maturity level?
- What is my solution's current maturity level?
- What are the mechanisms and processes that will take my solution's maturity from its current state to its target state?

Implementing an IIoT security program

A vital aspect of IIoT security governance is implementing a security program that is practical and actionable. In a constantly evolving threat landscape, it is a challenge for industrial adopters of IIoT to decide where and how to invest their limited security resources. Defining a security program by considering models such as SMM and C2M2 (USE-C2M2) can help organizations to right-size security mechanisms and investments.

The IIoT security program decides the resilience and reliability of the production environment, which directly impacts business goals, reputation, and the financial fate of an organization. That's why an organization's business-level stakeholders should directly engage and approve the security program. Many organizations may already have an IT security program, which is typically governed by the enterprise IT team. An IIoT security program involves both IT and OT environments and should either align with or build on top of existing IT security programs.

Many IIoT deployments involve "system of systems" architectures, where data flows across multiple organizational and geo-political domains. In such cases, ownership and accountability of a security program could get blurred and may require a supervisory domain for a "system of systems" level of governance.

The next section primarily focuses on implementing a security program in an industrial enterprise and presents the various functions involved in doing so.

Establishing an IIoT security team

Security is sustained by accountability. A security team takes responsibility for defining and executing a security program. IIoT security team members should include both IT and OT security professionals, and also management- and executive-level stakeholders. Depending on an organization's size and resources, the team members may be either dedicated or part-time. Some organizations may want to engage third-party security consultants during the formative stages of a security program or may partner with an external security organization.

The security team needs to clearly define the roles and responsibilities of individual members. The team is also accountable for assessing the end-to-end security posture during the planning and pre-production stages, and defining and enforcing security policies, controls, compliance, and incident response once the IIoT system is in the production environment.

A security program plan can be defined as an overarching governance document for an organization, which defines security policies, compliance requirements, and practice guidelines. The program plan also documents mechanisms to implement, track progress on, and revision control the security program.

Deciding on regulatory compliance

The security program plan needs to document the security standards and regulations to be complied with. Security policies, vendor selection, and operational policies need to align with the compliance requirements. An internal and external audits schedule for compliance should be planned accordingly.

Assessing and managing risks

The proper assessment of the threats and risks an organization faces provides the foundation for choosing and implementing the appropriate security controls. The risk assessment process should identity:

- Threats to an organization's industry vertical
- Regulatory and compliance requirements
- The vulnerabilities and risks unique to an operational environment
- The organization's threat profile

Considering resource availability, risks should be managed and prioritized. The current security posture of an organization, its target state, and the threats to maintain its target state can help in prioritizing risks. Security measures in accordance with the security maturity model can be used to devise a risk mitigation plan.

In the case of IIoT systems, risk assessment and mitigation should utilize both cybersecurity and domain expertise to produce the intended outcomes.

Managing third-party security

The complex ecosystem of the industrial internet involves several vendors and suppliers. Multiple products and services in an IIoT deployment may be based on an **as-a-service** subscription model. An organization's security program must take into account both purchased assets and subscription-based assets. Some third-parties, such as public and hybrid cloud vendors, employ a shared security responsibility model.

Insufficient security measures in third-party practices and infrastructure can expose an organization to threats that it cannot control. The security program must define ways an organization can track external vendors, and control how vendors access and manage an organization's assets. The evaluation criteria to assess third-party security practices and regulatory compliance should also be documented. A service level agreement with a third party should depend on successful compliance with an organization's third-party evaluation criteria. The security program should be able to track any changes in security policies of the third party throughout the duration of the contractual agreement.

Enforcing the security policy

Security policies embed intelligence in an organization's security operations. For ease and effectiveness, the policies should be consistent across the organization.

Security policies involving personnel, supply chain, and physical controls can be defined and enforced in alignment with enterprise IT guidelines, configurations, and infrastructure.

Device or machine policies normally can affect a group of devices. A device security policy should enumerate identity and access control policies for new device onboarding, device provisioning, secure software and firmware update policies, patching specifications, and security monitoring policies. These policies can be structured by defining baseline policies applicable to a broad set of devices, and then gradually narrowing those down to finer granularities with device-specific settings.

To scale to a large number of devices and avoid the human error associated with manual deployment, automated policy management is desirable. However, such a process should also allow a human operator to intervene and be able to interpret security policies. Based on security event analysis and changes in safety and reliability requirements, security policies should be periodically reviewed and updated.

Continuous monitoring and analysis

In security monitoring and analysis, security-related event data is collected, aggregated, and correlated for analytics. Asset visibility is vital for implementing continuous monitoring and analysis. Any new network-connected assets should be discoverable for monitoring. However, the IIoT security team should be able to define which assets are to be monitored and to what extent.

Some practical considerations in implementing continuous security monitoring are: performance should not be impacted, it should be generic and consistent for various endpoints and network resources, and it should minimize the cost of data transport, analysis, and storage.

The security monitoring policy needs to specify the minimum dataset to be monitored and its frequency. Collecting the minimum amount of data also reduces the risk of its exposure. It is highly possible that after a successful intrusion, all events and activities are erased, leaving no audit trail. As a countermeasure, monitored data can be securely transmitted to an external monitoring system. The logs can also be signed with a running hash to detect alteration.

In cases requiring the collection of user data, asset owners should ensure they have SLAs that adhere to data privacy and integrity regulations. Legacy industrial systems lacking modern logging and reporting capabilities are not always upgradable due to cost barriers, for example recertification. Data from legacy systems can be collected using gateways connected to them, or by using passive network monitoring systems for legacy communications (IIC-IISF).

Conducting security training

Misconfigurations and human error are very common causes of vulnerabilities. After all, the protection of industrial assets depends on the security awareness and training of the operational workforce. The convergence of state-of-the art IT technologies in OT environments has not only introduced complexity (and hence higher risk of human error), it has also introduced new workflows that demand new skills.

Ongoing security education, training, and certification for employees, operators, and consultants involved in both the IT and OT sides of the house should be part of security governance. Certain security training, standard compliance workshops, and certification programs may need to be mandated to sustain a secured operational life cycle.

Implementing incident management

Even with the best security measures and controls in place, incidents do happen. The security program plan should identify and define steps to contain the severity of an incident. The IR team is usually responsible for implementing the steps in order to respond to incidents before, during, and after an incident. Root cause analysis and incident resolution often depends on cross-functional collaboration with legal, communications, and third-party vendors.

It is also desirable to automate certain functions of incident management, such as generating alerts and notifications, and periodic report generation.

The incident response workflow needs to comply to regulations; for example, notifying all affected stakeholders of an incident. Any other regulatory mandates must be factored in as well while implementing an incident response program.

Forensic investigations and security audits are integral components of incident management. Insights from forensics and audits help evaluate and revise security policies. Publicly sharable forensic insights can also be shared with the security community to bolster overall threat intelligence.

Defining security audits

The security program plan needs to identify and document mandatory internal and external audits for regulatory compliance. In addition to compliance, the program plan document should clearly enumerate the frequency of internal audits to assess security operations in an IIoT deployment. The security assessment guidelines during a regular audit and when an audit is triggered by a security incident should also be documented.

The frequency and scope of security audits following device configuration changes, the authenticity of digital certificate and secrets stored in the device, tamper-proofing, and the device state following a firmware or software update should also be clearly enumerated and enforced.

The operational environment must be configured with secured monitoring, analysis, and event logging to provide audit trails. The result-and-report templates following a security audit can be standardized to provide clear and consistent audit-based insights.

Security revisions and maturity

The IIoT security program implementation is not a one-time activity. Compared to IT, industrial systems typically have a long operational lifespan; the industrial infrastructure and threat landscape are more dynamic and keep evolving. This necessitates a living security program; the security policies and security program elements should adapt to the changing threat environment.

A revision can be triggered following an incident and forensic analysis. Revisions can also be planned on an annual basis. Threat intelligence, vulnerability monitoring, audit reports, and periodic security gap analysis should be used to determine the current security state and plan revisions to meet the next target maturity state.

Figure 7.7 summarizes this section by illustrating the interplay for the various considerations of a living and proactive security program:

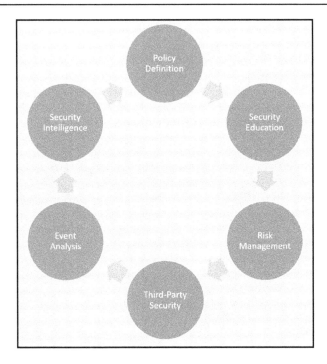

Figure 7.7: The moving wheel of a proactive security governance program

Summary

This chapter presented an actionable roadmap to implement the multi-layered IIoT security model. Readers are now able to utilize practical insights on securing IIoT life cycle processes, security roles and responsibilities, the various elements of an IIoT security governance program, and how an organization can implement a practical and adaptive security governance program. The necessity of right-sizing security by setting the IIoT security objectives in the context of safety and reliability, an introduction to the security maturity model, and an evaluation of security roles were also discussed in this chapter.

In Chapter 8, *IIoT Security Using Emerging Technologies*, a few promising technologies that are still in the early phases of development are presented to help readers gain a basic understanding of their relevance and applicability.

IIoT Security Using Emerging Technologies

8

"Security-enabled data, and the language of AI, will drive our future connected, driverless world."

— Sudha Jamthe, Author and CEO of IoT Disruptions

In the present century, we are thriving in a technology hotbed. Every industry—be it consumer, retail, or manufacturing—is embracing disruptive innovations that challenge our operational status quo. Just consider how fast we have digitally traveled from smartphones to smart homes, smart farming, and smart cars. Today, we rely on technology to solve any problem, be it individual, social, national, or industrial.

In the earlier chapters of this book, we discussed various technologies to arrive at a framework for industrial IoT security. The framework is by no means fixed and final. It needs to evolve, with newer innovations and attack vectors. After all, new technologies serve as hotbeds for new threats, as well. Just as the threat landscape never stops evolving, it is important that we continue to evolve the security architecture, as well, using innovative methodologies and overarching technologies.

In the context of technology evolution, right now, we are witnessing a convergence of physical sciences, such as physics, chemistry, and mathematics, with engineering and computing. This convergence is giving rise to game-changing innovations, such as quantum computing, deep learning, blockchain, and so on. In this chapter, we will review some of these trending technologies and explore their relevance and applicability to the problem of IIoT security.

The technologies discussed in this chapter will be segmented into the following topics:

- Blockchain to secure IIoT transactions
- Cognitive countermeasures – AI, machine learning, and deep learning
- Time-sensitive networking – next-gen industrial connectivity
- Other promising trends

Blockchain to secure IIoT transactions

IoT communications predominantly use broker or brokerless publish-subscribe models. Standards such as MQTT and DDS support these communication models. In the case of MQTT, the broker serves as the central supervisory entity, which can be either on-premise or in the cloud. This centralized, supervisory *modus operandi* is highly scalable. However, any attack on the central node (such as a denial of service) can potentially melt down communication in its entirety. From a security standpoint, the main promise of distributed ledger technology, or blockchain, is to overcome the vulnerabilities related to the single point of failure in centrally controlled architectures.

Decentralized identity management, tamper-proofing the supply chain, and so on, are supported by blockchain, as well.

Blockchain essentially provides a distributed transaction environment where-in, just like the DNA in every cell, a complete copy of the blockchain is held by every participant in the network. To initiate a transaction, the sender creates a digital message outlining the transaction, which is then broadcast to the entire network. Each participant represents a node in this network.

All transactions completed within a period of time are combined and fused into a block, which is then appended to the chain. Instead of being stored in one location, a copy of the ledger is distributed and stored at every node. A **block** comprising of a set of transactions is appended to the ledger only after the transactions are confirmed by using a cryptographic hash algorithm, a process referred to as **mining**.

Mining is a resource-intensive process. In the public Bitcoin blockchain, mining takes place every 10 minutes. *Figure 8.1* shows a relative measure of how difficult it is to find a new block. The difficulty is adjusted periodically, as a function of how much hashing power has been deployed by the network of miners (BLO-INF):

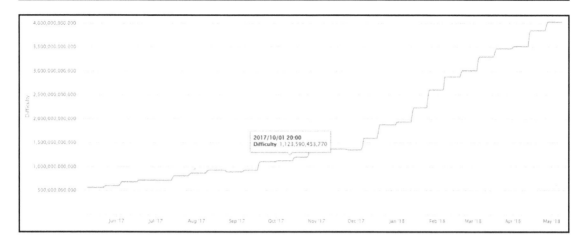

Figure 8.1: Non-linear increase in hashing power; source: blockchain.info

Every participant, or node, verifies and approves the transaction before it is added to the ledger. This chain of digital ledgers is immutable, and the data is cryptographically signed to preserve and secure the entire chain of transactions.

The time to approve and add a block to the ledger is in the order of minutes. However, individual transactions can take a few hundred milliseconds. This can still provide real-time performance in time-sensitive M2M communications, where a transaction is not necessarily dependent on a block to be approved and added to the blockchain.

Public and private blockchains

Private and public blockchains are both grounded on similar operational principles; namely:

- Decentralized peer-to-peer networks
- A synchronized copy of the append-only ledger maintained by each participant
- Guaranteed immutability and transparency of the ledger
- The use of pseudonymous identities of participants

The essential divergence between private and public blockchains is in the way that they are deployed and managed, which impacts the level of privacy and security. A public blockchain uses open source protocols; the network is open to anyone to join and participate in the blockchain transactions. Bitcoin and Ethereum are two currently widely used public blockchains. Due to unrestricted access, public blockchains grow in size rapidly, thereby bloating the time and computing resources needed for every transaction.

Private blockchain requires permissioned access and enforces access control and governance rules, which participants must comply with. The access control mechanism can vary, based on use cases. For example, existing participants, or a consortium, may democratically approve future entrants, or a regulatory authority may issue licenses for new entrants. After approval, the blockchain transactions are maintained in a decentralized manner. Transactions are accessible to all participants, and are hence vulnerable to **insider threats**.

Private blockchains are more suitable for industrial enterprises, where standards and regulations in managing the blockchain matter. Hyperledger (HYP-BLK) is a leading enabler of private blockchains for the industrial IoT.

Digital identity with blockchains

Decentralized identity management promises to overcome key and certificate management challenges, when scaled to millions of machines and human users. Vulnerability, errors, and single points of failure, associated with a centralized root of trust, are also addressed by a decentralized identity scheme.

Public blockchains, such as Bitcoin, use a consensus algorithm, which is replicated across participating nodes. Each transaction is digitally signed by the originator using a private key, and is chained to prior transactions with a digital hash. These cryptographic controls vouchsafe the public key associated with its owner within the blockchain. At the time of this writing, W3C is standardizing an address associated with the public key, called the **decentralized identifier** (**DID**), to be used in the emerging **decentralized PKI** (**DPKI**) infrastructure.

Interested readers can learn more about blockchain-based global public identity in (SOV-IDN).

Securing the supply chain

The immutability of each transaction in a blockchain can provide a stamp of authenticity, and track service provenance along the supply chain. In industries such as pharmaceutical, advertising, precious metals, or anything of high value, blockchain has already been used for authenticity and provenance. Industrial devices usually go through multiple changes in guard. For a device leaving the manufacturing shop, in transit, after sale, and throughout its life cycle, the transparency of blockchain transactions can potentially provide an audit trail and a proof of records.

As of the time of writing, a blockchain start-up by the name of Chronicled (`https://chronicled.com/`) has completed a technical pilot, demonstrating how multiple parties can verify a device identity and provenance by using its **Serialized Global Trade Item Number** (**SGTIN**), without directly interacting with one another (COI-JOU).

A SGTIN is a globally recognized identifier that enables us to identify an item as it moves through a multi-stage supply chain involving multiple custodians and geographic locations. The pilot applied **Zero Knowledge Succinct Non-Interactive Argument of Knowledge** (**zk-SNARK**), a cryptographic verification model developed by researchers at UC Berkeley and MIT to enable, an anonymous transfer of custody within multi-party supply chains.

Blockchain challenges

Industrial IoT involves scaled numbers of endpoints, transactions, and extended operational lifespans. The cryptographic workflow of a blockchain demands extensive computing and network resources, and this demand increases as the number of nodes and the size of the blockchain grows. This is a major viability concern in blockchain adoption for IIoT.

Figure 8.2 shows the trend in the number of terahashes per second that the Bitcoin network performed over a 10 month period:

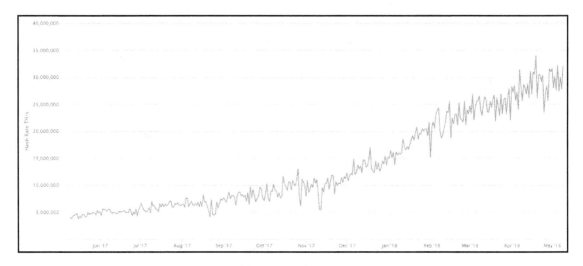

Figure 8.2 Estimated number of terahashes per second (trillions of hashes per second) that the Bitcoin network performed; source: blockchain.info

Current state of the art does not position blockchain as a practical alternative to centralized cloud-based models for IIoT deployments. While organizations can consider blockchain to gradually offload their low-latency M2M transactions, cloud-edge intelligence can continue to provide device management, telemetry, and related analytics functions.

At an industry level, several new consortia and research initiatives involving blockchain start-ups, universities, and technology companies are opening new possibilities within blockchain and IoT. Although blockchain could potentially be as pervasive as the internet and smartphones, its large-scale adoption depends on standards, legal frameworks, and regulatory environments that are yet to take shape. But, just like the internet, the disruptive power of blockchain could transform businesses sooner than we expect.

Cognitive countermeasures – AI, machine learning, and deep learning

Cognitive computing is highly relevant and increasingly indispensable to industrial IoT use cases, where machines can make autonomous decisions based on IoT device data, and can also protect themselves against external threats and malicious attacks. This may not be merely sci-fi imagination, as it was a decade ago.

Computer visionaries such as Alan Turing were optimistic about **artificial intelligence (AI)** since the 1950s. However, the recent spike in interest and research on AI owe to faster, cheaper, and more powerful parallel processing using GPUs, coupled with a steady growth in data sciences. Pure AI—where machines and robots can operate and decide with full autonomy—is still a long way away. However, practical AI, where cognitive computing augments human expertise, is already a reality. Machine learning and its specialized branch, called deep learning, are currently the main drivers behind cognitive IoT and practical AI.

Cognition generally refers to our ability to think. While machines may not yet "think" like humans, using certain computing abilities, they may still be able to perform the three underlying functions involved in thinking: understanding, reasoning, and learning (IBM-CIOT).

Few common terminology outlining the realm of cognitive computing are mentioned here:

- **Understanding**: A machine's ability to ingest large volumes of structured and unstructured data, and to derive meaning from the data by building models of concepts, relationships, and so on.
- **Reasoning**: A machine's ability to dynamically derive inferences by using the models. This is an essential element of autonomy, as compared to automation software using static, preprogrammed logic.
- **Learning**: A machine's ability to infer new knowledge from data either training data or **live** operational data. This new knowledge enables adaptive intelligence and improved intelligence. Learning often involves combining sensor data with other contextual data, to optimize processes and systems:

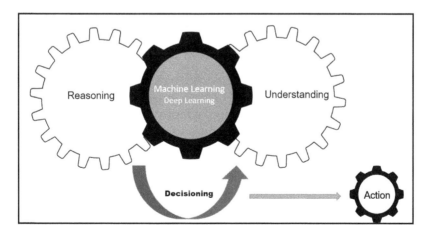

Figure 8.3: Functional components of cognitive IoT

Machine learning can be generalized as a data analytics discipline, where a use case specific model is derived by using algorithms and training datasets. The performance of this machine learning model improves with exposure to more data. Machine learning can be either supervised or unsupervised. In supervised learning, a model is trained using a known set of input and output data, so that the model can predict an output based on new data. In unsupervised learning, hidden patterns and implicit structures within data are learned to draw inferences (such as clustering) without any exposure to labeled outputs (MATH-ML).

Deep learning is a specialized branch of machine learning, where models are trained by using large sets of labeled data and neural network architectures that learn features directly from the data (such as images, text, or audio) without requiring manual feature extraction. Deep learning techniques deliver a very high level of accuracy in inferences, by minimizing false positives and negatives:

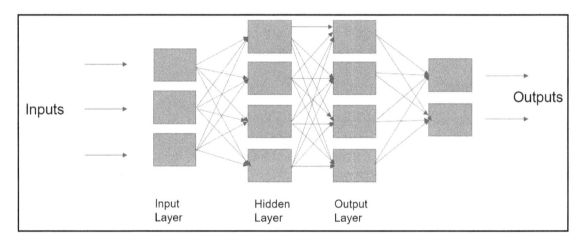

Figure 8.4: Neural network based deep learning

An industrial IoT application involves multiple, often disparate, data sources and data types, such as digital sensor data, GPS location data, unstructured text, imaging, and acoustic sources. In machine and deep learning, adaptive algorithms and models are used to harness these industrial big data, gain insights and to make autonomous decisions.

Machine health monitoring, predictive maintenance, drone-based surveillance, robotics for automated factories, autonomous vehicles, and so on, are some common industrial applications of practical AI using machine learning and deep learning. Malware identification, spam and anomaly detection, risk scoring, and so on, are some of the IIoT security applications of supervised machine learning, as illustrated in *Figure 8.5*:

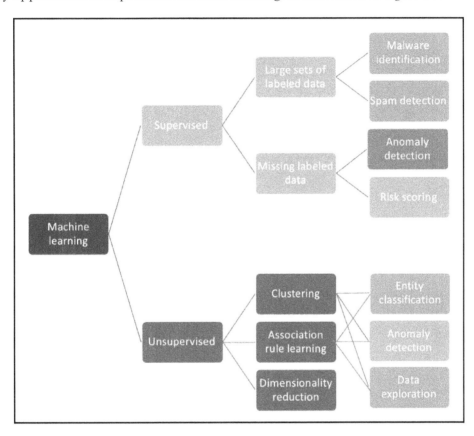

Figure 8.5: A taxonomy of machine learning and its applications; source: https://towardsdatascience.com/ai-and-machine-learning-in-cyber-security-d6fbee480af0

Practical AI, though not a silver bullet, has many promises to secure IIoT. Using observation and pattern recognition algorithms, it is possible to detect and stop cyberattacks in progress, at a scale and speed that far exceeds human analysis and manual processes. Predictive models and analytics can be used to predict and adapt to future threats, and to identify and remediate existing vulnerabilities (AI-FOR).

Practical AI may not replace cybersecurity personnel, but it can assist them. The skill gap of cybersecurity is well known. Cyber-physical security in industrial environments is still a nascent discipline, where the skill gap is quite prominent. AI can aid security professionals with its ability to analyze massive volumes of security data, constantly adapt to evolving threats and attack patterns, and present insights, alerts, and data visualization for human experts.

Practical considerations for AI-based IIoT security

The timely detection of a malware or an ongoing attack is a top challenge for organizations, as sometimes, a malicious intrusion may escape detection for months, or even a year.

Machine learning applications can significantly reduce these delays. Currently, there are multiple AI-based security products in the marketplace, to reliably detect malicious files, events, and activities. Some products can even predict and mitigate attacks before an attack actually initiates. To integrate machine learning in an IIoT security program, organizations should take note of a few practical considerations (AI-FOR):

- With a variety of AI tools, each with a unique set of offerings, it is important for organizations to identify the exact elements of the security program where AI-based applications are more suitable. Before starting a POC, specific goals and outputs should be clearly identified. Specific areas can be identified where ML-based applications can assist security personnel.
- False positive and false negative percentages for certain AI-based tools are as high as 89-90% (NULL-CON). This may, in fact, defeat the point of assisting human experts. Many deep learning based security solutions are able to achieve false positive rates below 50%. So, it is advisable to set an acceptable false positive limit.

- Any industrial IoT application involves multiple, often disparate, data sources and data types, such as digital sensor data, GPS location data, unstructured text, imaging, and acoustic sources. Identifying and clearly defining these data types and sources is key to the proper utilization of an ML strategy.
- A lack of context knowledge may impact the desired outcomes. Context adds meaning to the data. In the case of a device, the context includes its role, location, and owner. POCs need to evaluate how an AI-based solution should incorporate context in anomaly detection. For example, a DNS server is always expected to respond to DNS queries. But, for any other device, responding to DNS queries can be a sign of an attack (ML-CHA). The context performance of an AI product can be evaluated during POCs, to reduce false positives and negatives in deployment.

Time-sensitive networking – Next-gen industrial connectivity

Time-sensitive networking (**TSN**) is an evolution of the IEEE 802.1 Ethernet standard (IE3-TSN). TSN is not an IIoT-security-specific protocol, but its design offers multiple security benefits (and a few challenges). TSN is still in an early adoption phase. In this section, we will discuss the relevance of TSN as an emerging technology in secured IIoT deployments.

IEEE 802.1 Ethernet, although a widely deployed low-cost layer 2 technology, fails to match the deterministic performance requirements of industrial automation and control applications. To achieve deterministic performance, most industrial enterprises still continue to use fieldbus technologies and their proprietary enhancements to Ethernet (such as EtherCat, PROFINET, or SERCOS III). These proprietary protocols are not built for security and interoperability. The result has been fragmented industrial networks that are incapable of integrating with advanced analytics services of the Industrial Internet and Industrie 4.0.

As the next-generation Ethernet standard, TSN is designed for deterministic packet delivery with low latency and jitter. This provides a solid ground for industrial automation and control networks to adopt TSN and leverage the benefits of standard-based connectivity, interoperability, and advanced innovations. TSN enhancements are at layer 2; as such, higher-layer communication standards remain unaffected by these enhancements.

Figure 8.6 shows the suite of standards enhanced for TSN. TSN's key capability standards for time synchronization, scheduled delivery, and software-defined configuration have been highlighted in the diagram. Together, these capabilities provide a practical solution for secured IIoT:

Standard	Area
IEEE 802.1ASrev, IEEE 1588	Timing & Synchronization
IEEE 802.1Qav	Queue Management and Bandwidth Reservation for Deterministic Flows (Credit Based Shaper)
IEEE 802.1Qbv	Scheduling to Provide Fast Deterministic Cyclic Flows
IEEE 802.1Qbu & IEEE 802.3br	Frame Preemption for Lower Latency of Prioritized Flows
IEEE 802.1Qch	Simple Scheduling and Bandwidth Reservation for Deterministic Flows (Peristaltic Shapers)
IEEE 802.1Qcr	Queue Management and Bandwidth Reservation for Deterministic Flows (Asynch Traffic Shaping)
IEEE 802.1Qat	Distributed Protocol for Simplified Set-up (SRP)
IEEE 802.1Qcc	System Configuration for Simplified Set-up (Centralized Config and Improved SRP)
IEEE 802.1Qcp	Support for Standardized Systems Management (YANG)
IEEE 802.1CB	Seamless Redundancy for Critical Flows
IEEE 802.1Qci	Time Aware Ingress Policing for Reliability

Figure 8.6: IEEE 802.1 suite of standards enhanced for Time-Sensitive Networks (image partially adapted from (IIC-TSN))

Time synchronization

TSN is designed to establish a common concept of time between communicating devices, as specified in IEEE 802.1AS. The IEEE 1588 **Precise Time Protocol** (**PTP**) standard is used to distribute an accurate timing reference between devices and switches in the network. The specific IEEE 1588 profile for TSN is IEEE 1588ASrev. The standard also allows for time synchronization based on an external reference, such as a GPS.

Certain pilot testbeds have already reported having achieved time synchronization with less than 100-nanosecond accuracy.

Traffic scheduling

TSN achieves traffic prioritization for deterministic delivery by using time-aware shaper, as defined in IEEE 802.1Qbv. Time-aware shaper separates the communication into fixed-length, repeating time cycles. Peers agree on TSN communication to divide these cycles into time slots, as shown in *Figure 8.7*. Each time slot can be assigned to one or more of the eight Ethernet priorities (TSN-CS).

TSN defines three traffic types; namely, scheduled traffic, best-effort traffic, and reserved traffic. Industrial automation and control traffic requiring bounded latency and zero congestion loss are examples of scheduled traffic. Best-effort traffic is the general Ethernet traffic, with no specific **quality of service** (**QoS**) requirements. The reserved traffic type is frames allocated in different time slots, with a specified bandwidth reservation:

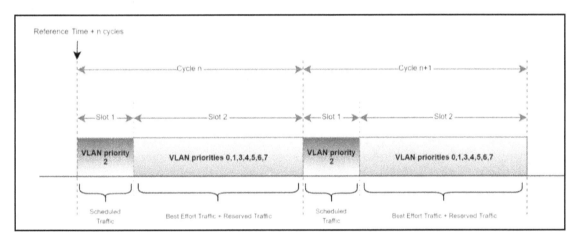

Figure 8.7: Time slot divisions in each cycle

Specific time slots and queues are reserved for scheduled traffic associated with a predefined timing of when the originating end node sends out data, and when the destination end node receives it. Intermediate switches know when to expect the traffic from a specific end node and schedule a time slot accordingly, so that the time to reach the destination end node is guaranteed.

Network and system configuration

TSN utilizes a software-defined networking concept for the automated setup and configuration of devices and network equipment. TSN system configuration is defined in IEEE 802.1Qcc. TSN configurations for timing, scheduling, and QoS metrics are agreed on in advance, among peers. These configurations, required for each switch and end node, are then passed on to respected devices. Automated configuration reduces management complexity and human error related attack surfaces, and promotes the scalability of IIoT deployments.

TSN security

Legacy industrial networks using Ethernet fieldbus technologies mainly rely on perimeter defense for security. If an intrusion can cut through the firewall, it can easily infect the legacy control networks that lack native cybersecurity defenses. TSN is designed with native security controls (such as access control), and, as such, extends the defense capabilities up to the device level, which significantly improves the strength of defense in industrial networks. TSN deployments can benefit from higher-layer security controls (IPSec, TLS, and so on).

Traffic scheduling gives priority to control traffic, which prevents an attacker from flooding the network with denial-of-service traffic. Deterministic delivery removes the chances of tampering with the cyclic flows.

On the downside, to achieve time synchronization, TSN relies on IEEE 1588, which has multiple vulnerabilities. Subsequent versions and industry proposals have attempted to address the vulnerabilities of 1588 implementations, to protect against complex cyberattacks. To secure the clock synchronization phase, adequate protection of all participating endpoints is expected. For high-priority scheduled traffic, providing cryptographic protections, authentication, and integrity of all messages at wire speed is a challenge. To meet the real-time deterministic requirements, messages cannot be fully analyzed before being re-sent. As such, non-authenticated traffic could be injected into the network for malicious purposes (TSN-CS).

The foundational promise of TSN is to provide industries with a cost-effective, standard-based interconnectivity framework, to leverage the benefits of IoT without compromising the real-time performance capabilities. New devices with the TSN stack are already being developed. For legacy devices using fieldbus protocols, gateways can be used for protocol translation. Early testing has demonstrated that fieldbus networks can successfully communicate over a TSN infrastructure without losing their deterministic characteristics. Integrations of industrial application layer protocols, such as OPC-UA, EtherCAT-IP, PROFINET, and IEC 61850, are already in progress.

Other Promising Trends

It is perhaps worthwhile to note that there are other disruptive concepts, such as **quantum computing** and **Artificial General Intelligence (AGI)**, that will redefine how we treat security today. Quantum computing, although rather nascent at present, uses the concept of quantum mechanical paradigms that could render current cryptography algorithms ineffective in several instances. The importance of hardware-based trust is now well acknowledged for industrial networks. MIT's **physical unclonable function** (**PUF**) is one of the emerging technologies to tamper-proof devices at the silicon level.

As noted earlier in this chapter, security is a dynamic discipline, where threats and countermeasures evolve with time. As such, product developers need to ensure that their solutions can stand the test of time-not just for a year or two, but for the foreseeable future. Emerging technologies and their impact on the security landscape in the **years to come** is a vital consideration in any security technology evaluation and adoption.

Summary

This chapter presented a few emerging concepts and enabling technologies for IIoT security. The current state of the art and practical viability of these technologies were also discussed. Intense research and development and pilots are in progress, as these technologies continue to mature. To gain an in-depth understanding and to keep up with the evolutionary track of these enablers, the interested reader is encouraged to utilize the references provided in this chapter.

The next chapter presents real-world scenarios to analyze the anatomy of an industrial cyberattack and to see how enterprises are implementing IIoT security best practices to protect their connected assets and infrastructures.

Real-World Case Studies in IIoT Security

9

"It's not that we use technology; we live technology."
- Godfrey Reggio

The acceleration of IIoT adoption depends on many enabling factors. Of those, safety and security are the foremost. Many technology vendors have started to recognize security as the *elephant in the room* for IIoT business cases. However, there are still a large number of industrial enterprises who are yet to prioritize security in their IoT adoption strategies, deterred mainly by its associated cost, complexity, and resource implications. Oftentimes, IT security controls are perceived as impediments in highly reliable and deterministic OT environments.

As more and more industrial organizations digitally connect their control systems and OT infrastructures, IIoT security countermeasures are no longer a matter of choice. The Stuxnet incident has already proved the inadequacy of the **security by obscurity** approach. There are, of course, certain industrial organizations where business leaders recognize the urgency of securing their connected OT operations and assets. These organizations are exemplary, and their case studies can help us gain practical insights on securing connected industrials.

In this chapter, three real-world case studies have been presented to highlight practical strategies for securing critical infrastructure and operations. The dangerous fallouts of inadequate OT security are showcased in the first case study.

The three main sections of this chapter are as follows:

- Analysis of a real-world cyber-physical attack
- Case study 2 – Building a successful IIoT security program
- Case study 3 – ISA/IEC 62443 based industrial endpoint protection

Analysis of a real-world cyber-physical attack

On December 23, 2015, three Ukrainian heat and electricity distribution companies (oblenergos) underwent a concurrent cyberattack that caused 225,000 customers to lose their power (ISAC-SANS). The cyber adversary remotely sabotaged the SCADA **distribution management system (DMS)**, maliciously took control of the HMIs, and subsequently launched destructive attacks to disable communications with the field. At least 27 substations were reported to have been taken offline.

This Ukrainian incident is a good example to understand the dynamics of a bold and successful cyber attack. The attack was the first of its kind, considering that it targeted a nation's critical infrastructure. It impacted physical assets, people, reliability, and reputation. Although third-party cloud providers (a typical component of IIoT architectures) were not involved in this use case, this study still showcases how the adversaries remotely hijacked the grid's operations; and also the mitigation techniques that could have prevented the incident.

Background and impact

In the Ukrainian electricity system, the attacks targeted the regional distribution level, as shown in *Figure 9.1*. Although the impacted utility companies recovered the normal power supply within six hours, damages from the attack reportedly forced the distribution units to operate in a constrained mode for many months following the incident:

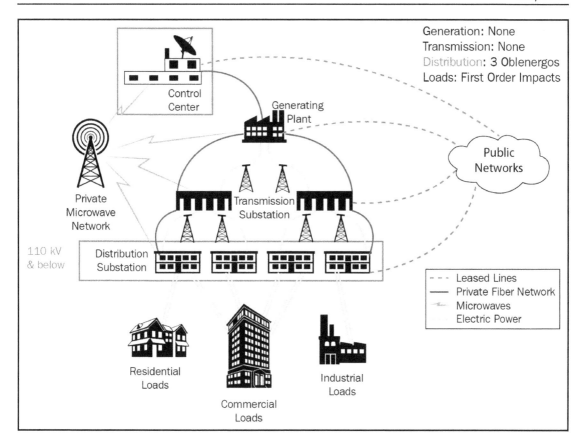

Generation: None
Transmission: None
Distribution: 3 Oblenergos
Loads: First Order Impacts

Figure 9.1: Electricity distribution overview; Source: (ISAC-SANS)

In response to the incident, investigators in the Ukraine, private companies, and the US government performed forensic analysis to evaluate the attack's root cause. This case study is based on publicly available information and a joint report on this attack published by E-ISAC and SANS ICS (ISAC-SANS).

The sequence of events

Based on forensic analysis, the incident involved multiple preparatory events that could have started five to eight months ahead of the attack-with-impact. The attack followed through stages 1 and 2 of the ICS Kill Chain, as shown in *Figure 9.2*:

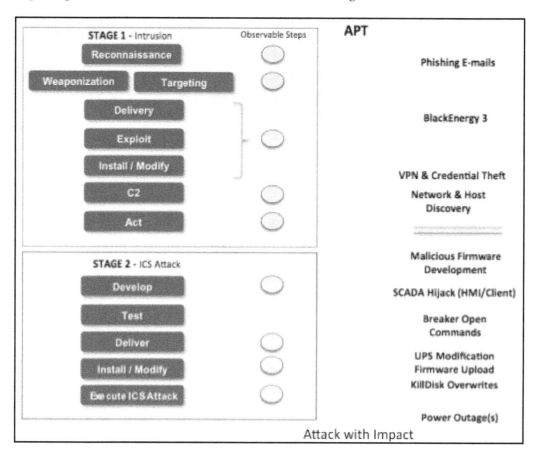

Figure 9.2: Sequence of events mapped to ICS kill chain diagram; Source: ISAC-SANS

The overall incident and the actions taken by the adversary can be decomposed into three distinct trails, described in the following sections.

Exploit loopholes to perform the attack

The Ukrainian power grids had implemented certain security measures, mostly perimeter defenses, for example, corporate and OT network segmentation. The adversary, through extensive reconnaissance, developed and delivered exploits to break through those defenses. They launched spear phishing attacks to inject BlackEnergy 3 malware, and harnessed credentials to gain remote access into the workstations and HMIs by exploiting trusted VPN connections.

Trigger the attack with impact

By gaining control of the ICS and HMI, and by locking out operators from their workstations, the adversaries took control of the field devices, remotely opened circuit breakers of the substations, and shut off power across a broad region.

Impair operations and delay recovery

A power grid involves many distributed field devices that are centrally controlled by the SCADA DMS using various connectivity and automation tools. The adversaries destroyed these automation capabilities. The Windows systems were rendered unrecoverable by installing the KillDisk malware. The serial-to-Ethernet converters were rendered non-functional through the use of a malicious firmware. As a result, SCADA communication failed, and it was no longer possible to control and communicate with the field units. Manual operation and recovery was the only option.

Inside the attack anatomy

In this section, let us analyze the sequence of events leading to the attack. The analysis can provide valuable insights into how the adversaries exploited the security loopholes of an energy infrastructure. *Figure 9.3* shows the broad steps of the attack:

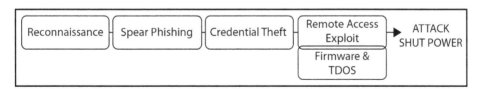

Figure 9.3: Attack anatomy—steps leading up to the attack

Reconnaissance

The orchestration of the attack suggests extensive reconnaissance, planning, and development. The three regional distribution companies had a high degree of SCADA automation, which allowed for remote operation of the breakers in the substations. The companies had certain security controls already in place, such as segmentation of corporate and OT networks using firewalls, robust system logging, and so on (ICS-WIR). The adversary exhibited sufficient insider knowledge to exploit the loopholes inherent in the system architecture.

Spear phishing

To gain access to the infrastructure, the adversary resorted to social engineering techniques. Spear phishing emails were sent to workers of the three companies with a malicious Microsoft Word document attached. Upon clicking the attachment, email recipients were prompted to enable macros for the document; compliance led to the installation of BlackEnergy 3 malware. This infected their machines and paved the way for the attackers to gain a foothold in the corporate network.

It is interesting to note that, instead of exploiting existing vulnerabilities, the attackers exploited a Microsoft Word feature to gain access to the systems.

Credential theft

Gaining access to the corporate network was not enough to control the grid. Since the SCADA network was segmented behind the firewall, the adversary resorted to harnessing credentials to exploit trusted connections. Extensive reconnaissance helped them to access the Windows Domain Controllers, which stored the user accounts, and to obtain worker credentials for VPN access into the SCADA networks. This was crucial for the attackers to remotely and reliably launch the attack on the power grid.

Data exfiltration

After securing their foothold in the grid communication infrastructure, the next step was to discover and exfiltrate information regarding the hosts and devices, to subsequently sabotage the SCADA DMS, open the breakers, and thus, shut off electricity. Workstations, servers, and embedded devices connected to the distribution substations were compromised.

Remote access exploit

Using the credentials of authorized users, the adversaries tunneled into the ICS/SCADA network using VPNs, bypassing the firewalls. The adversaries' next step was to take control of the operators' workstations and to lock the operators out of their systems. It was a crucial stage of the attack before the attackers could remotely operate the HMIs to trigger power outages in at least, 27 substations. While the attack was in progress, the attackers remotely injected KillDisk malware across the entire environment. KillDisk rendered the Windows systems inoperable by corrupting the master boot record, affecting the boot integrity. On other systems, it deleted log and system event files (this further emphasizes the rationale behind moving logs to a remote location, as discussed in `Chapter 7`, *Secure Processes and Governance*).

Impair recovery – Malicious firmware, TDOS, and UPS failure

The SCADA system used serial-to-Ethernet converters to remotely send control commands to operate the power circuit breakers. The adversaries remotely downloaded and installed malicious firmware updates to compromise these converters. Using operation-specific malicious firmware to render the converters inoperable and unrecoverable was an unprecedented step in ICS attacks. This prevented the operators from reclosing the breakers remotely after the blackout was triggered, which considerably increased the recovery time to restore power. The operators were left with the option to manually close the breakers. A malicious firmware update is irreversible. The compromised converters had to be replaced by new hardware to restore normal operation.

In the case of at least one company, the **uninterruptible power supply** (**UPS**) was reconfigured as an aggressive move to deny power to even the grid operators during the attack.

When the attack was in progress, the adversaries launched a remote **telephonic denial of service** (**TDOS**) by flooding the energy companies' call centers with fake calls. This prevented the impacted customers from reporting the outage. However, subsequent forensic evidence indicated that the motive behind the TDOS attack was probably more than just to block the power grid customers; there could have been socioeconomic reasons for it, as it frustrated the subscribers and their confidence in the energy service providers.

Cyber-physical defense – Lessons learned

This case study showcases the high degree of planning and orchestration that materializes a cyber-physical attack on critical infrastructure. The adversaries are usually well-versed and highly invested to successfully launch these attacks. Industrial IoT use cases and connected critical infrastructures must be well protected, to counter and minimize the fallout of similar sophisticated incidents. The three Ukrainian power companies had mostly perimeter protections in place, such as segmentation, firewalls, and so on. *Figure 9.4* shows a list of countermeasures that could have deterred the attack and its impact:

Reconnaissance	Limit public availability of architecture, sub-system versions, network diagrams etc. Detect anomalous behavior by passive monitoring of insider and third-party activities such as device access, browsing history, timestamps etc. Regularly leverage security intelligence and forensics.
Social Engineering	Personnel training to combat malicious social engineering. Segment functional network domains. Use proxy servers and gateways to monitor and control inbound and outbound communication paths. Deep packet inspection and malware detection tools to prevent malware proliferation across network segments.
Credential Theft	Directory segmentation ((e.g., Active Directory, Domain, eDirectory, and LDAP), ability to detect various forms of Trojans, user account activity monitoring.
Data Exfiltration	Maintain a vaulted copy of known good project files, control and safety logic, and firmware. Network Security Monitoring (NSM) can be used to detect exfiltration of ICS and IT data
Remote Access Exploit	Allow a bare minimum number of trusted remote connections. Use SoC to monitor VPN connections and activities. Two-factor authentication for remote users. Disable split tunneling. Application level logic that requires operator confirmation to trigger any high-risk actuation command (e.g. UPS, Circuit breaker operations).
Firmware Updates	Secure firmware updates of endpoints using digital signatures and hardware-based root of trust.
Response and Recovery	A solid incident response plan enables remediation well before the adversaries have performed the intended attack to impact. Active and passive monitoring, alarms and response from the IR team together detects malicious activity, minimizes impact of the final attack and expedites recovery.

Figure 9.4 Ukrainian power grid attack—Defense lessons learned

Case study 2 – Building a successful IIoT security program

This section has been adapted from `https://www.sans.org/webcasts/case-study-developing-innovative-ics-security-program-real-time-ot-monitoring-capability-oil-gas-infrastructures-103562`.

In `Chapter 7`, *Secure Processes and Governance,* we discussed the various components of an IIoT security program. This case study presents how an offshore drilling company implemented a security program from the ground up, for their connected offshore platforms. The security program for their automated fleet and **industrial automation control system** (**IACS**) was operationalized to protect valuable assets and ensure the safety of rig personnel.

Background

The drilling company had an automated fleet, spread at offshore locations around the globe, with 700 million USD worth of connected assets. The senior business leadership recognized the safety and reliability risks associated with a fleet IACS, as well as the business imperative to protect customer assets and data. As new automated rigs were being added, the need to communicate field data with other rigs and with onshore control centers kept adding to the system complexity. The company was also under pressure from its customers, who demanded stringent security measures, such as 24/7 event and activity monitoring, in their RFPs and contracts.

Defining the security program

For many industrial enterprises, having an OT security program is a new concept. This offshore drilling company had no precedence of coherent policies to secure their IACS. The company created a team accountable for defining and enforcing a security program from scratch. The team collaborated with an external security consulting firm to develop the industrial security program document. The document had 13 modules, covering the following:

- Risk management, architecture, local and remote access processes, subcontractor processes

- Processes for portable devices, wireless devices, and physical security related to the automation system
- Security awareness for crew and personnel aboard the vessels

The document defined the audit process and procedures for ongoing policy updates.

The team used risk management practices to identify and prioritize the major security capabilities. This is always a recommended step to right-size security controls and investments. The company focused its resources on the following areas:

- **Asset inventory and discovery**: This was important, as the company lacked the capabilities to determine which assets to monitor or protect.
- **Secure remote access**: To perform maintenance, troubleshooting, configuration, and so on, vendors were allowed to connect remotely to their systems housed in the vessel offshore. There were no systems in place to control or monitor activities during third-party remote access.
- **Configuration and patch management**: In offshore drilling environments, where the vessels operate 24/7/365, upgrades or patches can be performed only when the vessels are brought back to the shipyard, usually every five years. To schedule and have servers available to perform the upgrades during this *window of opportunity* was a major deal. The new security program defined a process to track PLC firmware versions, the availability of newer versions, and a process to plan vessel downtime for the updates. Processes were also defined to maintain a central repository in the vessel. This central repository kept track of the various patches and Microsoft Windows updates for machines operating in the control network.
- **Asset visibility, anomaly detection, and security intelligence**: Policies for continuous security monitoring were defined to discover and alert any new device connecting to the network, along with its MAC and IP address. The program also documented a list of activities, such as configuration downloads from laptops to PLCs, and PLC state changes from stop-to-run, run-to-stop, and so on, to be monitored, in order to detect anomalies.

Implementation

The components of the IACS, such as VF drive controls, dynamic positions, power management, drilling control systems, BOP controls, and so on, came from various vendors. The multi-vendor environment posed a major challenge to enforcing policies and verifying the enforcement. The security team had no visibility into the multi-vendor IACS assets and networks, except for some outdated network diagrams. So, they decided to go for a managed security solution vendor that could deliver integrated security services appropriate for the multi-vendor environment.

To implement 24/7 security monitoring technology appropriate for the OT networks was also a challenge. Control networks are deterministic, where IP-based network monitoring solutions may disrupt or interfere with the systems critical to the operation and safety of the vessel, personnel, and environment. A passive monitoring solution was selected, to minimize the risk of compromising system reliability. A single monitoring technology was used for the entire IACS network, from layer 0 to 3. A global **security operations center (SOC)** was built onshore, for real-time monitoring of multi-functional security data from management systems, live video feeds, and so on. Remote access for vendors was routed through the SOC.

Cybersecurity training videos for the crew and other third-party or customer personnel on the vessel were released to onboard them into the program, making them aware of the security policies regarding both corporate and industrial systems.

The managed IACS security program was subsequently enforced across the globe, in multiple connected vessels.

Concluding remarks

The definition and deployment of a security program involves several use-case-specific variables and challenges; hence, the security program needs to be custom-built, to optimize investment and to get the most value out of it. Risk management and risk-based prioritization are key to right-sizing resources and security expenditures, and also to prioritize the most critical vulnerabilities. This case study demonstrates how these important facets were dealt with in a real-world industrial use case.

Case study 3 – ISA/IEC 62443 based industrial endpoint protection

Multiple security breach reports have highlighted the inadequacy of perimeter-based protection in connected industries and critical infrastructures. Security defenses need to extend beyond the perimeter, all the way to the field devices, and the endpoints should be protected, as well.

In March 2016, in a recorded cyber incident, a water utility's control system was infiltrated, and the levels of chemicals used to treat tap water were altered to unsafe levels (WAT-CAS). The water utility's operational control system was connected to the internet. The control system managed the **programmable logic controllers** (**PLCs**) to regulate the valves and ducts controlling the flow of water and chemicals to treat the water. Using SQL injection and phishing, the attackers could obtain the login credentials of the control system, gain access to the PLCs, and alter the level of chemicals. Fortunately, the system was equipped with an alert functionality that enabled early detection and prevented further damage.

In the backdrop of this incident, let's consider the next case study, where a city's water and waste management facility recognized similar threats and improved their security posture. The city protected its control system/PLCs by implementing an ISA/IEC 62443 based security architecture (BEL-CAS).

Adapted from source: `https://www.belden.com/hubfs/resources/knowledge/case-studies/plc-security-for-water-wastewater-systems.pdf`.

Background

The waste management facility operated 24 hours a day, treating 13 million gallons of wastewater on each day, and was spread across 24 buildings, housing 500 pieces of equipment to run the various processes. This mission-critical plant's SCADA network was part of the city's IT infrastructure, and, as such, it was highly vulnerable to traffic storms, human errors, and attacks. The operations team wanted to secure the wastewater operations without losing the ability to easily share data among the various departments, maintain remote support capabilities, and so on.

Solution

The waste management company collaborated with a cyber security services group and a product vendor to embed security not just in the network perimeter, but throughout the system. The team followed the ISA/IEC 62443 standard to partition the critical plant infrastructure into zones, secured through conduits (these concepts were discussed in `Chapter 3`, *IIoT Identity and Access Management*). Each zone was protected by a specialized industry security appliance (a field-level firewall). This firewall was transparent to the network (no IP address), and was capable of deep packet inspection for industrial protocol communications, to protect against all malformed packet attacks. Each PLC and microprocessor unit was protected by the firewall.

Concluding remarks

Many industrial plants have connected control systems and assets without robust defenses to protect them. Considering the increasing sophistication of cyberattacks, air gaps or perimeter-based defenses are inadequate. It is important for organizations to protect connected end devices, such as PLCs and microcontrollers, against threats, coupled with 24/7 monitoring and alerting mechanisms.

Summary

In this chapter, three case studies were presented to highlight a few foundational IIoT security concepts in a real-world context. The first case study described (based on publicly available forensic reports) the anatomy of a successful cyberattack on a nation's critical infrastructure. It analyzed the trail of activities that led to the attack of impact, and it discussed countermeasures that could have averted the attack.

The second case study presented the business drivers and technical solutions used by an industrial enterprise to develop a security program to protect its connected OT environment. The security program was grounded on several practical considerations, discussed in earlier chapters of this book.

The third case study highlighted an industrial security standard-based approach to extend robust security defenses up to the endpoints.

In `Chapter 10`, *The Road Ahead*, we will sum up our discussions by focusing on the road ahead, to build a secure and connected brave new world.

10
The Road Ahead

"The Industrial IoT is more of an evolution than a revolution."
– Paul Didier, IoT Architect, Cisco

The industrial revolution of the 1800s unveiled the tremendous power of machines. Subsequent developments in industrial automation and ICS/SCADA systems steered industrial operations to new heights of efficiency and optimization. Presently, the transformative power of the industrial IoT is shaping a new era of industrial connectivity and autonomy.

In this chapter, we will highlight the tasks ahead of us in the IIoT security journey. This chapter will cover the following topics:

- An era of decentralized autonomy
- Endpoint security
- Standards and reference architecture
- Industry collaboration
- Interoperability
- Green patches in brownfield
- Technology trends

An era of decentralized autonomy

Industrial automation was founded on centralized supervision and management of industrial processes, field devices, and networks. Software-defined technologies and ubiquitous connectivity are quickly transforming that centralized model. Consider the case of time-sensitive network (or TSN, discussed in `Chapter 7`, *Secure Processes and Governance*), where endpoints **collaboratively** determine their necessary configurations, to synchronize in time. This autonomy addresses the complexity and inefficiencies associated with manual setup, teardown, and so on. An autonomous vehicle is essentially a robot (an AI specimen) on-the-wheels that dynamically learns, decides, and maneuvers without any central supervision.

The industrial internet is ushering in a new era of autonomous operations and decentralized control.

Meaningful evolution and the sustenance of an autonomous world depends on many foundational principles. Security is a prime one among them. As already elaborated in this book, security in the context of industrial IoT covers much more ground than cybersecurity. IIoT security ensures the trustworthiness of an autonomous ecosystem. The expansive scope of trustworthiness was discussed in `Chapter 2`, *Industrial IoT Dataflow and Security Architecture*. Secured endpoints, protocols, and connectivity are critical in ensuring human and environmental safety and reliability in autonomous industries.

As the majority of decision making (computing) and control is performed by edge devices, the principles of trustworthiness need to encompass the endpoints. Today, most industrial deployments that use the Purdue reference model-based architectures (PRA) primarily rely on perimeter defenses, such as segmentation and firewalls. Concepts of continuous security monitoring, and anomaly detection are gradually gaining momentum. However, these are only peripheral defenses added on top of the infrastructure and endpoints.

Endpoint security

To ensure the reliability of a hyperconnected and decentralized autonomous ecosystem, adequate security controls must be ingrained in every endpoint. Security must extend across the architecture, from the edge to the cloud. This requires arduous orchestration across various industry stakeholders. Certain industrial protocols have been updated to secure identities using digital certificates or crypto keys. Security vendors are working on tamper-proofing, hardware RoT, digital identity, key management, and so on. However, we may have to tread a long path before these proliferate across industrial deployments to a reasonable degree.

In `Chapter 7`, *Secure Processes and Governance*, we discussed how each phase of the product development life cycle needs to adhere to security and safety controls. The responsibility involves multifunctional stakeholders. System developers, integrators, OEMs, and architects all have a role in creating security built into device and network endpoints.

Standards and reference architecture

A practical scheme to standardize and regulate IIoT security practices is in need of much attention. Today, there exists an enormous body of safety and security standards for industrial systems. Many of these standards are vertical-specific, and, even within one industry, there are multiple overlapping standards. Secure coding, for example, has standards from MISRA to DISA, CWE, CERT, and more. Efforts to comply with an overlapping set of standards can be suboptimal. Besides, security standards and regulations often emerge with new technologies, such as machine learning, cloud security, and so on.

As the horizon of our autonomous future gets demystified, standard bodies must leverage the increasing visibility to define comprehensive, overarching security governance standards for the industrial internet. While defining such standards, sufficient care should be exercised to optimize them. Industrial IoT innovations are happening at a rapid pace.

Security standards should not be shunned as deterrents in terms of time to market, cost, and so on. New industry standards often take several years before they can be enforced. So, efforts to develop consolidated standards need to be made now.

As interconnected industries foster subscription-based business models, the data now traverses across multiple organizations and regional boundaries. This inherently involves many security implications that we alluded to in earlier chapters of the book. Industrie 4.0 has devoted its efforts to this cross-organizational aspect. But this new dynamic calls for greater focus in IIoT standard-based initiatives. Data ownership, data governance, and data management have assumed a heightened significance in the context of IIoT-enabled economies, where efforts need to be directed to adequately define and streamline their secured operation.

Safety and security must reside in architectural designs for software, systems, and edge-cloud deployments. To ensure security by design, reference architectures are a great place to start building usecase specific architectures. In `Chapter 2`, *Industrial IoT Dataflow and Security Architecture*, we discussed the IIC reference architectures for IIoT deployments. Reference architectures are also being developed by other technology-centric consortia, such as openFog and OpenFMB, which need to be leveraged whenever applicable:

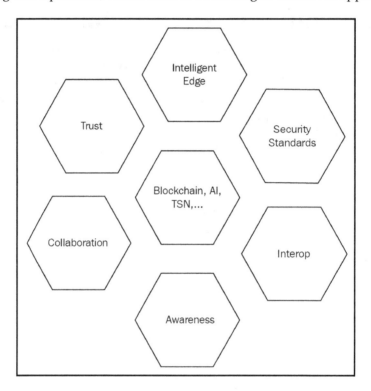

Figure 10.1: Industrial IoT security—the road ahead

Industrial collaboration

Industrial IoT deployments typically involve several vendors. In `Chapter` `9`, *Real-World Case Studies in IIoT Security*, the challenges associated with vendor complexity in the case of an automated offshore drilling IACS were discussed. For an industrial user of IIoT, it is a daunting task to coordinate the security postures of the solutions. In addition, there are complexities related to installation, confirmation, and device management that further increase the chances of human errors and insider threats. An overarching collaborative model for pre-deployment security testing of multi-vendor solutions, to coherently define, enforce, and monitor security policies, can minimize risks.

The IIC has an interesting platform for collaboration among IoT vendors, through their testbed program. At the time of this writing, there are nearly thirty testbeds, where any new IIoT technology, service, or product is incubated and rigorously tested to verify its utility before being released to the market. Each testbed is owned by a specific member company, where other vendors can collaborate to jointly test various proof of concepts. IIC's security evaluation testbed is part of this initiative, and is described as, *"An open and easily configurable cybersecurity platform for evaluation of endpoint, gateway, and other networked components' security capabilities"* (IIC-TEST).

It is important to note that, even within an organization, we expect to greater collaboration between the IT and OT stockholders to realize a practical IIoT security strategy.

Interoperability

Industrial technologies have evolved along each industry vertical over the years. For example, the energy sector is guided by a specific set of standards and regulations, which may be divergent from manufacturing. These verticals were never designed to interoperate. The industrial internet is driving a massive convergence of these industry verticals, to materialize new IIoT use cases, such as the smart city. IIoT interoperability anchors on security and scalability. We are still at too early a stage to define the necessary mechanics of interoperability, such as protocol gateways and reference architectures.

In `Chapter` `5`, *Securing Connectivity and Communications*, we discussed the **IIC Industrial Internet Connectivity Framework (IIC-IICF)**, published by the IIC. This framework document provides an important foundation and guidance for building interoperable systems and architectures.

In the power industry, the OpenFMB project is making significant progress in defining nonproprietary and standards-based reference architecture for intelligent power system field devices. The openFMB interoperability framework involves IP networking, IoT messaging protocols, and standardized semantic models, to enable communications and peer-to-peer information exchange (openFMB).

Green patches in brownfield

The lifespan of high-value industrial systems is measured in decades. As the industrial internet penetrates into OT environments, the legacy systems may continue to coexist for the foreseeable future. These legacy systems, though connected using gateways, were never built for ubiquitous connectivity, and are thus weak links in the security chain. Any IIoT use case involving brownfield deployments should take special considerations with respect to these legacy systems, and plan for event and activity monitoring, secure updates, and so on, at a minimum.

Greenfields with state of the art IIoT devices and equipment are evolving from being simple patches, becoming more pervasive. As the number of new, modern devices increases, industrial deployments may hit an inflection point in this migration path. Since these new industrial OT systems are also high-value and are meant to last for many years, new device manufacturers should cautiously build these with hardware-based trust, secured identity controls, and secure updates.

IIoT security certification for both products and personnel is also an area that needs to further develop and systemize.

Technology trends

In `Chapter 8`, *IIoT Security Using Emerging Technologies*, we discussed a few trending technologies, such as blockchain and machine learning, and their promises to secure the industrial internet.

Currently, we are at an early adoption phase of blockchain for IIoT security applications. The decentralized decision-making model of blockchain is relevant to an autonomous ecosystem. Blockchain also provides an immutable ledger, which can enable tamper-proofing. As a maturing technology, blockchain is yet to address IIoT specific concerns related to computing resources, scalability, data privacy etc. Lot of research and industry consortia efforts, such as the Hyperledger project, may make blockchain a viable IIoT security enabler.

Machine learning based security monitoring and anomaly detection applications are already in the marketplace. ML and robotics are evolving areas, where a lot of research is being directed to develop automated and adaptive security solutions. **Cognitive IoT (cIoT)** applications (such as drones) are trending upwards. These cIoT applications are introducing new safety and security paradigms that we must adequately understand, evaluate, and prioritize.

In many IIoT use cases, homomorphic encryption can help improve data privacy. Homomorphic encryption allows cloud computing platforms to perform difficult computations on ciphertext without accessing the unencrypted data, or to securely chain together different services without exposing sensitive data.

Quantum computing platforms, though still in incubation labs, are making steady progress as a cloud-based offering. The adoption of quantum computing could potentially render the current cryptography framework brittle. It may still take a while for quantum computing to evolve beyond the incubation phase, but the way it impacts the classical computing platforms and algorithms must be carefully monitored.

Time-sensitive networking (TSN) is in its early adoption phase. TSN is a promising IEEE connectivity standard. Although it is not a security standard, TSN can benefit the IIoT security framework in multiple ways, as already discussed in `Chapter 8`, *IIoT Security Using Emerging Technologies*. We can expect TSN to overlap with the migration roadmaps of many industrial networks, as they adopt IIoT.

The rise of edge intelligence and edge technologies to support edge computing is also a notable trend. Security investments should focus on the edge more. Edge intelligence, being close to the field devices, significantly reduces latency, as compared to centralized core or cloud intelligence. Edge intelligence does not rely on WAN (internet) connectivity, and, as such, it can provide uninterrupted service in low-power industrial networks. Most market-leading cloud providers realize the value of edge computing and have rolled out edge-cloud security solutions. Fog computing is a similar concept, and its reference architecture was recently published by the OpenFog consortium (Fog-ORA).

The significant impact of 5G on IIoT connectivity and in securing cellular communications was discussed in `Chapter 5`, *Securing Connectivity and Communications*.

Summary

Based on my (the author's) discussions with various industrial practitioners, it is evident that industrial business leaders now recognize the vital role of IIoT in defining their organizations' futures. However, the investment risks and complexities associated with IIoT have made them cautious in the adoption journey. Several organizations are performing POCs while actual adoption ramps up.

Top analyst firms expect significant investments in IIoT security in the near future. However, in many industrial sectors, there are still some challenges in sizing up the role of security as an IIoT success factor.

Cybersecurity, managed by enterprise IT teams, is often considered an impediment in the OT environments, especially when there is a service outage due to an IT system crash. An organization's IIoT security strategy needs to drive alignment and integration between the enterprise IT and OT teams. Many traditional enterprises still believe IIoT security myths, such as security by obscurity, security by using non-IP fieldbus protocols, and so on. These myths must be debunked through proper dialogue.

In this book, various concepts, standards, best practices, and practical tools were laced together to present the reader with a comprehensive treatment of IIoT security. We hope that this book will take the reader many steps ahead in building resilient industrial solutions, as we move towards our digital destiny.

- **ATT-NB**: AT&T NetBond® User Guide, `https://www.synaptic.att.com/assets/us/en/home/NB_User_Guide_AWS_Priv_Pub.pdf`
- **AMQP-SPEC**: `http://docs.oasis-open.org/amqp/core/v1.0/os/amqp-core-overview-v1.0-os.html`
- **AMQP**: `https://en.wikipedia.org/wiki/Advanced_Message_Queuing_Protocol`
- **AI-FOR**: Artificial Intelligence Will Revolutionize Cybersecurity, a whitepaper from Forrester
- **AWS-IOT**: `https://aws.amazon.com/iot-core/`
- **AWS-IAM**: `https://www.slideshare.net/AmazonWebServices/best-practices-with-iot-security-februart-online-tech-talks/4`
- **BAYNET**: Bayshore Networks® Defends against ICS/SCADA Malware, `https://www.bayshorenetworks.com/news/2016/08/bayshore-networks-defends-against-icsscada-malware`
- **BEL-CAS**: `https://www.belden.com/hubfs/resources/knowledge/case-studies/plc-security-for-water-wastewater-systems.pdf`
- **BLO-INF**: `https://blockchain.info`
- **CYDATA**: Not All Machine Learning Is Created Equal: Why Cylance Beats the Competition When It Comes to Endpoint Protection
- **CSC-FAC**: Advancing automation – Cybersecurity in Industrial Environments Volume VII, `http://www.automation.com/`
- **COI-JOU**: `https://coinjournal.net/chronicled-completes-pilot-blockchain-enabled-supply-chain-system/`
- **CSC-FOG**: `https://www.cisco.com/c/dam/en_us/solutions/trends/iot/docs/computing-overview.pdf`
- **CSCC**: Cloud Customer Architecture for Securing Workloads on Cloud Services, `http://www.cloud-council.org/deliverables/CSCC-Cloud-Customer-Architecture-for-Securing-Workloads-on-Cloud-Services.pdf`
- **CSA-API**: Cloud Standards Customer Council 2017, Cloud Customer Architecture for API Management, `http://www.cloud-council.org/deliverables/cloud-customer-architecture-for-api-management.htm`
- **DHS-NCCIC**: ICS CYBERSECURITY FOR THE C-LEVEL, `https://ics-cert.us-cert.gov/sites/default/files/FactSheets/NCCIC%20ICS_FactSheet_ICS_Cybersecurity_C-Level_S508C.pdf`

- **DOT-VHC**: `https://www.transportation.gov/briefing-room/us-dot-issues-federal-guidance-automotive-industry-improving-motor-vehicle`
- **DIG-HLT**: WannaCry impact on NHS considerably larger than previously suggested, `https://www.digitalhealth.net/2017/10/wannacry-impact-on-nhs-considerably-larger-than-previously-suggested`
- **DARKT-THREAT**: DARKTRACE Global Threat Report 2017, `https://www.darktrace.com/resources/wp-global-threat-report-2017.pdf`
- **DEF-IPSEC**: Introduction to Cisco IPSec Technology, `https://www.cisco.com/c/en/us/td/docs/net_mgmt/vpn_solutions_center/2-0/ip_security/provisioning/guide/IPsecPG1.html#wp1030249`
- **DDS-DEF**: `https://www.rti.com/products/what-is-a-databus`
- **DDS SECURE**: DDS Security Specification Version 1.1. BETA, `https://www.omg.org/spec/DDS-SECURITY/About-DDS-SECURITY/`
- **draft-KTM**: `https://tools.ietf.org/html/draft-keoh-tls-multicast-security-00`
- **ENER-SYMT**: `http://www.symantec.com/content/en/us/enterprise/media/security_response/whitepapers/targeted_attacks_against_the_energy_sector.pdf`
- **ETN-WRD**: `http://www.wired.co.uk/article/what-is-eternal-blue-exploit-vulnerability-patch`
- **ESec-BP**: IIC Endpoint Security Best Practices, IIC:WHT:IN17:V1.6.3:ID:20180129 Steve Hanna, Srinivas Kumar, Dean Weber
- **EST-CERT**: PKI—Simplify Certificate Provisioning with EST, Whitepaper Cisco, `https://www.cisco.com/c/dam/en_us/about/doing_business/trust-center/docs/public-key-infrastructure-provisioning-with-est.pdf`
- **ETH-BLK**: `https://www.ethereum.org/`
- **FSV-IoT**: CYBER SECURITY IN THE ERA OF INDUSTRIAL IOT, A Frost & Sullivan White Paper, `https://ww2.frost.com/frost-perspectives/cyber-security-era-industrial-iot/`
- **FDA-MED**: FDA approves pill with sensor that digitally tracks if patients have ingested their medication, `https://www.fda.gov/NewsEvents/Newsroom/PressAnnouncements/ucm584933.htm`
- **Fog-ORA**: `https://www.openfogconsortium.org/wp-content/uploads/OpenFog_Reference_Architecture_2_09_17-FINAL.pdf`
- **FIPS-180**: FIPS PUB 180-4, `https://ws680.nist.gov/publication/get_pdf.cfm?pub_id=910977`
- **GE-IIoT**: `http://www.geautomation.com/industrial-internet`
- **GART-IOT**: Gartner IoT Glossary, `https://www.gartner.com/it-glossary/`

- **GART-IIoT**: Cybersecurity Myths of the Industrial IoT, `https://www.gartner.com/smarterwithgartner/cybersecurity-myths-of-the-industrial-iot/`
- **GART-CL**: `https://www.gartner.com/newsroom/id/3616417`
- **HOM-WIK**: `https://en.wikipedia.org/wiki/Homomorphic_encryption`
- **IEEE-IOT**: `https://iot.ieee.org/images/files/pdf/IEEE_IoT_Towards_Definition_Internet_of_Things_Revision1_27MAY15.pdf`
- **ISP-4IR**: `https://www.i-scoop.eu/industry-4-0/`
- **ISP-IIoT**: `https://www.i-scoop.eu/internet-of-things-guide/industrial-internet-things-iiot-saving-costs-innovation/industrial-internet/`
- **IOT-WLD**: Industry of Things World Survey Report 2017, `https://industryofthingsworld.com/`
- **ICS-WIKI**: `https://en.wikipedia.org/wiki/Industrial_control_system`
- **IOT-SEC**: *Practical Internet of Things Security* by Brian Russell, Drew Van Duren, Packt Publishing.
- **ITU-IOT**: `ITU-T Rec. Y.2060 (06/2012) Overview of the Internet of things;` `https://www.itu.int`
- **IIC-IISF**: INDUSTRIAL INTERNET SECURITY FRAMEWORK TECHNICAL REPORT, `https://www.iiconsortium.org/IISF.htm`
- **IIC-IIRA**: INDUSTRIAL INTERNET REFERENCE ARCHITECTURE v 1.8, `https://www.iiconsortium.org/IIC_PUB_G1_V1.80_2017-01-31.pdf`
- **ISA-SECURE**: `www.isasecure.org`
- **IBM-MSS**: Attacks Targeting Industrial Control Systems (ICS) Up 110 Percent, `https://securityintelligence.com/attacks-targeting-industrial-control-systems-ics-up-110-percent/`
- **IIC-IICF**: Industrial Internet of Things Connectivity Framework, `www.iiconsortium.org/IICF-faq.htm`
- **IISF**: Industrial Internet Security Framework
- **INS**: Industrial Network Security Authors: Eric D. Knapp and Joel Langill(`https://www.elsevier.com/books-and-journals`). Learn more about Industrial Network Security from Syngress (`https://www.elsevier.com/books/industrial-network-security/knapp/978-0-12-420114-9`).
- **INCIBE**: Protocol and Network Security in ICS Infrastructures, INCIBE, `https://www.incibe.es/extfrontinteco/img/File/intecocert/ManualesGuias/incibe_protocol_net_security_ics.pdf`
- **IIoT-DATA**: `http://industrial.embedded-computing.com/articles/five-keys-to-securing-the-iiot-data-pipe/`

- **ICO-DEF**: Embedded Firewall, `https://www.automationworld.com/article/technologies/security/embedded-firewall`

- **IoT Security Maturity Model (IIC-SMM)**: Description and Intended Use, IIC:PUB:IN15:V1.0:PB:20180409, `https://www.iiconsortium.org/pdf/SMM_Description_and_Intended_Use_2018-04-09.pdf`

- **ISA-95**: Enterprise-Control System Integration, `https://www.isa.org/isa95/`

- **IBM-CIOT**: `http://www.ibmbigdatahub.com/blog/what-cognitive-iot`

- **IIC-TSN**: IIC Webinar—Modernizing your Industrial Networks, Time Sensitive Networks Readiness, `http://www.iiconsortium.org/webinars/index.htm`

- **IE3-TSN**: Time-Sensitive Networking Task Group, `http://www.ieee802.org/1/pages/tsn.html`

- **ISAC-SANS**: `https://ics.sans.org/media/E-ISAC_SANS_Ukraine_DUC_5.pdf`

- **ICS-WIR**: `https://www.wired.com/2016/03/inside-cunning-unprecedented-hack-ukraines-power-grid/`

- **IoT Security Maturity Model (IIC-SMM)**: Description and Intended Use, IIC:PUB:IN15:V1.0:PB:20180409, `https://www.iiconsortium.org/pdf/SMM_Description_and_Intended_Use_2018-04-09.pdf`

- **INETNW**: `http://www.internetnews.com/xSP/article.php/3603256/Chambers+The+Network+Is+The+Platform.htm`

- **JSRS**: Identity Fraud Hits Record High with 15.4 Million U.S. Victims in 2016, `https://www.javelinstrategy.com/press-release/identity-fraud-hits-record-high-154-million-us-victims-2016-16-percent-according-new`

- **LoRA-DEF**: `https://lora-alliance.org/about-lorawan`

- **MST-TRM**: `https://msdn.microsoft.com/en-us/library/ff648644.aspx`

- **MST-STR**: Internet of Things Security Architecture—Security in IoT, 2016-June-3, `https://azure.microsoft.com/en-us/documentation/articles/iot-hub-securityarchitecture/`

- **MS-DREAD**: `https://docs.microsoft.com/en-us/windows-hardware/drivers/driversecurity/threat-modeling-for-drivers`

- **MS-DXL**: `https://www.slideshare.net/McAfee/tech-talk-the-data-exchange-layer-dxl`

- **Massachusetts Institute of Technology-Kerberos (MIT-Kerb)**: The Network Authentication Protocol. MIT, 2016-Apr-20, retrieved 2016-09-26, `http://web.mit.edu/kerberos/`

- **MOC-TRUST**: WHITE PAPER Hardening the IoT Stack, `www.mocana.com`

- **MRA-DOC**: Bayshore Whitepaper SECURING OPERATIONAL TECHNOLOGY IN THE PHARMACEUTICAL AND CHEMICAL MANUFACTURING INDUSTRIES.
- **MQTTv3.1.1-OASIS**: `http://docs.oasis-open.org/mqtt/mqtt/v3.1.1/mqtt-v3.1.1.pdf`
- **MQTT-SN**: `http://mqtt.org/new/wp-content/uploads/2009/06/MQTT-SN_spec_v1.2.pdf`
- **MATH-ML**: `https://www.mathworks.com/discovery/machine-learning.html`
- **ML-CHA**: `https://towardsdatascience.com/ai-and-machine-learning-in-cyber-security-d6fbee480af0`
- **MIT-PUF**: `https://people.csail.mit.edu/devadas/pubs/rfid_puf_08.pdf`
- **MIT-PUF**: `https://people.csail.mit.edu/devadas/pubs/rfid_puf_08.pdf`
- **MS-DEF**: `https://smartbear.com/learn/api-design/what-are-microservices/`
- **NIST-800-82r2**: Guide to Industrial Control Systems (ICS) Security, `https://nvlpubs.nist.gov/nistpubs/specialpublications/nist.sp.800-82r2.pdf`
- **NIST-SMG**: Technologies to Enable a Smart Grid, NIST, `https://www.nist.gov/sites/default/files/documents/2017/05/09/energy_wp_10_28_10.pdf`
- **NIST-CPS**: Framework for Cyber-Physical Systems , Release 1.0, `https://s3.amazonaws.com/nist-sgcps/cpspwg/files/pwgglobal/CPS_PWG_Framework_for_Cyber_Physical_Systems_Release_1_0Final.pdf`
- **NIST-PE**: NIST Special Publication, 800-53, Revision 4, Security and Privacy Controls for Federal Information Systems and Organizations
- **NIST-800-53**: Security and Privacy Controls for Federal Information Systems and Organizations, `https://nvlpubs.nist.gov/nistpubs/SpecialPublications/NIST.SP.800-53r4.pdf`
- **NULL-CON**:NullCon `https://nullcon.net/website/`
- **OWA-IoT**: `https://www.owasp.org/index.php/OWASP_Internet_of_Things_Project#tab=IoT_Attack_Surface_Areas`
- **OWA-TRM**: `https://www.owasp.org/index.php/Threat_Risk_Modeling`
- **OWA-IOTP**: `https://www.owasp.org/index.php/OWASP_Internet_of_Things_Project#tab=Main`
- **OASIS-OPEN**: `http://docs.oasis-open.org/mqtt/mqtt/v3.1.1/os/mqtt-v3.1.1-os.html`
- **OAUTH-SEC**: `http://www.oauthsecurity.com`
- **OAUTH-SANS**: `https://www.sans.org/reading-room/whitepapers/application/%20attacks-oauth-secure-oauth-implementation-33644`

- **OMG-DDS**: http://portals.omg.org/dds/
- **ONE-M2M**: http://www.onem2m.org/
- **OPC-WP**: https://opcfoundation.org/wp-content/uploads/2016/04/OPC-UA-Security-Advise-EN.png
- **OPCF**: OPC Foundation, https://opcfoundation.org/
- **openFMB**: http://www.greenenergycorp.com/2016/03/17/naesb-ratifies-openfmb/
- **OWASP-SEC**: The Open Web Application Security Project ("OWASP"). OWASP Secure Coding Practices, https://www.owasp.org/images/0/08/OWASP_SCP_Quick_Reference_Guide_v2.pdf
- **PRA**: Purdue Enterprise Reference Architecture, https://en.wikipedia.org/wiki/Purdue_Enterprise_Reference_Architecture
- **PDX-BRF**: https://www.predix.com/sites/default/files/predix-the-industrial-internet-platform-from-ge-digital-brief.pdf
- **PDX-IO**: https://docs.predix.io/en-US/content/platform/get_started/predix_overview/
- **PDX-ARC**: Predix Architecture and Services, Technical Whitepaper, https://www.predix.com/sites/default/files/ge-predix-architecture-r092615.pdf
- **RIE-GERT**: Rieger, C.G.; Gertman, D.I.; McQueen, M.A. (May 2009), Resilient Control Systems: Next Generation Design Research, Catania, Italy: 2nd IEEE Conference on Human System Interaction.
- **RFC-6749**: The OAuth 2.0 Authorization Framework, https://tools.ietf.org/html/rfc6749
- **RFC-7252**: The Constrained Application Protocol (CoAP), https://tools.ietf.org/html/rfc7252
- **RFC-6347**: Datagram Transport Layer Security Version 1.2, https://tools.ietf.org/html/rfc6347
- **RFC-6819**: OAuth 2.0 Threat Model and Security Considerations, https://tools.ietf.org/html/rfc6819
- **RFC 4122**: A Universally Unique Identifier (UUID) URN Namespace, https://tools.ietf.org/html/rfc4122
- **RFC2**: RFC 5280, https://tools.ietf.org/html/rfc5280
- **RFC 7030**: https://tools.ietf.org/html/rfc7030
- **RFC-6090**: https://tools.ietf.org/html/rfc6090

- **RFC-TLS**: RFC 4346, `https://www.ietf.org/rfc/rfc4346.txt`
- **RFC-UDP**: `https://tools.ietf.org/html/rfc768`
- **RFC 6347**: `https://tools.ietf.org/html/rfc6347`
- **RFC 7252**: `https://www.rfc-editor.org/rfc/rfc7252.txt`
- RFC 4301: `https://tools.ietf.org/html/rfc4301`
- **STN-REP**: Stuxnet Worm Attack on Iranian Nuclear Facilities, Michael Holloway, July 16, 2015, `http://large.stanford.edu/courses/2015/ph241/holloway1/`
- **SANS-1**: Identification with Zero Knowledge Protocols, Annarita Giani, `https://www.sans.org/reading-room/whitepapers/vpns/identification-zero-knowledge-protocols-719`
- **SASL-OATH**: The OAuth 2.0 Internet of Things (IoT) Client Credentials Grant, `https://tools.ietf.org/id/draft-tschofenig-ace-oauth-iot-01.html#I-D.ietf-kitten-sasl-oauth`
- **SEC-IIoT**: Jacob Wurm, Khoa Hoang, Orlando Arias, Ahmad-Reza Sadeghi and Yier Jin. Department of Electrical and Computer Engineering, University of Central Florida and Technische Universität Darmstadt, Germany
- **SYM-ECC**: Symantec Corporation—Elliptic Curve Cryptography (ECC), Certificates Performance Analysis, whitepaper, `https://www.websecurity.symantec.com/content/dam/websitesecurity/digitalassets/desktop/pdfs/whitepaper/Elliptic_Curve_Cryptography_ECC_WP_en_us.pdf`
- **SIF-ODF**: Firewall: On-demand Virtual Firewall and IPS Services, `http://www.cloudinfinit.com/products/IaaS/cloud/security/firwl`
- **SOV-IDN**: `https://sovrin.org/wp-content/uploads/Sovrin-Protocol-and-Token-White-Paper.pdf`
- **SEI-SEC**: Software Engineering Institute, Carnegie Mellon University. SEI CERT Top 10 Secure Coding Practices, `https://www.securecoding.cert.org/confluence/display/seccode/Top+10+Secure+Coding+Practices`
- **Tschofenig-ace**: Authentication and Authorization for Constrained Environments (ACE), `https://tools.ietf.org/html/draft-ietf-ace-oauth-authz-09`
- **TCGG-29**: *TCG Guidance for Securing Network Equipment Using TCG Technology*, Version 1.0 Revision 29 Jan 17, 2018 Published
- **TIA**: ANSI TIA-942-A, `http://www.tia-942.org/`
- **TSN-CS**: **Time-Sensitive Networking** (TSN) in the Electric Sector—Security, a paper by Dr. Armando Astarloa and Mikel Rodriguez, `https://soc-e.com`
- **TSN-BEL**: `https://www.belden.com/blog/industrial-ethernet/what-is-tsn-a-look-at-its-role-in-future-ethernet-networks`

- **TSN-AUT1**: https://www.automationworld.com/article/industry-type/all/4-reasons-why-time-sensitive-networking-matters
- **TSN-CSC**: https://www.cisco.com/c/dam/en/us/solutions/collateral/industry-solutions/white-paper-c11-738950.pdf
- **TSN-AUT2**: https://www.automationworld.com/video/how-time-sensitive-networks-are-transforming-industrial-networks-today
- **USG-WS**: THE STORY OF WATERFALL SECURITY & UNIDIRECTIONAL GATEWAY TECHNOLOGY, https://static.waterfall-security.com/Company-Profile_Waterfall-Security.pdf
- **USE-C2M2**: Office of Electricity Delivery and Energy Reliability—Cybersecurity Capability Maturity Model (C2M2), http://energy.gov/sites/prod/files/2014/03/f13/C2M2-v1-1_cor.pdf
- **USE-C2M2**: Office of Electricity Delivery and Energy Reliability–Cybersecurity Capability Maturity Model (C2M2), http://energy.gov/sites/prod/files/2014/03/f13/C2M2-v1-1_cor.pdf
- **VPN-DEF**: Wikipedia, https://en.wikipedia.org/wiki/Virtual_private_network
- **WLT-ICS**: An Executive Guide to Cyber Security for Operational Technology, https://www.ge.com/digital/cyber-security
- **WAVE-1609**: IEEE 1609.2™-2016, *Standard for Wireless Access in Vehicular Environments—Security Services for Applications and Management Messages. T. M. Kurihara, Chair, IEEE 1609 Working Group, W. Whyte, Vice-Chair, IEEE 1609 Working Group ITU-T CITS Tokyo, Japan July 5, 2016*
- **WSN**: Wireless Sensor Network Security, https://www.sciencedirect.com/science/article/pii/S2452414X16301029
- **W3C**: http://www.w3.org/TR/2004/NOTE-ws-gloss-20040211/#webservice
- **WSS-SEC**: https://en.wikipedia.org/wiki/WS-Security
- **WATERSEC**: https://waterfall-security.com/
- **WAT-CAS**: https://www.theregister.co.uk/2016/03/24/water_utility_hacked/

Security standards – quick reference

Standards related to Industrial IoT security discussed in this book are summarized here for quick reference.

Device endpoint security

- **CWE**: Common Weakness Enumeration
- **FIPS 140-2**: Security Requirements for Cryptographic Modules
- **FIPS 180-4**: NIST-CSRC Secure Hash Standard (SHS)
- **ISO/IEC 197702**: Specification on Software Tagging
- **ISA 62443-1-1**: Security for Industrial Automation and Control Systems Part 1 – Terminology, Concepts, and Models
- **ISA/IEC 62443-3-3**: Security for Industrial Automation and Control Systems Part 3-3 – System Security Requirements and Security Levels
- **ISO/IEC 15408**: Common Criteria for Information Technology Security Evaluation
- **NIST SP 800-155**: Boot-process integrity measurement
- **NIST SP 800-53**: Security and Privacy Controls for Federal Information Systems and Organizations

Industrial connectivity infrastructure security

- **ISA95**: Purdue Enterprise Reference Architecture Enterprise-Control System Integration
- **ISA-99**: Industrial Automation and Control Systems Security (https://www.isa.org/isa99/)
- **IEC 62443**: Industrial Network and System Security
- **IEC 62541**: OPC Unified Architecture Specification

- **IEC 61850**: Substation Automation Protocols
- **IEEE 1588**: IEEE Standard for a Precision Clock Synchronization Protocol for Network Measurement and Control Systems
- **NIST SP 800-53 Rev 4**: Recommended Security and Privacy Controls for Federal Information Systems and Organizations
- **NIST SP 800-82 Rev 2**: Guide to Industrial Control Systems (ICS) Security, May 2015
- **NIST SP 800-52**: Guidelines on the Selection and Use of Transport-Layer Security
- **TIA-942-A** (`http://www.tia-942.org/`): ANSI/TIA-942-A: Telecommunications Infrastructure Standard for Datacenters (`http://blog.siemon.com/standards/ tia-942-and-tia-942-a-%E2%80%9Cdata-center-infrastructure%E2%80%9D- standards`)

Edge-cloud security

- **ISO/IEC 27001**: A high-level management systems standard and its associated cloud-service-specific standards: ISO/IEC 27017 (for security) and ISO/IEC 27018 (for protection of personal data)
- **Standards addressing specific aspects of cloud computing**: ISO/IEC 27033 for network security, ISO/IEC 27034 for application security, ISO/IEC 19086 for cloud service SLAs
- **Technology-specific security standards**: Such as OASIS KMIP (key management), FIPS 140-2 (approved cryptographic modules), and OASIS SAML 2.0 (security assertions, used in IdAM implementations)
- **ISO/IEC 20889**: Standardizes de-identification techniques
- **US National Institute of Standards and Technology (NIST) Special Publication 800-175B**: Provides guidance on strong cryptographic methods
- **NIST SP 800-144**: Guidelines on Security and Privacy in Public Cloud Computing

Some useful documents on cloud security include the following:

- **CSCC white paper Cloud Security Standards**: What to Expect and What to Negotiate V2.0 (`http://www.cloud-council.org/deliverables/CSCC-Cloud-Security-Standards-What-to-Expect-and-What-to-Negotiate.pdf`)
- **Cloud Control Matrix**: `https://downloads.cloudsecurityalliance.org/initiatives/ccm/CCM_v3_Info_Sheet.pdf`
- **Cloud Customer Architecture for Securing Workloads on Cloud Services**: Published by Cloud Security Council
- **SAFEcode/CSA**: Practices for Secure Development of Cloud Applications
- **Cloud computing – Benefits, risks, and recommendations for information security**: Published by European Union Agency for Network and Information Security (ENISA)

Other Books You May Enjoy

If you enjoyed this book, you may be interested in these other books by Packt:

Practical Internet of Things Security - Second Edition
Brian Russell, Drew Van Duren

ISBN: 978-1-78862-582-1

- Discuss the needs of separate security requirements based on the IoT device
- Apply security engineering principles on IoT devices
- Focuses on operational aspects to plan, deploy, manage, monitor and detect remediation and disposal of IoT systems
- Use Blockchain Solutions for IoT Authenticity and Integrity
- Explore additional privacy features emergent in the IoT industry such as anonymity, tracking issues and countermeasures.
- Design a Fog Computing Architecture to support IoT Edge Analytics
- Detect and respond to IoT security incidents and compromises

Enterprise Internet of Things Handbook
Arvind Ravulavaru

ISBN: 978-1-78883-839-9

- Connect a Temperature and Humidity sensor and see how these two can be managed from various platforms
- Explore the core components of AWS IoT such as AWS Kinesis and AWS IoTRules Engine
- Build a simple analysis dashboard using Azure IoT and Power BI
- Understand the fundamentals of Google IoT and use Google core APIs to build your own dashboard
- Get started and work with the IBM Watson IoT platform
- Integrate Cassandra and Zeppelin with Kaa IoT dashboard
- Review some Machine Learning and AI and get to know more about their implementation in the IoT domain.

Leave a review - let other readers know what you think

Please share your thoughts on this book with others by leaving a review on the site that you bought it from. If you purchased the book from Amazon, please leave us an honest review on this book's Amazon page. This is vital so that other potential readers can see and use your unbiased opinion to make purchasing decisions, we can understand what our customers think about our products, and our authors can see your feedback on the title that they have worked with Packt to create. It will only take a few minutes of your time, but is valuable to other potential customers, our authors, and Packt. Thank you!

Index

www.ingramcontent.com/pod-product-compliance
Lightning Source LLC
Chambersburg PA
CBHW080624060326
40690CB00021B/4804